California Interiors
Intérieurs californiens

Diane Dorrans Saeks

California Interiors
Intérieurs californiens

Edited by | Sous la direction de | Herausgegeben von
Angelika Taschen

TASCHEN

KÖLN LONDON MADRID NEW YORK PARIS TOKYO

Endpapers | Pages de garde | Vorsatzpapier:
David Hockney, Portrait of an Artist (Pool with Two Figures) | Portrait d'un artiste (piscine avec deux personnes) | Porträt eines Künstlers (Swimming-pool mit zwei Figuren), 1972
Acrylic on Canvas, 84 x 120" | Acrylique sur toile, 213,4 x 304,8 cm | Acryl auf Leinwand, 213,4 x 304,8 cm
© David Hockney

Illustration page 2 | Reproduction page 2 | Abbildung Seite 2:
In the home of Mary Sue Milliken and Josh Schweitzer, Los Angeles
Dans la maison de Mary Sue Milliken et Josh Schweitzer, Los Angeles
Im Haus von Mary Sue Milliken und Josh Schweitzer, Los Angeles
Photo: Edina van der Wyck/The Interior Archive

Illustration page 7 | Reproduction page 7 | Abbildung Seite 7:
Case Study House #22, Pierre Koenig, Los Angeles, 1959–60
Photo: Julius Shulman

© 1999 Benedikt Taschen Verlag GmbH
Hohenzollernring 53, D–50672 Köln
www.taschen.com

© 1999 for the works by Ray and Charles Eames:
Lucia Eames dba Eames Office, P.O. Box 268
Venice, CA 90294, www.eamesoffice.com

Edited by Angelika Taschen, Cologne
Text edited by Ursula Fethke, Cologne
Production by Ute Wachendorf, Cologne
German translation by Corinna von Bassewitz, Big Pine Key
French translation by Jacques Bosser, Paris

Printed in Italy

ISBN 3–8228–6610–5
ISBN 3–8228–6986–4 (Edition with French cover)

Contents
Sommaire
Inhalt

The California Dream

Text by Diane Dorrans Saeks
Photos by Julius Shulman

Le rêve californien

Texte de Diane Dorrans Saeks
Photos de Julius Shulman

Der kalifornische Traum

Text von Diane Dorrans Saeks
Fotos von Julius Shulman

Freeman House
Frank Lloyd Wright, Los Angeles, 1923

The California home of the popular imagination is the residential equivalent of a breezy convertible, all fresh air, good times, and sunshine. Blame Hollywood and almost a century of cosmetically-enhanced posters and movie sets that portray fantasies of palm-shaded pools, brightly-colored exotic gardens and the studied tranquillity of bikini-clad models basking beneath cloudless blue skies.

Los Angeles, always the exhibitionistic metaphor for the state of California, cannot wiggle free from its reputation as a free-thinking trendsetter, and the land of permanent sunshine. Swimming pools, icons of health and affluence, glimmer still. Glance from a plane high over Los Angeles on a summer afternoon and blue pools wink back from the verdant topography of Bel Air and Beverly Hills. Luscious, star-quality interiors and verdant terraces as comfortable as outdoor living rooms designed by the imperious decorator Elsie de Wolfe, and by Cedric Gibbons and William Haines for classic movies that are always in rerun, add luster to these sun-struck hedonistic dreams. Sketch into the California freeze-frame image a pair of pneumatic white sofas, unembellished steel and glass mid-century modernist architecture, and full-length windows overlooking a sunlit beach, and all the ingredients for the prototypical California house and garden in the universal consciousness fall into place. All conventions thrown aside, a perfect movie set awaits a director, stars, and a film crew.

And the California scenario traverses even more interesting territory. Speed north through Big Sur to San Francisco, where the Summer of Love, the psychedelic merry-go-round of the Haight Ashbury, and Northern California hippie tie-dyed lifestyles have all left their legacies. But times and mores change. The political idealists and hippies of today are more likely to be designing web sites and working in the biotech industry than practicing zazen or laboring over a bead necklace. A chic South of Market loft filled with Modernist furniture and flea-market treasures, has replaced the sweetly smoky macramé and tofufed Victorian interiors of the 60s and 70s. It's too cool for pools here in the north, so instead of cultivating a tan, San Franciscans meditate on the grey and green

Dans l'imagination populaire, la maison californienne est un peu l'équivalent d'un cabriolet décapoté qui filerait au vent sous le grand soleil. Tout cela est la faute d'Hollywood, de presque un siècle d'affiches retouchées et de décors de cinéma qui nous ont offert le portrait d'une vie au bord des piscines, sous les palmiers et dans de luxuriants jardins exotiques, où se prélassent dans des poses affectées de superbes mannequins en bikini sous un ciel d'azur.

Los Angeles, métaphore exhibitionniste de l'Etat de Californie, ne peut se dégager de sa réputation de lanceur de modes et de royaume du soleil éternel. Les piscines, symboles de santé et de richesse, miroitent toujours sous le ciel. Quand vous survolez Los Angeles par un bel après-midi d'été, des rectangles, des ronds et des haricots turquoise vous font des clins d'œil entre les frondaisons de Bel Air et de Beverly Hills. Les intérieurs luxueux et les terrasses verdoyantes aussi confortables qu'un salon de plein air, conçus par des décorateurs impérieux comme le furent Elsie de Wolfe, Cedric Gibbons et William Haines pour les classiques du cinéma ou leurs remakes ajoutent plus de lustre encore à ce rêve hédoniste et lumineux. Ajoutez à cette image immuable de la Californie une architecture moderniste des années 50 en verre et acier brut, de grandes baies vitrées donnant sur une plage baignée de soleil, et toutes les composantes de l'archétype de la maison californienne et de son jardin se mettent en place dans la conscience universelle. Toutes conventions mises à part, ce parfait décor de cinéma n'attend plus qu'un metteur en scène, les stars et une équipe de tournage.

Mais ce scénario californien nous entraîne sur des territoires encore plus intéressants. Dirigez-vous vers San Francisco en passant par Big Sur, où le «Summer of Love», cette période triomphale du style de vie psychédélique autour d'Haight Ashbury, et les hippies de Californie du Nord ont laissé leurs traces, même s'ils ont pour beaucoup disparu. Les temps et les mœurs ont changé, et les idéalistes et les hippies d'aujourd'hui sont probablement plus occupés à concevoir des sites pour le Web ou à travailler pour les biotechnologies que de pratiquer le zazen ou de monter un collier de perles. Au quartier de South Market, les lofts chics remplis de meubles moder-

Nach allgemeiner Vorstellung ist das kalifornische Haus das bewohnbare Äquivalent zu einem Cabriolet mit geöffnetem Verdeck: frischer Fahrtwind, Spaß und Sonnenschein. Hollywood und fast ein Jahrhundert retuschierter Plakate und Filmkulissen sind schuld daran, daß sich in unseren Köpfen palmenumstandene Pools, exotische, farbenfrohe Gärten und die einstudierten Posen der Models im Bikini unter wolkenlosem blauem Himmel festgesetzt haben.

Los Angeles war immer die exhibitionistische Metapher für Kalifornien, und von dem Image des freidenkenden Trendsetters und des ewigen Sonnenscheins kann es sich nicht befreien. Pools, die Götzen der Gesunden und Reichen, glitzern in der Sonne. Fliegt man an einem Sommertag über die grüne Landschaft von Bel Air und Beverly Hills, schimmern die vielen Pools wie blaue Tupfen. Luxuriöse Interieurs und begrünte Terrassen, so gemütlich wie ein Wohnzimmer im Freien, bringen Glanz in die sonnendurchfluteten, hedonistischen Träume. Entworfen wurden solche Wohnungen von der Design-Koryphäe Elsie de Wolfe, von Cedric Gibbsons und William Haines für Filmklassiker, die immer wieder gezeigt werden. Versetzen Sie sich in dieses kalifornische Stilleben und stellen Sie sich dazu die modernistische Stahl- und Glasarchitektur der 50er Jahre vor sowie Fenster, die vom Boden bis zur Decke reichen und auf einen sonnigen Strand blicken. Und voilà! Die Elemente des prototypischen kalifornischen Hauses und Gartens machen auf einmal Sinn. Weitab von allen Konventionen wartet der perfekte Set nur noch auf Regisseur, Stars und Crew.

Das kalifornische Szenario bietet allerdings weitere interessante Facetten. Fahren Sie nach Norden über Big Sur nach San Francisco. Hier hinterließen der »Summer of Love«, das psychedelische Karussell in Haight Ashbury und der Lifestyle der batikenden, nordkalifornischen Hippies ihre Spuren. Aber Zeiten und Sitten ändern sich. Die politischen Idealisten und Hippies von heute entwerfen Webseiten und arbeiten in biotechnischen Laboren. Zazen und Perlenketten sind passé. Im Viertel von South Market wurden die viktorianischen Wohnungen mit ihrer Atmosphäre der 60er und 70er Jahre – Räucherstäbchen, Makramee und Tofu – in schicke Lofts mit

Leiser Residence
Marvin Leiser, Santa Monica,
1965

Case Study House #8
(Eames House)
Ray and Charles Eames,
Pacific Palisades, 1945–49

waters of San Francisco Bay and watch wisps of white fog billowing around the Golden Gate Bridge.

North and South are like separate kingdoms. History-revering San Francisco, like the serious sister who went to France and studied art and architecture, pays little attention to Los Angeles, her glitzy sister further south who thrills to the moment, who pursues youth and youths, and seems much too colorful and carefree. Living in narrow houses with bay windows – of course – and vertiginous streets gives San Francisco residents a quirky sense of permanence and enhances their well-being, to the clang of cable car bells. Strict city codes prescribe architectural styles, limiting forever the experimentation and bravado that gives Los Angeles its chaotic geometry, hill-defying engineering stunts, and six generations of blockbuster architecture.

The grape-infused Napa Valley and oak-scented reaches of the northern wine country, have become the new real-estate gourmand's dream destination. California's lyrical new country architecture is rising on rocky hillsides where once Wappo Indians wandered. Excavations for valley villas often turn over arrowheads, and signs of early nomadic life are revealed.

The California dream does exist. It's alive and well and living in a remodeled Richard Neutra or John Lautner house in the Hollywood Hills. Long neglected, many 40s, 50s and 60s classics are being revived, repaired and restored to life. Hollywood's young creatives, a new generation of directors, musicians and actors, furnish their interiors with patiently collected Eames chairs, and wander through rooms that seem utterly modern and cool again.

Head north of San Francisco over the Golden Gate Bridge and into Marin County and the ideals of the late 60s are still evident in Arts and Crafts cottages, organically-grown market gardens, yeasty artisanal bakeries, and weekend farmers' markets. There within sight of Mount Tamalpais, green, open spaces have been preserved and protected for all time.

In Big Sur, along the Central Coast, use of the land and existing sight lines are guarded so proudly that hardly a house is to be seen. Even the black night sky and the Milky Way are protected there. Come

nistes et de trouvailles de marchés aux puces ont remplacé les intérieurs victoriens bourrés de macramé et fleurant la cuisine au tofou des années 60 et 70. Ici, au nord, il fait trop frais pour les piscines, et les San Franciscains, plutôt que de cultiver leur bronzage, méditent sur les eaux vertes et grises de la baie de San Francisco et contemplent des écharpes de brouillard tournoyer autour du Golden Gate Bridge.

Le Nord et le Sud sont comme des royaumes séparés. San Francisco, sensible à l'histoire, c'est un peu la grande sœur sérieuse qui est allée en France pour y étudier l'art et l'architecture, et se soucie peu de sa cadette glamoureuse du sud qui ne vit que dans l'instant et lui semble beaucoup trop délurée et inconsciente. Vivre dans des maisons étroites éclairées par de grandes baies donnant sur des rues vertigineuses donne aux habitants de San Francisco un sens prégnant de la permanence, et la cloche des tramways à crémaillère rythme ce sentiment de bien-être. Une réglementation municipale stricte prescrit les styles architecturaux, et limite à jamais les expérimentations et les provocations qui donnent justement leur caractère aux rues de Los Angeles.

La Napa Valley au nord de San Francisco envahie par la vigne et les plantations de chênes de cette région viticole sont devenus le rêve des amateurs d'immobilier de qualité. La nouvelle architecture californienne de caractère bucolique s'implante sur des pentes rocailleuses, jadis territoire des Indiens Wappo.

Le rêve californien existe bien. Il est même en pleine forme et a pris ses quartiers dans une maison rénovée de Richard Neutra ou de John Lautner dans les Hollywood Hills. Longtemps négligés, les classiques des années 40, 50 et 60 sont ramenés à la vie, réparés, soignés. Les jeunes créateurs d'Hollywood – une nouvelle génération de réalisateurs de films, de musiciens et d'acteurs – meublent leurs résidences de fauteuils Eames réunis avec patience, et vivent dans des pièces qui semblent avoir renoué avec la modernité et la décontraction.

Au nord de San Francisco, au-delà du Golden Gate Bridge et dans le Marin County, les idéaux de la fin des années 60 sont encore bien vivants dans les cottages néo-Arts and Crafts, les jardins biologiques,

modernistischen Möbeln und Schätzen vom Flohmarkt verwandelt. Hier oben im Norden ist es zu kalt
für Pools. Statt Sonnenbräune zu pflegen, meditieren
die Bewohner von San Francisco am graugrünen
Wasser der San Francisco Bay und beobachten die
Nebelschwaden über der Golden Gate Bridge.

Der Norden und der Süden Kaliforniens sind
wie zwei verschiedene Königreiche. San Francisco
gleicht der seriösen Schwester, die Kunst und Architektur in Frankreich studierte. Sie schenkt ihrer extra-
vaganten, spontanen und leichtsinnigen Schwester
Los Angeles kaum Beachtung. Die Bewohner San
Franciscos leben in engen Häusern mit Blick auf die
Bucht. Die steilen Straßen vermitteln ein seltsames
Gefühl von Beständigkeit ebenso wie das Klingeln der
Straßenbahnen. Strenge Bauvorschriften grenzen die
Architekturstile ein. Dadurch gehen aber auch die Ex-
perimentierfreude und der provokative Geist verlo-
ren, die Los Angeles prägen.

Diejenigen, die noch ihre Traumimmobilie suchen, haben bereits ein neues Zielgebiet gefunden:
das nördlich von San Francisco gelegene Winzer-
Dorado Napa Valley, ein nach Wein und Eichen duf-
tendes Hügelland. Auf den Hügeln, über die einst die
Wappo-Indianer zogen, stehen heute romantische
Landhäuser. Wenn in den Tälern Fundamente für Villen ausgehoben werden, finden sich oft Pfeilspitzen,
Zeichen einer frühen Nomadenkultur.

Den kalifornischen Traum gibt es wirklich. Er
ist höchst lebendig und wohnt in einer umgebauten
Richard-Neutra-Residenz oder einem John-Lautner-
Haus in den Hügeln von Hollywood. Viele Klassiker
aus den 40er, 50er und 60er Jahren, die lange Zeit
vernachlässigt wurden, werden jetzt repariert und
restauriert. Hollywoods junge Kreative, die neue Generation der Regisseure, Musiker und Schauspieler,
richten ihre Häuser mit geduldig zusammengetra-
genen Eames-Stühlen ein und bewegen sich in
Räumlichkeiten, die wieder höchst modern und kühl
wirken.

Fährt man über die Golden Gate Bridge in
Richtung Norden nach Marin County, wird man von
den Idealen der späten 60er Jahre empfangen: Arts-
and-Crafts-Cottages, ökologische Gärten, Feinbäcke-
reien mit Hefeprodukten und am Wochenende Bau-

Kramer House
Richard Neutra, Norco, 1953

Case Study House #22
Pierre Koenig, Los Angeles, 1959

Frey House II
Albert Frey, Palm Springs,
1963/64

darkness, barely-there lighting must be directed earthward. Summer fog whistles and soars over the dry-grass hillsides. From Highway One, little of the real Big Sur is visible. Access to the coast is limited. But, oh, the locals are there. Undisturbed, they're writing music, designing furniture, crafting paintings, sweeping oak leaves from dusty terraces, running on damp, gray Pfeiffer Beach, and lolling in hammocks awaiting inspiration for the next book or movie script.

It's a deft balancing act living on earthquake fault lines, but Californians are used to living on the edge. Dwelling in paradise requires a certain bravado. A tremor or temblor may rattle the nerves once or twice a year, but earthquakes, residents assure themselves, are rare. A human-induced power-outage is more common than a full-scale, rock'em, sock'em 'quake. Still, somewhere in storage is a fully-equipped Earthquake Kit packed with mineral water, granola bars, batteries, pet food – most Californians live with a dog or a cat – and perhaps a bottle or two of Napa Valley Chardonnay.

Geography is destiny. California is a state with many borders, coastlines and corners: Palm Springs was built in a desert. Squaw Valley's snow-white winters draw skiers from all over the world. Sausalito clambers over sheltered hillsides, embraced in permanent springtime. San Diego glances over the border into Mexico. And the terrain, with its impossible beauty, mysterious deserts, rocky beaches, and mist-swirled stands of native oaks, seems to tower over any man-made configuration.

Architects who dream of making a statement here have their work cut out. While the didactic Case Study Houses of the 40s by such architects as Raphael S. Soriano, Pierre Koenig, and Richard Neutra attempted to draw new homeowners into a dialogue with steel and simple lines, many Californians are in thrall to the familiar. Ranch houses were the 50s ideal, and generations of children grew up in open-plan houses which broke down the barriers between indoors and out.

The most rigorous and thoughtful architects, such as Cliff May or Jim Jennings or Ned Forrest take their cues from old Mission dwellings of centuries ago, or look to 19th-century California farm buildings

les boulangeries artisanales de pain au levain, et les marchés de paysans le week-end. Là, en vue du Mount Tamalpais, les grands espaces d'un vert intense sont préservés et protégés depuis toujours.

A Big Sur, sur la Central Coast, l'utilisation de l'espace est si étroitement surveillée, que l'on aperçoit à peine les maisons. Même le noir du ciel et la voie lactée sont protégés. Lorsque le soleil disparaît, les quelques sources lumineuses doivent être orientées vers le sol. Le brouillard estival se lève et se répand sur les collines d'herbes sèches. De l'Highway One, on ne voit pratiquement rien du vrai Big Sur. L'accès à la côte est limité. Mais les autochtones sont bien là. Sans risque d'être dérangés, ils composent de la musique, dessinent des meubles, peignent, balayent les feuilles de chêne de leurs terrasses, courent le long de la plage grise de Pfeiffer Beach, et paressent dans des hamacs en attendant l'inspiration pour leur prochain livre ou scénario.

Il est toujours délicat de vivre sur des lignes de failles telluriques mais les Californiens ont l'habitude de ce genre de vie. Un tremblement ou une vibration peuvent titiller les nerfs une ou deux fois par an, mais les vraies catastrophes sont rares, se disent les habitants pour se rassurer. Une panne de courant est plus fréquente qu'une bonne vieille secousse bien sérieuse, bien médiatisée. On n'en conserve pas moins toujours dans un coin un kit «Tremblement de terre», bourré d'eau minérale, de barres de céréales, de piles électriques, de nourriture pour les animaux – la plupart des Californiens vivent avec un chien ou un chat – et peut-être une ou deux bouteilles de chardonnay de la Napa Valley.

La géographie est un destin. La Californie est un Etat avec des frontières, des côtes et des paysages extrêmement variés. Palm Springs est en plein désert. Squaw Valley attire des skieurs du monde entier. Sausalito escalade ses collines ombragées, bénie par un printemps éternel. San Diego regarde d'un œil la frontière mexicaine. Et la nature, avec ses mystérieux déserts, ses plages de rochers et ses forêts de chênes noyées de brume semble plus délirante encore que n'importe quelle création de l'homme.

Les architectes qui rêvent de marquer leur passage sont ici soumis à rude compétition. Si les cé-

ernmärkte. Die offenen, grünen Flächen beim Mount
Tamalpais wurden für alle Zeit unter Naturschutz ge-
stellt.

In Big Sur an der Zentralküste werden Boden-
nutzung und Bebauung so vehement überwacht, daß
kaum ein Haus zu sehen ist. Selbst der Nachthimmel
und die Milchstraße sind hier geschützt. Bei Einbruch
der Dunkelheit müssen die ohnehin spärlichen Lichtquellen nach unten gerichtet werden. Sommernebel
wabert über die trockenen Grashügel. Vom Highway
One aus ist Big Sur kaum auszumachen. Es gibt wenige Straßen, die zur Küste führen. Aber die Bewohner sind da. Ungestört komponieren sie, entwerfen
Möbel, fegen Eichenlaub von staubigen Terrassen,
laufen auf dem feuchten Pfeiffer Beach und schaukeln
in ihren Hängematten, in der Hoffnung auf Inspiration für das nächste Buch oder Skript.

Es ist freilich ein Drahtseilakt, im Erdbeben-
gebiet zu wohnen. Aber die Kalifornier sind es ge-
wohnt, am Rand der Gefahr zu leben. Vielleicht zwei-
mal pro Jahr stellen kleine Erschütterungen die
Nerven auf die Zerreißprobe, doch Erdbeben, so sagen sich die Einwohner, sind selten. Ein Stromausfall
wegen menschlichen Versagens kommt häufiger vor
als ein Beben auf der höchsten Stufe der Richterskala.
Trotzdem horten sie irgendwo in ihrer Wohnung ein
Überlebensset mit Mineralwasser, Müsliriegeln,
Batterien und Tiernahrung – die meisten Kalifornier
haben einen Hund oder eine Katze – und wahrscheinlich einer Flasche Napa Valley Chardonnay.

Geographie ist Schicksal. Kalifornien hat un-
endlich viele Grenzen, Küsten und Landschaften.
Palm Springs wurde auf Wüstensand gebaut. Die
schneereichen Winter im Squaw Valley locken Skifah-
rer aus aller Welt an. Sausalito bietet hinter geschütz-
ten Hügeln ewigen Frühling. San Diego blickt über
die Grenze nach Mexiko. Die mysteriösen Wüsten,
felsigen Strände und nebelverhüllten Eichen ziehen
alle Aufmerksamkeit auf sich vor jeder menschlichen
Schöpfung.

Architekten, die davon träumen, hier einen
Meilenstein zu setzen, müssen sich große Mühe geben. Während die berühmten Case Study Houses der
40er Jahre von Raphael S. Soriano, Pierre Koenig und
Richard Neutra neue Hausbesitzer für Stahl und klare

Frey House I
Albert Frey, Palm Springs, 1947–53

with their archetypal barns and hand-hewn timbers for appropriate references.

Los Angeles, more than San Francisco, has always supported experimental architecture. The precise and unpretentious houses by Los Angeles architects Rudolf M. Schindler and Richard Neutra, along with Ray and Charles Eames, built in the first half of the 20th century have been some of the great and enduring achievements of Southern California architecture, and most of them still please. There are the iconoclasts such as the muscular John Lautner and his predecessor Frank Lloyd Wright who crafted houses of great originality.

No one place or time represents the California zeitgeist. A quick design tour of California might also take in the historical wine country town of Healdsburg. A pretty, shaded town square with a fretwork Victorian-style bandstand is surrounded by neat old-fashioned shops, and tidy houses that range from prim Edwardians to ivy-covered adobes and Arts and Crafts bungalows. Further south in the sunny upper reaches of the Napa Valley, a glider hovers above the Palisades, and Carlo Marchiori's witty Palladian-style villa, which began life as a barn, hovers into view.

A trip through San Francisco starts, perhaps, in Pacific Heights where the bay-view Edwardian mansions of railroad barons and sugar millionaires pose grandly beside new boxy Modernist residences chosen by high-tech billionaires and idealists who believed that architecture should be of its time. The coastal highway winds south through the fog. Between San Francisco and Los Angeles, a distance of some 560 km, most of the land is unbuilt: space enough for building the California dream.

lèbres Case Study Houses pédagogiques des années 40 dues à des architectes comme Raphael S. Soriano, Pierre Koenig et Richard Neutra tentaient d'entraîner de nouveaux propriétaires dans un dialogue avec l'acier et la simplicité des lignes, de nombreux Californiens restent attachés à leur environnement familier. Le style Ranch fut l'idéal des années 50, et des générations d'enfants ont grandi dans ces maisons à plan ouvert qui avaient abattu les barrières entre l'intérieur et l'extérieur. Les plus rigoureux et les plus réfléchis des architectes, comme Cliff May, Jim Jennings ou encore Ned Forrest ont trouvé leur inspiration dans d'anciennes constructions de style Mission, ou se sont penchés sur les bâtiments de ferme du 19e siècle aux granges et ossatures de bois typiques.

Los Angeles, plus que San Francisco, a toujours soutenu l'architecture expérimentale. Les maisons d'architectes angéliniens comme Rudolf M. Schindler, Richard Neutra, ou Ray et Charles Eames, toutes édifiées à la fin de la première moitié du 20e siècle font partie des plus grandes et plus durables réussites de l'architecture de la Californie du Sud. On trouve aussi des iconoclastes comme John Lautner, ou plus avant, Frank Lloyd Wright.

Aucun endroit ou lieu ne peut à lui seul symboliser le «Zeitgeist» californien. Un rapide voyage dans cet Etat peut, par exemple, vous faire découvrir la petite cité viticole et historique de Healdsburg, avec son kiosque à musique victorien et ses petites maisons proprettes qui vont d'un style edwardien pimpant à des constructions en adobe recouvertes de lierre ou à des bungalows Arts and Crafts. Plus au sud, dans les vallonnements ensoleillés de la Napa Valley, un planeur s'enfuit à tire d'ailes au-dessus des Palisades, et l'amusante villa néo-palladienne de Carlo Marchiori, qui fut jadis une grange, attire le regard.

Une promenade dans San Francisco peut commencer dans le quartier de Pacific Heights où les demeures edwardiennes, avec vue sur la baie, des «barons» des chemins de fer et des magnats du sucre posent avec suffisance à côté des «boîtes» modernistes. Entre San Francisco et Los Angeles, environ 560 km, la nature est presque encore vierge, autant d'espace encore libre pour édifier le rêve californien.

Linien begeisterten, blieben viele Kalifornier beim
Althergebrachten. Ranches waren das Ideal der 50er
Jahre, und Generationen von Kaliforniern wuchsen in
diesen offenen Häusern auf, in denen die Grenze zwischen innen und außen verschwamm. Kühne und be-
dachte Architekten wie Cliff May, Jim Jennings oder
Ned Forrest inspirierten sich an jahrhundertealten
Missionssiedlungen oder orientierten sich an kalifornischen Farmhäusern des 19. Jahrhunderts mit den
typischen Scheunen und handbearbeiteten Balken.

    Los Angeles, eher als San Francisco, hat im-
mer schon die experimentelle Architektur gefördert.
Die funktionalen Gebäude der Architekten Rudolf M.
Schindler, Richard Neutra, Ray und Charles Eames,
die alle in der ersten Hälfte des 20. Jahrhunderts in
Los Angeles entstanden, gehören zu den wichtigsten
Errungenschaften der südkalifornischen Architektur.
Auch Pioniere wie zum Beispiel John Lautner oder
Frank Lloyd Wright schufen höchst originelle Häuser.

    Es gibt keinen Ort und keine Epoche, die re-
präsentativ für den kalifornischen Zeitgeist stehen.
Eine schnelle »Tour de Design« durch Kalifornien
könnte beispielsweise in die historische Weinstadt
Healdsburg führen. Der hübsche schattige Dorfplatz
mit dem Musikpavillon im viktorianischen Laubsäge-
Stil ist von adretten, altmodischen Läden umgeben.
Die gepflegten Häuser sind züchtige edwardianische
Bauten, efeubewachsene Adobe-Häuser oder Arts-
and-Crafts-Bungalows. Ein Segelflugzeug schwebt
über die Palisades in den sonnigen Hügeln des Napa
Valley weiter im Süden. Und plötzlich taucht Carlo
Marchioris neopalladianische Villa auf, die ursprüng-
lich ein Schuppen war.

    Ein Gang durch San Francisco fängt wahr-
scheinlich im Viertel von Pacific Heights an. Dort
protzen die edwardianischen Herrenhäuser der
Eisenbahnbarone und Zuckermillionäre neben den
neuen, schachtelförmigen Residenzen der Moderni-
sten, die High-Tech-Milliardäre und Idealisten für
sich gewählt haben. Der Coastal Highway schlängelt
sich durch den Nebel nach Süden. Zwischen San
Francisco und Los Angeles, auf einer Strecke von
ungefähr 560 km, ist das meiste Land immer noch
unbebaut – hier ist genug Platz für den kalifornischen
Traum.

Malin Residence (Chemosphere)
John Lautner, Hollywood, 1960

Malin Residence (Chemosphere)
John Lautner, Hollywood, 1960

Metropolitan Life:
Los Angeles

Lorsque Stephen Chin, juriste diplômé de Yale devenu réalisateur de films indépendant, acheta cette maison moderniste dans les Hollywood Hills, ses amis furent atterrés. Pour lui, c'était une icône de l'architecture angélinienne du milieu de siècle, pour eux, un garage à voitures exigu et vide. «La maison était en très mauvais état et ils pensaient que j'allais la démolir», se rappelle ce natif de Toronto. Sa découverte, une construction de verre audacieusement maintenue par de fins bandeaux d'acier, avait été conçue par l'architecte Allyn E. Morris dans les années 50. Ce diplômé de Stanford qui avait reçu une formation beaux-arts voulait susciter une nouvelle architecture californienne en s'appuyant sur la technologie et l'optimisme moderniste. Il voulait exprimer la culture de l'époque avec la même liberté que le jazz, la danse moderne et l'art contemporain. De 110 m² de surface et 9 m de large, la maison à peine visible de la rue est perchée sur une colline plantée d'eucalyptus. Sa façade spectaculaire domine le terrain et fait penser à une boîte à lumière géante.

Stephen Chin

When Yale graduate attorney-turned-independent film-maker Stephen Chin acquired his modernist house in the Hollywood Hills, his friends were aghast. Chin saw it as an icon of mid-century Los Angeles architecture. His friends saw a poky carport, with bare floors. "The house was in disarray and they thought I should just tear it down" recalled Chin, a native of Toronto. His trophy, all glass and bravado wrapped in thin bands of steel, had been designed by architect Allyn E. Morris in the 50s. Morris, a Stanford graduate, was Beaux-Arts-trained, but wanted to reveal a new California architecture which capitalized on technology and optimistic modern thinking. He wanted to express the culture in the same free-form way as jazz, modern dance, and contemporary art had done. The 110 sq.m., 9 m-wide house, which perches on a eucalyptus-wooded hillside, is barely visible from the street. Its dramatic façade looms over the site and looks for all the world like a giant light box.

Als der ehemalige Rechtsanwalt mit Hochschulabschluß der Elite-Uni Yale und heutige unabhängige Filmemacher Stephen Chin sein modernistisches Haus in den Hügeln Hollywoods kaufte, waren seine Freunde schockiert. Für Chin war das Haus eine Ikone der Architektur der 50er Jahre in Los Angeles, für seine Freunde war es eine abgetakelte Garage mit blanken Fußböden. »Das Haus war heruntergekommen, und alle rieten mir, es abzureißen«, erinnert sich Chin, der aus Toronto stammt. Seine Trophäe aus Glas und dünnen Stahlbändern war von dem Architekten Allyn E. Morris entworfen worden. Morris, Absolvent der Stanford University, hatte an der Kunstakademie studiert. Sein erklärtes Ziel war eine neue kalifornische Architektur, die von Technologie und optimistischem modernem Denken geprägt sein sollte. In ihr sollte sich der gleiche freie Geist ausdrücken wie in Jazz, Modern Dance und zeitgenössischer Kunst. Von der Straße aus ist das 110 m² große, 9 m breite Haus an einem mit Eukalyptusbäumen bestandenen Hügel kaum zu sehen. Die spektakuläre Fassade gleicht einer gigantischen, erleuchteten Schachtel.

Film-maker Stephen Chin, an ardent modernist, is among the new wave of creative types who are snapping up modernist houses around the Hollywood Hills. His house is all pure lines and structure. Still, there is the enrichment of dark turquoise glass tile detailing. The neatly arranged brickwork has complex rythms, somewhat reminiscent of Frank Lloyd Wright's textile blocks. The joyous interior vibrates with bursts of color. A steel stairway edged with dark turquoise tiles spirals up the center of the house. The living room, kitchen and terrace are on the second level. The lowest level has the studio.

Le réalisateur Stephen Chin, amateur passionné d'art moderne, fait partie de cette nouvelle vague de créateurs qui achètent des maisons modernistes dans les Hollywood Hills. La maison de Stephen est un exercice de style en structures et épuration de lignes. On y trouve cependant quelques surprises presque chaleureuses comme des carreaux de verre turquoise foncé. L'appareil de brique aux rythmes complexes, rappelle un peu l'approche «textile» de Frank Lloyd Wright. Joyeux, l'intérieur vibre de multiples éclats de couleur. Un escalier de métal revêtu de carreaux turquoise foncé grimpe en spirale au centre de la maison. Le séjour, la cuisine et la terrasse se trouvent à l'étage. Le rez-de-chaussée abrite l'atelier.

Der Filmemacher Stephen Chin gehört zu der Riege von Kreativen, die überall in den Hollywood Hills die modernistischen Häuser aufkaufen. Sein Haus kennzeichnen klare Linien und Strukturen. Den letzten Schliff erhält es durch blaue Glaskacheln. Die makellose Ziegelbauweise zeigt einen komplexen Schwung und erinnert an Frank Lloyd Wrights »textile blocks«. Innen explodieren die Farben förmlich. Eine Stahltreppe, die mit blauen Kacheln abgesetzt ist, schraubt sich im Zentrum des Hauses nach oben. Wohnzimmer, Küche und Terrasse befinden sich im ersten Stock. Im Erdgeschoß liegt das Atelier.

Above and right: Throughout the house, steel beams and rails are painted jazz-hot colors. The kitchen cabinets are faced with blue Formica. Chin is on the search for furniture and lighting by the likes of Ray and Charles Eames, Arne Jacobsen, and Eero Saarinen, and often makes felicitous finds at the Rose Bowl Flea Market, Pasadena.
Facing page: The bedroom of Stephen Chin's funhouse is on the top floor, beneath the concrete slab roof. The platform bed is raised on brick pedestals. In the restoration, Chin stripped away poorly conceived additions to his 50s house, and the house today is true to the architect's original plan.

Ci-dessus et à droite: La poutraison d'acier est uniformément peinte en couleurs jazzy. Les meubles de cuisine sont en Formica bleu. Stephen recherche le mobilier et les luminaires de créateurs comme Ray et Charles Eames, Arne Jacobsen et Eero Saarinen et fait souvent d'heureuses trouvailles au marché aux puces du Rose Bowl, à Pasadena.
Page de droite: La chambre-repaire de Stephen se trouve à l'étage, sous la dalle de béton du toit. Le lit repose sur des piédestaux de brique. Au cours de la restauration, Chip a éliminé certains ajouts malheureux, et la maison des années 50 a retrouvé son plan d'origine.

Oben und rechts: Im ganzen Haus sind die Stahlträger und Geländer in knallbunten Farben gestrichen. Die Küchenschränke sind mit blauem Formica, einem hitzebeständigen Kunststoff, verblendet. Chin ist stets auf der Suche nach Möbeln und Lichtquellen von Designern wie Ray und Charles Eames, Arne Jacobsen und Eero Saarinen. Fündig wird er oft auf dem Rose Bowl Flohmarkt in Pasadena.
Rechte Seite: Das Schlafzimmer befindet sich im obersten Stockwerk von Stephen Chins witziger Behausung, direkt unter dem Flachdach aus Beton. Das Bett ruht auf Ziegelsteinsockeln. Chin ließ verschiedene Anbauten abreißen, so daß das Haus heute wieder so dasteht, wie es in den 50er Jahren geplant worden war.

Imaginez-vous rouler la nuit sur une freeway de Los Angeles, tandis que les panneaux des sorties défilent les uns après les autres avant de se fondre dans l'indigo foncé du ciel. Vous manipulez les commandes de votre autoradio et tombez par hasard sur la bonne station. La voix séduisante du critique gastronomique Merrill Shindler descend du ciel et vous aide à vous sentir mieux ... Non seulement elle est rassurante, mais elle vous guide vers les meilleurs restaurants. Lorsque Shindler s'est acquitté de cette tâche quasi civique, il regagne sa délicieuse résidence nichée dans un canyon tranquille près du quartier de Brentwood. Merrill et son épouse, Merri Howard, productrice de «Star Trek Voyager», vivaient auparavant dans une Case Study House de Raphael S. Soriano. Leur nouvelle maison, conçue par l'architecte Finn Kappe, reprend les principes d'épure et de logique des plans des années 40 de Soriano. Vers l'ouest, la maison n'est que verre.

Merri Howard and Merrill Shindler

Imagine this: You're speeding along a Los Angeles freeway at night, the destination just a dream as exit after exit looms and recedes in the darkness. Blindly stabbing at the radio controls, you hit by chance exactly the right number. The mellifluous voice of Los Angeles restaurant critic, Merrill Shindler, comes across the airwaves and all is well with the world. Not only is Shindler's voice reassuring, he also steers you toward his pick of the hottest restaurants. When Shindler's finished this civic duty, he drives himself home to a delicious residence in a quiet canyon near Brentwood. Shindler and his wife, Merri Howard, supervising producer of "Star Trek Voyager", previously lived in a Case Study house designed by Raphael S. Soriano. Their new house, by architect Finn Kappe, follows the same simple lines and ruling logic of Soriano's 40s plan. To the west, the house is all glass.

Stellen Sie sich vor, Sie fahren nachts auf einem Freeway in Los Angeles, das Ziel so weit weg wie der Mars. Sie passieren eine Ausfahrt nach der anderen, die dann wieder im Dunklen verschwindet. Sie zappen sich durch die Radiosender, und plötzlich landen Sie bei dem richtigen Kanal. Sie lauschen der melodiösen Stimme von Merrill Shindler, dem unangefochtenen König der Restaurantkritiker von Los Angeles. Sie folgen den hypnotisierenden Worten und landen garantiert in einem der angesagtesten Gourmet-Tempeln der Stadt. Wenn Shindler seine öffentlichen Auftritte beendet, fährt er in sein wunderbares Haus in einem ruhigen Canyon in der Nähe des Stadtteils Brentwood. Früher lebten Shindler und seine Frau Merri Howard – sie ist Supervising Producer der Serie »Star Trek Voyager« – in einem Case Study House von Raphael S. Soriano. Ihr neues Domizil, gebaut von dem Architekten Finn Kappe, zeigt dieselbe Konsequenz und dieselben klaren Linien wie Sorianos Bau aus den 40er Jahren. Die Westseite des Gebäudes ist völlig verglast.

First pages, left: Restaurant critic Merrill Shindler and the Los Angeles cityscape; detail of the entrance.
First pages, right: The walnut "Ivar" mirror reflected in the glass-topped Alvar Aalto dining table is by Los Angeles interior designer Michael Berman.
Previous pages: Michael Berman also designed the "Hudson" sofa in the living room. The curvy upholstered armchairs are 40s originals by Gilbert Rohde.
Right and below: Walls of books are lavished on Shindler's study, which is furnished with 40s and 50s furniture.

Premières pages, à gauche: Le critique gastronomique Merrill Shindler devant le panorama de Los Angeles; détail de l'entrée.
Premières pages, à droite: Le miroir en noyer «Ivar» se reflète sur la table à dîner à plateau de verre d'Alvar Aalto. Il est signé du décorateur angélinien Michael Berman.
Double page précédente: Michael Berman a également dessiné le canapé «Hudson» du salon. Les fauteuils tout en courbes sont des modèles originaux des années 40 de Gilbert Rohde.
A droite et ci-dessous: Les murs du bureau, meublé dans le style des années 40 et 50, sont recouverts de bibliothèques.

Erste Doppelseite, links: Der Restaurantkritiker Merrill Shindler vor der Stadtlandschaft von Los Angeles; Detail des Eingangsbereiches.
Erste Doppelseite, rechts: Der »Ivar«-Spiegel aus Walnußholz des Interior-Designers Michael Berman aus Los Angeles spiegelt sich in der Glasplatte des Eßtisches von Alvar Aalto.
Vorhergehende Doppelseite: Michael Berman entwarf auch das »Hudson«-Sofa im Wohnzimmer. Die kurvenreichen Polstersessel von Gilbert Rohde sind Originale aus den 40er Jahren.
Rechts und unten: Bücher über Bücher in Shindlers Arbeitszimmer. Die Einrichtung stammt aus den 40er und 50er Jahren.

Merri Howard and her husband, Merrill Shindler, love to cook and entertain. Their updated kitchen includes granite counters, cherry-wood cabinets, and verdant canyon views. A stainless-steel topped table is useful for food preparation. Open shelves are used for cook books, and condiments. The shiphape shelves keep everything accessible, and enliven the walls without looming large.

Merri Howard et Merrill Shindler adorent cuisiner et recevoir. Leur cuisine modernisée est équipée de plans de travail en granit, de meubles en cerisier et, de plus, donne sur la coulée verte d'un canyon. Une table à plateau d'acier inoxydable sert à la préparation des repas. Des étagères ouvertes et bien rangées reçoivent les livres de cuisine et les condiments; elles laissent tout à portée de main et animent les murs sans prendre trop de place.

Merri Howard und ihr Mann Merrill Shindler laden gerne zum Abendessen ein. Ihre moderne Küche mit einem unvergleichlichen Blick auf den grünen Canyon verfügt über Arbeitsflächen aus Granit und Kirschholzeinbauten. Der Tisch mit der Platte aus rostfreiem Stahl dient der Zubereitung der Mahlzeiten. Kochbücher und Gewürze stehen griffbereit auf den offenen Regalen, die die Wände gliedern, ohne sie zu erschlagen.

Above: *German artist Karl Dietz crafted the bookcase which serves also as a desk and is accompanied by a fiberglass chair by Charles Eames, one of Dietz's design icons. A Karl Dietz watercolor, part of a series concerning site and space, hangs on the wall beside the desk.*
Left: *The couple's quiet Santa Monica outpost affords them privacy and space to pursue their work.*

Ci-dessus: *L'artiste allemand Karl Dietz a construit la bibliothèque qui lui sert également de bureau. Au premier plan, une chaise en fibre de verre de Charles Eames, l'une des icônes du design moderniste selon Karl. L'une de ses aquarelles, qui fait partie d'une série sur le thème du site et de l'espace, est accrochée au mur.*
A gauche: *Ce calme petit avant-poste moderniste à Santa Monica a offert au couple l'intimité et l'espace dont il avait besoin pour poursuivre ses recherches.*

Oben: *Der deutsche Künstler Karl Dietz schreinerte das Bücherregal, das gleichzeitig als Schreibtisch dient. Davor steht ein Fiberglas-Stuhl von Charles Eames, eines der großen Vorbilder von Dietz. An der Wand hängt ein Aquarell des Hausherrn aus einer Serie zum Thema »Ort und Raum«.*
Links: *Das ruhig gelegene Haus in Santa Monica erlaubt es dem Paar, ungestört seiner Arbeit nachzugehen.*

California Interiors   Katharina Ehrhardt and Karl Dietz

Venu de la lointaine Allemagne, le modernisme se bâtit une solide tête de pont à Los Angeles au cours des années 30 et 40. De la même façon, l'artiste Karl Dietz et son épouse, la styliste capillaire Katharina Ehrhardt franchirent en 1989 les 9 500 km qui séparent l'Allemagne de la Californie pour donner une expression plus entière à leurs idées et à leur art. Il n'est sans doute pas surprenant que le couple ait élu un appartement dans un immeuble moderniste aux lignes pures de Santa Monica, dessiné par Alice Gilman en 1966. «Mon travail artistique est lié au modernisme classique. L'architecture et le décor de l'appartement ne font donc qu'un avec ma philosophie», fait remarquer Karl. Ces deux Berlinois se sont tous deux senti inspirés par le climat édénique et le soleil permanent de Los Angeles, et l'esprit d'ouverture des Angéliniens aux idées nouvelles. Ils ont meublé leurs pièces beiges de classiques de Ray et Charles Eames. «J'utilise les murs comme des toiles, et mon art est ce qui compte le plus pour moi», commente le peintre.

Katharina Ehrhardt and Karl Dietz

Modernism traveled west from Germany and gained a strong foothold in Los Angeles in the 30s and 40s. In a similar fashion, artist Karl Dietz and his wife, hair stylist Katharina Ehrhardt, jetted 9 500 km from Germany to California in 1989 to find full expression for their ideas and art. Perhaps not surprisingly, the couple acquired an apartment in a clean-lined Modernist building in Santa Monica, designed by Alice Gilman in 1966. "My art work is related to classic Modernism, so the architecture and decor of the apartment follow my philosophy seamlessly," noted Dietz. The two former Berliners have both been inspired by the Edenic climate and bright year-round sunlight of Los Angeles, and by the easy acceptance of new ideas. They have furnished the cream-walled rooms with classic Ray and Charles Eames pieces. "I use the walls as my canvas and my art is the primary focus," said Dietz.

Die Bewegung des Modernismus kam in den 30er und 40er Jahren aus Deutschland nach Los Angeles. Ähnlich war es auch bei dem Künstler Karl Dietz und seiner Frau, der Haar-Stylistin Katharina Ehrhardt. Sie jetteten 1989 mehr als 9 500 km über den Atlantik, um in Los Angeles ihre Ideen und ihre Kunst leben zu können. Deshalb war es eigentlich nicht verwunderlich, daß die beiden ein geradliniges, modernistisches Gebäude in Santa Monica kauften, das Alice Gilman 1966 entworfen hatte. »Meine Kunst inspiriert sich an der klassischen Moderne. Die Architektur und der Dekor des Apartment sind ganz im Sinne meiner Philosophie«, sagt Dietz. Die beiden gebürtigen Berliner fühlten sich von dem paradiesischen Klima und dem ganzjährigen Sonnenschein in Los Angeles angezogen. Außerdem ist die lebendige Stadt viel offener für neue Ideen. Die cremefarbenen Räume wurden mit Klassikern von Ray und Charles Eames möbliert. »Die Wände sind meine Leinwand, meine Kunst steht immer im Vordergrund«, erklärt Dietz.

Karl Dietz, who pursued his classic fine arts education at the Art Academy in Frankfurt, crafted the Zen bed platform of solid maple with a plain satin finish. Japanese Shoji paper screens conceal the closet. Dietz's painted wood panels, an exercise in color, set up a lively rhythm on the bedroom wall.

Karl Dietz, qui a étudié les beaux-arts à l'Académie de Francfort, a fabriqué le lit zen sur une plate-forme en érable massif satiné. Les écrans japonais Shoji en papier masquent un placard. Les panneaux de bois peints par Karl – un exercice chromatique – créent un rythme animé sur le mur de la chambre.

Karl Dietz, der an der Frankfurter Kunstakademie studiert hat, baute die Bettplattform im Zen-Stil aus seidenmatt lackiertem Ahorn. Die japanischen Shoji-Paravents aus Papier verbergen die Toilette. Die bemalten Holzplatten von Karl Dietz, eine Farbstudie, rhythmisieren die Schlafzimmerwände.

In the living room, Dietz and Ehrhardt arrange their collection of classic Modernist furniture by Ray and Charles Eames. The table in the foreground was made by Dietz. The painted wood wall installation is part of a series exploring color variations by Karl Dietz.

Dans le séjour, Karl et Katharina ont disposé leur collection de classiques modernistes de Ray et Charles Eames. La table du premier plan est une réalisation de Karl. L'installation en panneaux de bois peints sur le mur fait partie d'une recherche de l'artiste sur la couleur.

Im Wohnzimmer. Dietz und Ehrhardt haben eine Sammlung von Möbeln der klassischen Moderne von Ray und Charles Eames zusammengetragen. Dietz baute den Tisch im Vordergrund. Die Wandinstallation aus bemalten Holzplatten stammt aus einer Serie von Karl Dietz, die Farbvariationen zum Thema hat.

Le seul nom d'Hollywood évoque des piscines bordées de palmiers bruissant sous le vent. Mais l'architecte Josh Schweitzer et son épouse, la restauratrice Mary Sue Milliken, sont allés beaucoup plus loin. Ils ont tout simplement acquis en 1985, en plein cœur de Los Angeles, un ancien club de natation pour en faire leur petit coin de paradis que Robinson Crusoé n'aurait pas dédaigné. Ce projet qui a duré plus de dix ans n'a pas été une totale partie de plaisir. Les sols de béton étaient bizarrement inclinés, et les vieux bâtiments en bois n'inspiraient guère confiance. L'architecte est un habitué des défis, et le «club house» comme le petit trio de trois pavillons ont gagné en cohésion sans rien perdre de leur côté amusant et ensoleillé. La nouvelle salle à manger et la cuisine ont été découpées dans les anciens bureaux, et les cabines de vestiaire transformées en salle de séjour décorée de mobilier années 50 décontracté, en gardant les pièces aussi ouvertes que possible.

Mary Sue Milliken and Josh Schweitzer

Mention Hollywood, and swimming pools surrounded by rustling palm trees often spring to mind. But architect Josh Schweitzer and his wife, chef Mary Sue Milliken, went one better. They acquired a former swimming club in 1985, and turned it into their own Gilligan's Island home right in the heart of urban Los Angeles. Not that the conversion, which has been a ten-year project, was a piece of cake. Old concrete floors were oddly sloped, and the post-and-beam buildings were an odd lot — dated and funky. The architect is used to diving right into challenges, and the "club house" and a trio of one-story pavilions now feel cohesive but still sunny and fun. The new dining room and kitchen were carved from the former office, and reconfigured changing rooms became a living room with relaxed 50s furniture. He kept the rooms as open as possible.

Denkt man an Hollywood, hat man sofort palmenumstandene Pools vor Augen. Der Architekt Josh Schweitzer und seine Frau, Chefköchin Mary Sue Milliken, setzten noch einen drauf. Sie kauften 1985 einen ehemaligen Schwimmclub im Herzen von Los Angeles und verwandelten ihn in ihre persönliche Robinson-Crusoe-Idylle. Der zehnjährige Umbau war nicht ganz einfach. Die alten Betonböden verliefen in merkwürdigen Schrägen, die gesamte Anlage mit den Gebäuden aus Pfosten und Balken sah bizarr, altmodisch und eigenwillig aus. Josh Schweitzer ist bekannt dafür, daß er keine Herausforderungen scheut. Er stellte einen Zusammenhang zwischen dem Clubhaus und einem Trio von einstöckigen Pavillons her, ohne daß Helligkeit und Leichtigkeit verlorengingen. Die Räume beließ er so offen wie möglich. Das neue Eßzimmer und die Küche entstanden aus dem ehemaligen Büro. Die umgestalteten Umkleidekabinen dienen heute als Wohnzimmer und sind mit legeren Möbeln aus den 50er Jahren ausgestattet.

Architect Josh Schweitzer said he gained his bold color schemes from the Saturday morning kid shows he watched on television, but perhaps it's simply the clear California light that begs splashes of bold color. The remodeled swimming club is now furnished with 50s furniture and has floors of Arizona flagstone. A polygonal soffit which hovers above the kitchen and dining area like an umbrella, is inset with a circular ceiling light. Blue and green tones mirror the pool outside.

L'architecte Josh Schweitzer affirme avoir hérité son goût des couleurs fortes des émissions de télévision du samedi matin qu'il regardait pendant son enfance, mais peut-être est-ce simplement la puissante lumière californienne qui attire ainsi les débauches de couleur. Le club de natation remodelé est maintenant meublé en style années 50, et les sols ont été refaits en dalles de l'Arizona. Un plafond polygonal a été suspendu au-dessus de la cuisine et du coin salle à manger, un peu comme une ombrelle. Une verrière circulaire y a été découpée. Les tonalités bleues et vertes rappellent les reflets de la piscine.

Die gewagten Farben, erzählt der Architekt Josh Schweitzer, habe er aus morgendlichen Kindersendungen im Fernsehen übernommen. Wahrscheinlich verlangt aber das klare kalifornische Licht einfach nach ungewöhnlichen Farben. Der renovierte Schwimmclub ist mit Möbeln aus den 50er Jahren eingerichtet. Die Böden wurden mit Steinplatten aus Arizona ausgelegt. Eine polygonale Zwischendecke schwebt wie ein Regenschirm über Küche und Eßzimmer. Das Licht kommt von einer ringförmigen Deckenleuchte. Die blauen und grünen Töne nehmen die Farben des Pools auf.

Josh Schweitzer, Mary Sue Milliken and their son, Declan. "The boy was able to swim virtually before he could walk," said Schweitzer proudly. "Since we were our own clients, I was able to take my time and experiment with finishes and materials," added the architect, who kept the rooms as open as possible. Schweitzer gained fame in Southern California for the Technicolor interiors of his wife's Border Grill restaurant, in Santa Monica, and for their desert house in Joshua Tree, in the California desert.

Josh, Mary Sue et leur fils Declan. «Le petit a pratiquement nagé avant de marcher», est fier d'annoncer Josh. «Comme nous étions nos propres clients, j'ai pu enfin prendre le temps de m'attacher aux détails, aux finitions et aux matériaux», ajoute l'architecte qui a laissé les pièces aussi ouvertes que possible. Il est réputé en Californie du Sud pour les intérieurs Technicolor du restaurant de sa femme – le Border Grill de Santa Monica – et leur maison de Joshua Tree, en plein désert.

Josh Schweitzer, Mary Sue Milliken und ihr Sohn Declan. »Der Junge konnte schwimmen, bevor er laufen lernte«, sagt Schweitzer stolz. »Da ich mein eigener Kunde war, konnte ich mir bei dem Projekt Zeit lassen und ausgiebig mit Ausführung und Materialien experimentieren«, berichtet der Architekt, der alle Räume so offen wie möglich hielt. Berühmt wurde Schweitzer mit der verrückten Gestaltung des Restaurants seiner Frau Mary in Santa Monica, des Border Grill, den er in Technicolor-Farben ausmalen ließ. Große Anerkennung gab es auch für die Gestaltung ihres Hauses in Joshua Tree, mitten in der kalifornischen Wüste.

Josh Schweitzer said that some of his subliminal inspiration is from classic cartoons, such as "The Jetsons", which he watched as a child. The master bedroom suite, formerly a changing room, looks as if it started its new life as a quick sketch. Schweitzer animated the open space with "cardboard cut-outs" for room dividers, and added broad swathes of shelves for books. He often sculpts new forms first from foam-core to get the spatial geometries right.

Josh affirme tirer une inspiration subliminale de dessins animés classiques, comme les «Jetsons» par exemple, qu'il regardait pendant son enfance. La chambre principale, un ancien vestiaire, a trouvé une nouvelle vie d'un coup de baguette magique. Josh a animé l'espace ouvert par des panneaux découpés qui font office de cloisons et ajouté de multiples étagères pour ses livres. Il sculpte souvent ses formes dans de la mousse de résine pour déterminer avec précision leur géometrie.

Josh Schweitzer sagt, daß einige seiner großartigen Einfälle aus den klassischen Comics seiner Kindheit wie »The Jetsons« stammen. Das Schlafzimmer des Hausherrn, eine ehemalige Umkleidekabine, sieht so aus, als ob es nach einer schnell hingeworfenen Skizze gestaltet sei. Schweitzer beseelte den offenen Raum mit Raumtrennern aus ausgeschnittenem Karton und Bücherregalen. Oft modelliert er neuen Entwürfe zunächst aus Schaumstoff, um die räumliche Geometrie zu verstehen.

Le producteur de films Joel Silver, un des pontes du cinéma hollywoo-dien, a mis les écrans à feu et à sang avec des succès comme «48 heures», la série de «L'Arme fatale», «Une journée en enfer», «La Conspiration» et «The Matrix». Il est aussi connu pour son goût pour le design. Connaisseur de longue date de l'œuvre de Frank Lloyd Wright, il a restauré et ramené à la vie la maison Storer à Los Angeles (voir pages 222–231) et restauré à grand frais l'Auldbrass Plantation, toujours de Wright, en Caroline du Sud. Pour la décoration de sa ca-ravane Teton, il a donc tout naturellement contacté un architecte et décorateur aussi perfectionniste que lui, Thierry Despont, Français établi à New York, qui compte parmi ses clients Bill Gates, Calvin Klein et Ralph Lauren. Les deux hommes se sont amusés à prendre pour point de départ les années 40, époque bénie du design qui vit s'illustrer les premiers grands designers industriels américains dont Raymond Loewy, Donald Deskey et Warren McArthur qui s'effor-çaient de créer le meilleur des mondes avec du mobilier fabriqué en série. Despont a réussi là une intéressante translation des principes modernistes et une réflexion sur les matériaux.

Joel Silver

Film producer Joel Silver, who set the big screen afire with such hits as "48 HRS.", the "Lethal Weapon" series, "Die Hard", "Con-spiracy Theory", and "The Matrix", is also known in Hollywood as a design-savvy movie mogul. A longtime connoisseur of the work of Frank Lloyd Wright, Silver restored and revived the Storer House in Los Angeles (see pages 222–231), and has painstakingly restored Wright's South Carolina plantation, Auldbrass. When the time came to design the interiors of his Teton trailer, Silver contacted the equally perfectionist architect and interior designer, New York-based Thierry Despont, who has worked with Bill Gates, Calvin Klein and Ralph Lauren. Silver and Despont cast their imaginations back to the 40s, a hallowed design era of groundbreaking Ameri-can industrial designers such as Raymond Loewy, Donald Deskey, and Warren McArthur, who created brave new worlds of factory-crafted furniture. Despont deftly translated the Moderne aesthetic, keeping the materials rich but light.

Der Filmproduzent Joel Silver, der mit Kassenschlagern wie »Nur 48 Stunden«, der »Lethal Weapon«-Reihe, »Conspiracy Theory« und »The Matrix« Furore machte, ist in Hollywood auch als designbe-wußter Filmmogul bekannt. Silver, der seit langem die Bauten von Frank Lloyd Wright schätzt, restaurierte das Storer-Haus in Los Ange-les (siehe Seite 222–231) und renovierte in mühsamer Kleinarbeit Wrights Auldbrass-Plantage in South Carolina. Als er dann endlich dazukam, sich um die Inneneinrichtung seines Teton Trailer zu küm-mern, kontaktierte er den gleichermaßen auf Perfektion bedachten New Yorker Interior-Designer Thierry Despont, der zu seinen Kunden Bill Gates, Calvin Klein und Ralph Lauren zählt. Silver und Despont ließen ihre Fantasie bis in die 40er Jahre zurückschweifen, einer ge-weihten Epoche des Design, in der bahnbrechende Industriedesigner wie Raymond Loewy, Donald Deskey und Warren McArthur neue Wohnwelten mit fabrikgefertigten Möbeln schufen. Despont über-setzte die Ästhetik der Moderne, indem er großzügige, aber leichte Materialien verwendete.

Facing page: the streamlined kitchen; the quilt-swathed bed, surrounded by light-controlling lined and inter-lined draperies, offers comfort and solace while on location.

Above and right: Joel Silver's movable command post stands at high noon on the Western set of the Warner Brothers lot in Los Angeles. His 1960 Facel Vega sportscar is an auto fantasy of luscious leather seats and lustrous walnut burl dashwood. On movie locations, Silver is surrounded by the trailer's state-of-the-art electronic equipment, including a television satellite system, and multi-line phones.

Page de gauche: la cuisine très «streamline»; la chambre au lit recouvert d'un quilt, est protégée par des rideaux doublés pour mieux contrôler la lumière et pouvoir se reposer en paix sur la route.

Ci-dessus et à droite: Le Q.G. mobile de Joel Silver parqué à midi sur un décor de la Warner à Los Angeles. Note de luxe encore plus éclatante, un superbe coupé Facel Véga de 1960, à profonds fauteuils de cuir et tableau de bord en noyer verni. Sur les tournages Joel dispose d'un équipement multimédia dernier cri, dont un système de télévision par satellite, et d'une multiplicité de lignes de téléphone.

Linke Seite: die stromlinienförmige Küche; das mit einem Quilt bedeckte Bett bietet Komfort, wenn Silver auf Location ist. Die doppelt gelegten Vorhänge halten den Raum dunkel.

Oben und rechts: Joel Silvers mobiler Kommandoposten um zwölf Uhr mittags auf dem Western-Set des Warner-Brothers-Geländes in Los Angeles. Der Facel-Vega-Sportwagen von 1960 mit seinen luxuriösen Ledersitzen und dem walnußfurnierten Armaturenbrett glänzt silbrig in der Sonne. An den Drehorten steht Silver in dem Trailer allerneuestes technisches Equipment zur Verfügung, darunter ein Satellitenfernseher und eine Telefonanlage mit mehreren Leitungen.

Above: Streamlined Moderne all the way: Silver's vintage 40s chairs and the coffee table were designed by Warren McArthur. The sofa is a refurbished Paul Theodore Frankl design.
Right: The bedroom has been meticulously fitted with a quilt-covered bed, a desk, and a Frank Lloyd Wright chair which was originally in one of the master's turn-of-the-century residences in Oak Park, Illinois.
Facing page: New York-based architect and interior designer Thierry Despont's achievement in Joel Silver's trailer was to make the sitting room feel substantial, comfortable and inviting – far from transitory.

Ci-dessus: Modernisme et «Streamline» omniprésents: les fauteuils des années 40 et la table basse ont été dessinés par Warren McArthur. Le canapé est un modèle restauré de Paul Theodore Frankl.
A droite: La chambre est quasiment remplie par un lit recouvert d'un quilt, un bureau et un siège de Frank Lloyd Wright qui se trouvait à l'origine dans une des résidences édifiées par l'architecte à Oak Park en Illinois, au tournant du siècle.
Page de droite: Basé à New York, Thierry Despont a réussi à créer un salon confortable, accueillant et de dimensions substantielles, qui fait oublier que l'on se trouve dans une caravane.

Oben: Wo man hinsieht, stromlinienförmige Moderne: Silvers Sessel aus den 40er Jahren und der Couchtisch sind Entwürfe von Warren McArthur. Das restaurierte Sofa ist von Paul Theodore Frankl.
Rechts: Das Schlafzimmer wurde sorgfältig eingerichtet mit einem quiltbedeckten Bett, einem Tisch und einem Stuhl von Frank Lloyd Wright, der ursprünglich in einem der Häuser stand, die der Architekt zur Jahrhundertwende in Oak Park in Illinois errichtete.
Rechte Seite: Dem New Yorker Architekten und Interior-Designer Thierry Despont gelang es, das Wohnzimmer in Joel Silvers Trailer gemütlich und einladend zu gestalten.

Le réalisateur de films Joel Schumacher est admiré et applaudi pour ses scénarios et ses longs métrages pleins d'originalité, dont «Batman Forever» et «Batman et Robin». Son œil pour le détail, la couleur, les textures, le souffle et le spectaculaire, comme son oreille pour les dialogues, ont fait de lui un auteur apprécié des critiques et célébré par le public. Dans sa maison située dans un canyon bucolique de Los Angeles, son sens visuel extraordinaire, la sûreté de son goût et son sens de l'assemblage de collections rassemblées depuis toujours transparaissent dans chaque pièce. Les tables, les étagères et les sols font office de scènes de théâtre pour des sculptures et des peintures religieuses mexicaines, de vieilles couvertures de cheval, des objets kitsch américains, des peintures d'amateurs, des vases pique-assiette, des portraits d'élèves d'écoles d'art, des peintures japonaises et des «serapes» du Nouveau-Mexique, des couvertures de laine colorées et tissées à la main. Ce choc culturel jubilatoire fonctionne, précise Joel, parce que ses collections réunissent essentiellement des objets faits à la main qui expriment honnêteté, inspiration et beauté intemporelle.

Joel Schumacher

Film director Joel Schumacher is admired and praised for his fine and original screenplays and movies. "Batman Forever" and "Batman and Robin" are among his many credits. Schumacher's expert calibration of detail, color, texture, dimension, and drama – and his quirky ear for dialogue – set him apart and have made his films critical and cult classics. At his house in a rustic Los Angeles canyon, Schumacher's extraordinary visual sense and his confident and muscular editing of lifelong collections are evident in every room, and on every surface. Cushions and throws made from vintage fabrics tumble on sofas, and shelves and tables and floors are landscapes of Mexican religious statuary and paintings, New Mexican serapes, antique trading blankets, kitsch Americana, village paintings by untutored artists, "pique-assiette" vases covered with broken pieces of porcelain, art-school portraits and Japanese paintings. This exalted culture clash works, says Schumacher, because his collections are mostly handmade. The hands of the artists imbue honesty, soul, and lasting beauty.

Der Regisseur Joel Schumacher wird hoch gelobt für seine hervorragenden, originellen Drehbücher und Filme. »Batman Forever« und »Batman und Robin« zählen zu seinen vielen Erfolgen. Schumachers meisterliches Gespür für Details, Farben, Textur, Raum und Spannung sowie sein feiner Sinn für Dialoge machen seine Filme zu Klassikern bei Kritikern und Publikum. Jedes Zimmer in seinem Haus in einem Canyon in Los Angeles beweist die außergewöhnliche visuelle Begabung von Schumacher, der sein Leben lang sammelte: Kissen und Überdecken aus antiken Stoffen liegen auf den Sofas. Regale, Tische und Böden gleichen Landschaften aus mexikanischen Heiligenfiguren, alten Pferdedecken, amerikanischem Kitsch, Werken von unbekannten Malern, mit Porzellanscherben dekorierten »pique-assiette«-Vasen, Porträts von Kunststudenten, japanischen Malereien und »serapes«, farbenfrohen, handgewebten Wolldecken aus New Mexico. »Diese exaltierte Kulturmischung funktioniert«, sagt Schumacher. Wahrscheinlich deshalb, weil die Stücke alle von Hand gefertigt sind und Ehrlichkeit, Lebendigkeit und Schönheit ausstrahlen.

Previous page: Cosmopolitan and handcrafted, his 25-year collections are stacked on shelves in the kitchen.
Above: Like many others in Los Angeles, Schumacher's house is a comfortable, easygoing piece of architecture – surrounded by verdant gardens and overgrown hillsides.
Right: the pool and "de rigueur" spa.
Facing page: Everyone's dream of California living: Schumacher's day-to-day "mise en scène" around the handsome, stone-flagged pool. Like banners of a fantasy paradise, vivid handwoven Mexican serapes are draped on teak pool chaises longues.

Page précédente: Cosmopolites et artisanales, 25 ans de collections s'étalent en strates variées sur les étagères de la cuisine.
Ci-dessus: Comme beaucoup d'autres à Los Angeles, la maison de Joel est d'une architecture simple et confortable, entourée d'un jardin verdoyant et nichée entre des collines envahies de végétation.
A droite: la piscine et le spa de rigueur.
Page de droite: Un rêve californien: mise en scène schumacherienne autour de la superbe piscine à bordure de pierre. Comme les drapeaux d'un paradis imaginaire, ses »serapes« mexicains de couleurs vives recouvrent les chaises longues de teck.

Vorhergehende Seite: In den Küchenregalen stapelt sich die kosmopolitische Sammlung von handgefertigten Stücken, die Schumacher in 25 Jahren zusammengetragen hat.
Oben: Wie viele Residenzen in Los Angeles ist Schumachers Haus gemütlich und unprätentiös, umgeben von üppigen Gärten.
Rechts: Pool und Jacuzzi.
Rechte Seite: eine Inszenierung à la Schumacher an dem steingefaßten Pool. Wie die Banner eines fantastischen Paradieses sind die mexikanischen »serapes« auf den Liegestühlen aus Teak drapiert.

Previous pages: *Artisans' studios, flea markets, junk shops and crafts galleries around the globe are among the worldly sources for Joel Schumacher's superb art-directed collections.*
Facing page: *In his attic, Joel has installed a gym and office.*
Above: *The Rolodex at Schumacher's bedside indicates that one key to the director's success is his keeping in touch.*
Right: *the bathroom.*

Double page précédente: *Les sources des superbes collections réunies par Joel sont les ateliers d'artisans, les marchés aux puces, les brocantes et les galeries d'artisanat d'art du monde entier.*
Page de gauche: *Dans son grenier, Joel a aménagé un bureau-gym.*
Ci-dessus: *Le Rolodex au chevet du lit du maître de maison montre bien qu'une des raisons de son succès tient à son sens du contact.*
A droite: *la salle de bains.*

Vorhergehende Doppelseite: *Künstlerateliers, Flohmärkte, Secondhand-Geschäfte und Kunsthandwerksläden in der ganzen Welt sind die Quellen, aus denen Joel Schumacher seine exzellente, kunstvoll präsentierte Sammlung bezieht.*
Linke Seite: *Den Speicher funktionierte er in Fitneßraum und Büro um.*
Oben: *Die Rolodex-Adreßdatei neben Schumachers Bett zeigt, daß einer der Schlüssel zum Erfolg in seinen guten Kontakten liegt.*
Rechts: *das Badezimmer.*

Artiste angélinien, Simon Toparovsky est certainement un pionnier à sa façon. Sa collection «United Labor» composée de pièces en bronze moulé à tirage limité, produites en collaboration avec le designer Randy Franks, annonce l'arrivée d'un nouvel âge du bronze fascinant. Mais c'est son audacieuse reconfiguration d'une clinique des années 50 dans le quartier de West Adams à Los Angeles qui lui vaut sa présence ici. Avec détermination, il a transformé un sombre labyrinthe de 20 petites pièces sur 280 m² en un atelier ensoleillé et une maison spacieuse. Le bâtiment n'était pas sans inconvénients. Il fallait, entre autres, débarrasser les murs de l'oxyde nitreux laissé par un dentiste disparu depuis longtemps. Les sols de béton ont été passés à la ponceuse à terrazzo pour retrouver leur aspect d'origine. Pour la cuisine, Toparovsky a mobilisé une pièce étriquée transformée par des portes-fenêtres. «Jamais, je n'aurais pu trouver autant d'espace pour vivre et travailler dans d'autres quartiers de L.A. C'est mon oasis, et elle m'inspire», commente l'artiste.

Simon Toparovsky

Los Angeles artist Simon Toparovsky might be considered a pioneer. He heralds an exciting new bronze age with his limited edition "United Labor" collection of cast-bronze sculptures, produced in collaboration with designer Randy Franks. But it's Toparovsky's brave new reconfiguration of a 50s medical clinic in the Los Angeles West Adams district that deserves a medal. Through determination he turned the 280 sq. m. building, a maze of 20 tiny rooms, into a sunny studio and spacious residence. The commercial building presented a few conundrums. One involved ripping out nitrous oxide lines from the walls, the dentist having long gone. Concrete floors had a quick once-over with a terrazzo grinder to restore the plain concrete. For a kitchen, the artist commandeered a former poky room, and added French doors. "I could never have found so much affordable raw space for living and working anywhere else in Los Angeles," said Toparovsky. "It's my own oasis, very inspiring."

Der Künstler Simon Toparovsky aus Los Angeles ist ein Pionier. Er initiierte eine neue »Bronzezeit« mit einer limitierten Auflage von Skulpturen, die er »United Labor« nennt und die in Zusammenarbeit mit dem Designer Randy Franks entstanden. Ungewöhnlich ist auch Toparovskys »Schöne Neue Welt«, die er sich in einer Klinik aus den 50er Jahren im West Adams District in Los Angeles eingerichtet hat. Dank seiner Entschlossenheit verwandelte er ein Labyrinth von 20 Zimmern auf mehr als 280 m² in ein sonnendurchflutetes Atelier und eine großzügige Residenz. Die ehemalige Klinik hatte ihre Tücken. Lachgasleitungen einer längst geschlossenen Zahnarztpraxis mußten herausgerissen werden, mit einer Terrazzo-Schleifmaschine wurden die ursprünglichen Betonböden wieder hervorgeholt. Eine alte Abstellkammer mutierte zur Küche, durch deren Glastüren das Licht hereinflutet. »Ich hätte nirgendwo sonst in Los Angeles soviel Raum zum Leben und Arbeiten gefunden«, sagte Toparovsky. »Dieses Haus ist meine Oase, es ist ungeheuer inspirierend.«

Previous pages: *Simon Toparovsky displays a series of cast-bronze sculptures on the terrace outside his kitchen. He extended the kitchen 1 m, and decided to leave the large resulting crack in the concrete floor as a decorative element and memory of Southern California earthquakes.*
Above: *An old sink from the clinic comes in handy in the new studio.*
Facing page: *Toparovsky's Jack Russell, Betty, snoozes on a slipcovered chair, one of a pair donated by a friend.*

Double page précédente: *Simon Toparovsky a mis en scène une série de sculptures en bronze moulé sur la terrasse de sa cuisine. Il a élargi celle-ci de 1 m et décidé de ne pas toucher à la fissure du sol de béton causée par ces travaux, en guise d'élément décoratif et de clin d'œil aux tremblements de terre californiens.*
Ci-dessus: *Un vieux bassin de la clinique a trouvé un nouvel emploi dans l'atelier.*
Page de droite: *Le jack-russell Betty sommeille sur un siège houssé, qui appartient à une paire empruntée à un ami.*

Vorhergehende Doppelseite: *Auf der Terrasse vor der Küche hat Toparovsky einige seiner Bronzeskulpturen aufgestellt. Er erweiterte die Küche um 1 m. Der dabei entstandene große Riß im Betonboden blieb als dekoratives Element, weil er an die Erdbeben in Südkalifornien erinnert.*
Oben: *das alte Krankenhauswaschbecken im neuen Atelier.*
Rechte Seite: *Auf dem Sessel schläft Toparovskys Jack-Russell-Terrier Betty. Zu dem Sessel gibt es noch ein Pendant – die Leihgabe eines Freundes.*

L'imagination délirante fait partie des composantes de l'esprit angélinien. Le décorateur Randy Franks s'est appuyé sur ses vastes talents
théâtraux pour insuffler un peu de «show» et de «romance» à deux
bungalows contigus que possèdent à Venice ses clients de longue date,
Kathleen Cornell, agent d'artiste, et Chuck Bennett, directeur artistique chez TBWA Chiat/Day, une célèbre agence de publicité. Bien
situés, non loin de la plage, les deux cottages des années 40 man-
quaient pourtant de distinction. Jay Griffith les a entourés d'un impressionnant jardin. Kathleen et Chuck ne craignent pas les couleurs
fortes, et Randy Franks a badigeonné les mur d'orange, de bleu
bleuet, de jaune citron, d'indigo et de vert cactus pour offrir un écrin
raffiné à un mobilier rare de série limitée. «J'ai recherché des éléments un peu osés, mais plutôt romantiques», précise-t-il. «Les cabinets de Fornasetti et la commode d'Elisabeth Garouste et Mattia
Bonetti ont fini par constituer l'architecture de chaque pièce ...»

Kathleen Cornell
and Chuck Bennett

Fantasy is the stock-in-trade of Los Angeles. Interior designer
Randy Franks leaned heavily on his considerable theatrical talents
to create drama and romance in two side-by-side Venice bungalows
for long-time clients, Kathleen Cornell, an artist's agent, and Chuck
Bennett, a creative director at TBWA Chiat/Day, an award-winning
advertising agency. The couple's pair of 40s stucco cottages were
well-located near the beach but lacked architectural distinction. Jay
Griffith designed a dramatic garden to make the houses sing in
unison. Bennett and Cornell are not afraid of strong colors so
Franks splashed tangerine, cornflower blue, lemon yellow, indigo,
and cactus on the walls as a fine foil for limited-edition furniture.
"I sought out bold but rather romantic pieces," said Franks. "In
the end, the Piero Fornasetti cabinets and the chest by Elisabeth
Garouste and Mattia Bonetti became the architecture for the
rooms."

Fantasie wird heiß gehandelt in Los Angeles. Interior-Designer Randy
Franks verließ sich auf seine theatralische Begabung, um Drama und
Romantik in die beiden nebeneinander stehenden Bungalows am Venice Beach einziehen zu lassen. Sie gehören seinen langjährigen Kunden, der Künstleragentin Kathleen Cornell und Chuck Bennett, Art-
Director bei TBWA Chiat/Day, einer vielfach ausgezeichneten
Werbeagentur. Die beiden mörtelverputzten Cottages aus den 40er
Jahren lagen nur ein paar Minuten vom Beach entfernt, ließen archi-
tektonisch allerdings zu wünschen übrig. Jay Griffith legte einen ein-
drucksvollen Garten an, der die beiden Häuser optisch zusammen-
faßt. Da Bennett und Cornell keine Angst vor kräftigen Farben haben,
tobte sich Franks aus: mit Orange, Kornblumenblau, Zitronengelb,
Indigo und Kakteengrün – ein perfekter Hintergrund für die Möbel
aus limitierter Auflage. »Ich suchte gewagte, aber romantische
Stücke aus«, sagt Franks. »Am Ende waren es das Schränkchen von
Piero Fornasetti sowie die Kommode von Elisabeth Garouste und
Mattia Bonetti, die die Raumarchitektur beherrschten.«

Previous pages: *Geraniums, bougainvillea and a lantern create a stage set in the garden, designed by Jay Griffith.*
Right: *Classic "Ox" chairs with matching ottomans, designed in the 6os by Hans J. Wegner, were crafted by Erik Jorgensen. A pair of solid white oak tables by Christian Liaigre accompany the chairs in the media room.*
Below: *A Piero Fornasetti "Sole" chair peeks over the dining table, crafted loosely after the traditional Portuguese farmhouse table style, in white gesso and black lacquer. Massimo Iosa Ghini's 8os airstream "Velox" chairs were crafted in maple, chrome and leather.*

Page précédente: *Des géraniums, des bougainvillées et une lanterne créent une petite scène dans le jardin dessiné par Jay Griffith.*
A droite: *Les classiques fauteuils «Ox» à pouf assorti ont été dessinés dans les années 6o par Hans J. Wegner et fabriqués par Erik Jorgensen. Une paire de tables de chêne massif de Christian Liaigre accompagnent les sièges du salon de télévision.*
Ci-dessous: *Une chaise «Sole» de Piero Fornasetti dont le soleil jette un œil par-dessus la table en plâtre blanc et laque noire, inspirée de celles des fermes portugaises traditionnelles. Les fauteuils aérodynamiques «Velox» de Massimo Iosa Ghini – années 8o – sont en érable, chrome et cuir.*

Vorhergehende Seite: *Geranien, Bougainvillea und eine Laterne bilden eine hübsche Szenerie im Garten, den Jay Griffith angelegt hat.*
Rechts: *Die klassischen »Ox«-Sessel mit passendem Hocker im Fernsehzimmer, Entwürfe aus den 6oer Jahren von Hans J. Wegner, sind Nachbauten von Erik Jorgensen. Die beiden weißen Beistelltische aus Eiche sind von Christian Liaigre.*
Unten: *Ein »Sole«-Stuhl von Piero Fornasetti lugt über den Rand des Eßtisches. Dieser wurde im Stil traditioneller portugiesischer Bauerntische in weißem Gips und schwarzem Lack gearbeitet. Die aerodynamischen »Velox«-Armlehnstühle von Massimo Iosa Ghini aus den 8oer Jahren sind aus Ahorn, Chrom und Leder.*

Above: In a superb design collaboration, Gio Ponti designed the elaborate "Architettura" secretaire, which was decorated as pure fantasy after a Genoese palace by Piero Fornasetti. In the dressing room background, a mid-80s "Peapod" chair is an indoor and outdoor piece crafted of powder-coated steel.
Right: A B&B Italia chaise longue of woven leather has custom-dyed Spinneybeck leather upholstery. The white and gold-leaf chest is one of a limited edition of eight by Elisabeth Garouste and Mattia Bonetti.

Ci-dessus: Superbe exemple de collaboration créative, ce complexe secrétaire «Architettura» dessiné par Gio Ponti a reçu un fabuleux décor de Piero Fornasetti, inspiré d'un palais gênois. Au fond du dressing-room, le fauteuil «Peapod» en acier poudré, du milieu des années 80, va aussi bien à l'intérieur qu'à l'extérieur.
A droite: une chaise longue B&B Italia en cuir tressé et ses coussins recouverts de cuir Spinneybeck teint sur commande. La commode blanche et dorée à la feuille d'Elisabeth Garouste et Mattia Bonetti fait partie d'une série limitée de huit exemplaires.

Oben: Der Sekretär »Architettura« ist das Ergebnis einer einmaligen Zusammenarbeit von Designern: Entworfen von Gio Ponti, wurde er von Piero Fornasetti fantasievoll nach dem Vorbild eines genuesischen Palazzo dekoriert. Der »Peapod«-Armlehnstuhl aus gepudertem Stahl im Ankleidezimmer im Hintergrund wurde Mitte der 80er Jahre entworfen und dient gleichzeitig als Innen- und Außenmöbel.
Rechts: Die Chaiselongue von B&B Italia aus geflochtenem Leder wurde mit handgefärbtem Spinneybeck-Leder bezogen. Die weiße, mit Blattgold verzierte Kommode ist eines von acht Stücken aus der limitierten Serie von Elisabeth Garouste und Mattia Bonetti.

Facing page: The balmy Los Angeles coastal weather means that bathroom windows can be left open and bathers may enjoy views of the garden. An aluminum "Klismos" chair stands on the concrete floor of the bathroom.
Above: Leopard-print velvet pillows recline on antique Belgian sheets on the bed. The bedside table, a flea-market find lacquered with silver for glamor, is draped with an antique linen cloth.

Page de gauche: Le temps clément de la côte de Los Angeles permet de laisser la fenêtre de la salle de bains ouverte, pour mieux bénéficier de la vue sur le jardin en prenant son bain. Une chaise d'aluminium «Klismos» est posée sur le sol en béton.
Ci-dessus: Des coussins en velours léopard contrastent avec les draps belges anciens en lin. Le chevet, découvert au marché aux puces et laqué argent pour plus de «glamour», est drapé d'une nappe de lin ancien.

Linke Seite: Das milde Küstenklima von Los Angeles erlaubt es, die Badezimmerfenster offen stehen zu lassen und beim Baden den Blick auf den Garten zu genießen. Auf dem Betonboden steht der »Klismos«-Stuhl aus Aluminium.
Oben: Samtkissen in Leopardenoptik liegen auf dem mit altem belgischem Leinen bezogenen Bett. Der Nachttisch vom Flohmarkt wurde in glitzerndem Silber lackiert und darauf ein antiker Leinenstoff drapiert.

Après une brillante carrière de directeur artistique et d'innombrables «dead-lines», David Cruz a finalement trouvé sa vocation. En 1993, ce personnage vif s'est associé à son ami Adam Blackman pour fonder Blackman/Cruz, une galerie d'antiquités très observée pas ses consœurs. Installée dans le Design Center de West Hollywood, elle est devenue incontournable pour le mobilier des années 50, les pendules françaises anciennes, les urnes antiques, les maquettes d'architecture fin de siècle et les tableaux et textiles de collection. Dans son appartement de Santa Monica, David a imposé son style. Originaire de Chihuahua au nord du Mexique, il s'est focalisé sur les souvenirs de Grand Tour, les urnes sculpturales, les textiles africains, les icônes, et les peintures coloniales mexicaines. Mais sa nouvelle orientation – il le jure – est le minimalisme. «Je vais essayer de conserver juste ce qu'il faut pour distraire un peu le regard», insiste-t-il, «je veux sentir une émotion vraie pour tout ce que je rapporte chez moi. Lorsqu'un siège, une lampe ou une peinture religieuse ne me dit plus rien, je les renvoie au magasin», ajoute le décorateur.

David Cruz

After a lively career and too many deadlines as an art director, David Cruz finally found his calling. In 1993, the kinetic Cruz joined forces with his friend Adam Blackman to open Blackman/Cruz. Their trend-setting antiques gallery, in the heart of the West Hollywood design center, has become Action Central for the best mid-century furniture, old French clocks, ancient urns, turn-of-the-century architectural models, and highly collectible paintings and textiles. In his Santa Monica apartment, Cruz sets his own tone. The designer, originally from Chihuahua, in Northern Mexico, zeroes in on Grand Tour souvenirs, sculptural urns, African textiles, religious icons, and Mexican colonial paintings. But his new direction, he swears, is minimalism. "I'm going to try to keep just enough things to keep my eyes entertained," he insists. "I have to have an emotional reaction toward anything I bring home. When I no longer get excited about my chairs or lamps or religious paintings, I send them back to the store."

Nach einer steilen Karriere als Art-Director und zu vielen Deadlines fand David Cruz schließlich seine wahre Bestimmung. 1993 tat sich der dynamische Cruz mit seinem Freund Adam Blackman zusammen und gründete die Firma Blackman/Cruz. Die Antikgalerie im Herzen des West Hollywood Design Center bestimmt nicht nur Trends, sondern ist auch die beste Adresse für Möbel der 50er Jahre, alte französische Uhren, antike Urnen, Architekturmodelle der Jahrhundertwende sowie Gemälde und Textilien mit hohem Sammlerwert. In seinem Apartment in Santa Monica lebt Cruz seinen eigenen Stil. Der Designer, der aus Chihuahua in Mexiko stammt, schwört auf Souvenirs, die er auf seinen Reisen sammelt: figürliche Urnen, afrikanische Stoffe, Heiligenbilder und mexikanische Gemälde aus der Kolonialzeit. Sein neuer Lebensstil allerdings, sagt er, sei der Minimalismus. »Ich werde versuchen, nur so viel zu behalten, daß mein Auge etwas zu gucken hat«, behauptet er. »Zu allem, was ich nach Hause bringe, muß ich eine emotionale Beziehung haben. Wenn ich mich nicht mehr über meine Stühle, Lampen oder religiösen Gemälde freuen kann, bringe ich sie zurück in den Laden.«

California Interiors   David Cruz

Above: Geometric-patterned Kuba cloth from Africa is draped over the sofa, which was unearthed at the Rose Bowl Flea Market in Pasadena. The rocker is 19th-century English, and "very comfortable".
Facing page: Cruz designs rooms without reference to geography. His 50s chairs were crafted in Los Angeles, and his large rusted metal urns on the terrace were discovered in Indiana. Cruz has a special fondness for the glass specimen jars on the tabletop, which were deaccessioned by the laboratories at the Kew Gardens study center near London.

Ci-dessus: Des étoffes africaines Kuba, tissées à la main et décorées de motifs géometriques, sont jetées sur le canapé, découvert au marché aux puces du Rose Bowl à Pasadena. Le siège à bascule est anglais, 19e, et très confortable, selon son propriétaire. Le paravent de bois provient d'un café français.
Page de droite: David conçoit ses pièces sans référence à la géographie. Ses chaises des années 50 ont été fabriquées à Los Angeles, et les grands vases en métal rouillé de la terrasse découverts dans l'Indiana. Il a un faible pour les bocaux de verre disposés sur la table, qui ont été achetés lors d'une vente aux enchères des laboratoires de Kew Gardens près de Londres.

Oben: Handgenähte afrikanische Kuba-Decken mit geometrischem Muster wurden auf dem Sofa drapiert, das Cruz auf dem Rose-Bowl-Flohmarkt in Pasadena aufgestöbert hat. Der Schaukelstuhl ist englisches 19. Jahrhundert und laut Cruz »sehr bequem«. Der hölzerne Paravent stand einmal in einem französischen Bistro.
Rechte Seite: Cruz richtet Räume ein, ohne sich im geringsten um Geographie zu kümmern. Seine 50er-Jahre-Stühle wurden in L.A. gefertigt, die großen, rostigen Metallurnen auf der Terrasse stammen aus Indiana. Cruz hängt besonders an den Laborgläsern auf dem Tisch, die er dem Laboratorium des Studienzentrums der Kew Gardens bei London abluchste.

Bub and Sis

Rimes No. 3

Après 40 ans passés à l'étranger, l'artiste américain Ronald B. Kitaj a emménagé avec son fils, Max, dans une maison de style Monterey du verdoyant quartier de Westwood à Los Angeles. En 1997, il a demandé à l'entreprise Israel Callas Shortridge Associates de transformer le garage en atelier de peinture. Après avoir vécu beaucoup d'années dans une maison victorienne de Chelsea à Londres, il trouvait assez surprenante l'idée de disposer d'une piscine. «On nous a demandé de transformer un garage à toit de tuiles mansardé en un atelier ouvert à la lumière du nord», explique Barbara Callas. «Il voulait en faire une sorte de maison du bonheur.» De Chelsea, Kitaj envoya ses références de couleurs – jaune de cadmium, jaune de chrome, ocre jaune, terre de Sienne – à partir desquelles les architectes ont créé leur palette. Kitaj ne sait pas encore jusqu'à quel point la fameuse lumière de L. A., le paysage californien et son nouvel environnement affecteront sa peinture. Mais six mois plus tard, les Marx Brothers apparaissaient déjà dans ses tableaux.

Ronald B. Kitaj

After 40 years abroad, the American artist Ronald B. Kitaj moved to a Monterey-style house in the leafy Westwood area of Los Angeles with his son, Max. In 1997, he engaged the architectural firm Israel Callas Shortridge Associates to convert the garage into a painting studio. After living in a Victorian house in Chelsea for many years, Kitaj found the swimming pool quite novel. "Our brief was to turn a stucco garage with a clay tile mansard roof into a painting studio filled with Northern light," said Barbara Callas. "He wanted to make this into a 'House of Life'." From Chelsea, Kitaj sent lists of oil paint colors – cadmium yellow, chrome yellow, yellow ochre, raw sienna – and the architects developed their color palette. Kitaj said that he was still uncertain how the famous Los Angeles light, Southern California streetscapes, and his new environment would affect his paintings. But even after six months, Hollywood – in the guise of the Marx Brothers – was creeping into his paintings.

Nach 40jährigem Auslandsaufenthalt zog der amerikanische Künstler Ronald B. Kitaj ins grüne Westwood-Viertel von Los Angeles. Dort lebt er mit seinem Sohn Max in einem Haus im Monterey-Stil. Im Jahr 1997 engagierte er das Architekten-Team Israel Callas Shortridge Associates, um die dazugehörige Garage in ein Studio umbauen zu lassen. Nachdem Kitaj lange in einem viktorianischen Haus in Chelsea, dem Künstlerviertel Londons, gelebt hatte, war es für ihn ziemlich überraschend, plötzlich einen Swimmingpool zu haben. »Unsere Aufgabe war es«, sagt Barbara Callas, »eine roh verputzte Garage mit ziegelgedecktem Mansardendach in ein Maleratelier mit Nordlicht zu verwandeln. Kitaj wollte ein ›lebendiges Haus‹ haben.« Von Chelsea aus schickte Kitaj eine Liste mit Farbwünschen: Kadmiumgelb, Chromgelb, Ocker und Ockergelb. Die Architekten mixten daraus ihre eigene Farbpalette. Kitaj war sich nicht sicher, inwiefern das berühmte Licht von Los Angeles, das südkalifornische Straßenbild und die neue Umgebung sich auf seine Gemälde auswirken würden. Doch schon nach sechs Monaten tauchte Hollywood in seinen Bildern auf: in den Personen der Marx Brothers.

Shades of Saint-Rémy-de-Provence and Arles: The cheerful sunflower yellow walls of the 56 sq.m. studio and the vibrant blue of the pool bring to mind Van Gogh's chrome yellow house and cobalt skies. Architects Barbara Callas and Steven Shortridge tilted the new roof and opened the north facade with a bank of clerestory windows, 1.8 m high and 6 m long. They retained the original door and tiny windows on the pool side. The building interior itself acts as a canvas for the artist who pins, hangs, and stands works in progress and completed paintings around the space. Collages of pictures are on the walls, which are clad in white-painted cork.

Souvenirs de Saint-Rémy-de-Provence et d'Arles: le chaleureux jaune tournesol des murs de l'atelier de 56 m² et le bleu vibrant de la piscine font penser à la maison jaune de chrome de Van Gogh et à ses ciels de cobalt. Les architectes Barbara Callas et Steven Shortridge ont incliné le nouveau toit et ouvert sur la façade nord un bandeau de fenêtres de 6 m de long sur 1,80 m de haut. Ils ont conservé la porte d'origine et les petites ouvertures côté piscine. Pour l'artiste, l'intérieur est une toile sur laquelle il épingle, tend et appuie ses œuvres en cours ou ses tableaux achevés. Des collages d'images qui l'inspirent sont punaisés aux murs recouverts de liège peint en blanc.

Erinnerungen an Saint-Rémy-de-Provence und Arles: Die fröhlichen, sonnenblumengelben Wände des 56 m²-Studios und das brillante Blau des Pools lassen an das gelbe Haus Van Goghs und den kobaltblauen Himmel auf dessen Gemälden denken. Die Architekten Barbara Callas und Steven Shortridge gaben dem neuen Dach mehr Schräge und öffneten die Nordfassade mit einem Band von klerikal wirkenden Fenstern, das 1,80 m hoch und 6 m lang ist. Die originale Tür und die winzigen Fenster an der Pool-Seite blieben bestehen. Der Innenraum dient dem Künstler als gigantische Leinwand, auf der er angefangene und vollendete Werke stellen, heften, verhüllen kann.

California Interiors   Ronald B. Kitaj

San Francisco

La penthouse au 25ᵉ étage d'une tour de San Francisco tient à la fois du belvédère, du club de nuit et du petit coin de paradis. «J'ai choisi cet espace pour ses vues et non son architecture», précise le propriétaire, un jeune restaurateur et homme d'affaires. «Le plan des années 50 était fondamentalement maladroit et laid». Les deux penthouses acquises étaient encombrées de petites pièces et de plafonds bas. «Rien ne pouvait inspirer quoi que ce soit, aussi avons nous dû inventer une architecture intérieure spectaculaire», poursuit-il, et il a demandé aux décorateurs Stephen Weaver et Craig Leavitt, de l'agence de Modesto Leavitt/Weaver, d'intervenir. Après avoir mis à nu la coquille de béton, ils ont doublé les mur d'écrans à la japonaise en fibre de verre, coulé des sols en béton teint à la main, tendu les murs de mohair, créé des rangements en médium peint, doré et texturé les murs, et apporté tout un mobilier sur roulettes. Ils ont parachevé leur œuvre par des juxtapositions habiles de somptueux velours couleur bronze et mousse, de bois noueux et de cuirs gris brouillard.

A Penthouse in San Francisco

The 26th-floor San Francisco penthouse is part super-sophisticated cloud club, part funhouse, and an entirely original "haute" haven. "I chose this space for the views, not for its original architecture," said the owner, a young restaurateur and businessman. "The 50s layout was so awkward and ugly in basics." The pair of penthouses he acquired had small rooms, low ceilings. "I wasn't handed anything inspirational, so we had to invent spectacular interior architecture," said the owner. He commissioned Stephen Weaver and Craig Leavitt, of the Modesto-based Leavitt/Weaver design firm, to craft his new digs. After carving out a bare concrete shell, they lined the walls with fiberglass shoji screens, and dreamed up hand-tinted concrete floors, kinetic furniture on casters, mohair-upholstered walls, painted particle-board cabinets, and rock-textured gilded walls. Leavitt and Weaver deftly juxtaposed lavish bronze and moss-colored velvets, with burl woods and fog-colored leather.

Das Penthouse im 25. Stock eines Hochhauses in San Francisco ist gleichzeitig ein kultivierter Club hoch über den Wolken und eine wirklich witzige Wohnung. »Ich lebe hier wegen der Aussicht, nicht wegen der originellen Architektur«, sagt der Besitzer, ein junger Restaurator und Geschäftsmann. »Der Grundriß aus den 50er Jahren war unbeholfen und unansehnlich«. Das Duplex hatte ursprünglich winzige Zimmer mit niedrigen Decken. »Als ich es übernahm, gab es gar nichts Inspirierendes hier. Wir mußten selber die atemberaubende Inneneinrichtung in Angriff nehmen«, sagt der Hausherr. Er beauftragte Stephen Weaver und Craig Leavitt von Leavitt/Weaver Design in Modesto mit der Umgestaltung der Räume. Sie schälten die nackten Betonwände heraus, zogen Wände aus Fiberglas mit Shoji-Effekt ein, gossen handgefärbte Betonböden, stellten Möbelstücke auf Rollen und bemalte Preßholzschränke auf. Die Wände wurden mit Mohair gepolstert oder mit Rauhputz versehen und in Gold gestrichen. Leavitt und Weaver kombinierten üppige, bronze- und moosfarbene Samtstoffe mit knotigen Hölzern und Leder in der Farbe des Nebels.

Previous pages, left: Craig Leavitt and Stephen Weaver.
Previous pages, right: The designers contrasted elegant leather and silk taffeta with hard-edge, machine-made aluminum fireplace mantels, olive and bronze-stained particle-board – an inexpensive composite commonly known as MDF.
Right: The oval-shaped library is filled with ancient volumes and witty trompe l'œil wooden "volumes" painted by Leavitt.
Below: On the south-facing side of the penthouse, a study, dressing rooms and a romantic bedroom all face city views and sunshine.

Double page précédente, à gauche: Craig Leavitt et Stephen Weaver.
Double page précédente, à droite: Les décorateurs ont joué les contrastes entre les cuirs, les taffetas de soie, les manteaux de la cheminée en aluminium à angles vifs produits industriellement, les panneaux en contreplaqué teinté olive et bronze – un support bon marché connu sous le nom de MDF.
A droite: La bibliothèque ovale est bourrée de livres anciens et de faux «volumes» en bois, peints par Leavitt.
Ci-dessous: Côté sud, un bureau, des dressing-rooms et une chambre à coucher romantique font face au soleil et à la ville.

Vorhergehende Doppelseite, links: Craig Leavitt und Stephen Weaver.
Vorhergehende Doppelseite, rechts: Die Designer schufen einen interessanten Kontrast aus elegantem Leder, Seidentaft, scharfkantigen, industriell gefertigten Kaminsimsen aus Aluminium sowie in Olivgrün und Bronze getönten Preßholztafeln – ein preiswertes Material, auch bekannt als MDF.
Rechts: Die Bibliothek ist bis an den Rand gefüllt mit antiquarischen Büchern und Buchrepliken aus Holz, die von Leavitt bemalt wurden.
Unten: Im Südbereich des Penthouse liegen ein Arbeitszimmer, die Ankleidezimmer und ein romantisches Schlafzimmer – alle sonnig und mit Blick auf die City.

Above: The bathroom, wrapped with faux stone walls, has a stone-mounted spa bath, positioned to catch the sunset. The open shower is on the right. From the tub, it is possible to view the Golden Gate Bridge, San Francisco Bay, Russian Hill, and the wooded reaches of the Presidio.
Right: In the south-east corner, floor-to-ceiling windows overlook the city and Telegraph Hill. The living room is a movable arrangement of tufted leather and chartreuse velvet sofas on custom-made, cone-shaped aluminium casters.

Ci-dessus: La salle de bains, aux murs enduits en fausse pierre, possède un bain à remous monté sur pierre, placé pour observer le coucher de soleil. De la baignoire, on aperçoit jusqu'au pont du Golden Gate, la baie de San Francisco, Russian Hill et les abords boisés du Presidio. A droite, la douche ouverte.
A droite: Côté sud-est, des baies toute hauteur donnent sur la ville et Telegraph Hill. Le salon est une mise en scène modulable de sièges de cuir garnis de glands, de canapés de velours chartreuse montés sur roulettes coniques en aluminium spécialement créées pour la pièce.

Oben: Im Bad, das mit imitiertem Stein verkleidet ist, steht eine in Stein gefaßte Badewanne. Sie ist so ausgerichtet, daß man von ihr aus den Sonnenuntergang beobachten kann. Wenn man in der Wanne liegt, blickt man auf die Golden Gate Bridge, die Bucht von San Francisco, Russian Hill und die bewaldeten Ausläufer des Presidio. Rechts die offene Dusche.
Rechts: In der Südostecke reichen die Fenster vom Boden bis zur Decke, und man blickt direkt über die Stadt und den Telegraph Hill. Im Wohnzimmer steht ein mobiles Arrangement aus dick gepolsterten Ledersofas und Sesseln, die mit grünem Samt bezogen sind. Sie ruhen auf maßgefertigten, konischen Aluminiumrollen.

«J'adore le design américain du milieu de ce siècle, en particulier le mobilier des années 50», annonce d'emblée Chris Baisa, décorateur et designer de meubles installé à San Francisco. Il cite d'ailleurs le légendaire designer George Nelson comme l'une des figures qui l'ont le plus influencé. Son pied-à-terre en ville est minuscule, et ses 46 m² comptent tout juste une pièce et demie. Il est meublé avec style d'un canapé «Steel Frame» de Nelson, de son fauteuil «Kangaroo» de 1958, d'une lampe de table «Half Nelson», d'une lampe «Bubble» et de nombreuses autres créations fameuses du maître. Chris, qui admire également des designers contemporains comme Ron Arad et Gae Aulenti, a lancé en 1995 sa propre agence de design de meuble, Delinear, et a récemment présenté sa première table basse. Sculptée avec vigueur, ce modèle à deux niveaux repose sur un piètement d'acier très nelsonien. Chris Baisa déteste le concept du marché de masse du «bon goût». «Tout le monde devrait pouvoir créer un environnement à son image», aime-t-il à dire.

Chris Baisa

"I love American mid-century design and especially 50s furniture," said Chris Baisa, a San Francisco interior and furniture designer. He cites American furniture design legend, George Nelson, as one of his major influences. Baisa's city pied-à-terre is just a slip of an apartment; 46 sq.m. and barely one and a half rooms. It's stylishly composed with Nelson's "Steel Frame" sofa, his 1958 "Kangaroo" armchair, a "Half Nelson" table lamp, a "Bubble" lamp, and as many other Nelson icons as Baisa can comfortably arrange. Baisa, who also admires contemporary designers such as Ron Arad and Gae Aulenti, started his own furniture design company, Delinear, in 1995 and recently introduced its first coffee table. Boldly sculpted, the two-level table is supported on Nelsonesque steel legs. Baisa dislikes the concept of mass marketing "good taste". "Everyone should challenge themselves to create an environment as a reflection of who they are," he said.

»Ich liebe amerikanisches Design der 50er Jahre, vor allem die Möbel«, sagt der Interior- und Möbel-Designer Chris Baisa aus San Francisco. Der legendäre amerikanische Designer George Nelson ist von allen Gestaltern dieser Epoche Baisas Idol. Baisas City-Absteige ist ein Mini-Apartment: gerade mal anderthalb Zimmer auf 46 m². Dennoch ist die Wohnung elegant eingerichtet mit dem berühmten »Steel Frame«-Sofa, dem »Kangaroo«-Sessel von 1958, der »Half Nelson«-Tischleuchte und der »Bubble«-Lampe: Nelson-Design, wohin man schaut. 1995 gründete Baisa, der auch zeitgenössische Designer wie Ron Arad und Gae Aulenti bewundert, seine Firma Delinear, und kürzlich brachte er seinen ersten Couchtisch heraus. Der Tisch mit den kühnen Formen verfügt über zwei Ebenen, die auf stählernen Beinen à la Nelson ruhen. Besonders verheerend findet Baisa die Massenvermarktung des sogenannten guten Geschmacks. »Jeder sollte die Herausforderung annehmen, seine Umwelt der eigenen Persönlichkeit entsprechend zu gestalten«, sagt er.

Previous pages, left: *Chris Baisa with his mid-century collections; the orange table is Baisa's new "Suspension" table, made of stainless steel and hand-rubbed lacquered wood.*
Previous pages, right: *The designer has made some lucky vintage furniture finds. He discovered the Isamu Noguchi dining table dating from 1952 in the cafeteria of a building which was about to be demolished. The Eero Saarinen dining chairs are from 1948.*
Facing page, above and right: *Baisa combined the strict geometries of George Nelson's work with the sensual curves of several Italian lighting designs.*

Double page précédente, à gauche: *Chris Baisa au milieu de sa collection des années 50; la table orange est le nouveau modèle «Suspension» qu'il a dessiné, en acier inoxydable et bois laqué frotté.*
Double page précédente, à droite: *Designer, Chris a fait quelques intéressantes trouvailles. Il a ainsi découvert la table à manger d'Isamu Noguchi de 1952 dans la cafétéria d'un immeuble que l'on allait démolir. Les chaises de table d'Eero Saarinen sont de 1948.*
Page de gauche, ci-dessus et à droite: *Chris a tempéré la stricte géométrie des créations de George Nelson par les courbes sensuelles de luminaires italiens.*

Vorhergehende Doppelseite, links: *Chris Baisa und seine 50er-Jahre-Sammlung; der orangefarbene Tisch aus rostfreiem Stahl und lackiertem Holz heißt »Suspension« und ist sein eigener Entwurf.*
Vorhergehende Doppelseite, rechts: *Der Designer hatte Glück und fand diesen Eßtisch von Isamu Noguchi von 1952 in der Cafeteria eines Gebäudes, das abgerissen werden sollte. Die Eero-Saarinen-Eßzimmerstühle stammen von 1948.*
Linke Seite, oben und rechts: *Chris Baisa lockerte die strenge Geometrie Nelsons durch die sinnlichen Formen italienischer Leuchtobjekte auf.*

Above left: Almost monastic in its simplicity, Baisa's bedroom is furnished with a steel-frame George Nelson bedside table, Nelson's iconic "Bubble" lamp and a steel-framed bed.

Above right: The somewhat sinister white lamp "La Ruspa" (the scraper) by Italian architect Gae Aulenti was designed in 1968. It stands on a George Nelson laminate and steel desk designed in 1954 for Herman Miller. The painting "Interiors" dating from 1946 is by Patricia Harris.

Facing page: In a corner of the living room, Baisa has placed a George Nelson steel-framed chair, designed for Herman Miller, a Flos lamp, and a George Nelson clock.

Ci-dessus, à gauche: Presque monastique dans sa simplicité, la chambre est meublée d'une table de chevet à structure d'acier de George Nelson, de sa célèbre lampe «Bubble», et d'un lit métallique.

Ci-dessus, à droite: L'assez sinistre lampe blanche «La Ruspa» (la râpe) de l'architecte italienne Gae Aulenti a été dessinée en 1968. Elle est posée sur un secrétaire d'acier lamifié de George Nelson créé en 1954 pour Herman Miller. La peinture «Interiors» de 1946 est signée Patricia Harris.

Page de gauche: Un coin de séjour est occupé par un fauteuil à structure d'acier de George Nelson pour Herman Miller, d'un lampadaire Flos et d'une pendule de George Nelson.

Oben links: Das Schlafzimmer ist klösterlich einfach gehalten mit einem Stahlrohr-Nachttisch von George Nelson, dessen berühmter »Bubble«-Lampe und einem Bett aus Stahlrohr.

Oben rechts: Der unheimlich wirkende weiße Leuchtkörper heißt »La Ruspa« (Der Schaber) und wurde 1968 von der italienischen Architektin Gae Aulenti entworfen. Er steht auf einem Schreibtisch aus Stahl mit Laminat, den Nelson 1954 für Herman Miller gestaltete. Das Gemälde »Interiors« malte Patricia Harris 1946.

Rechte Seite: In einer Ecke des Wohnzimmers schuf Baisa eine wohnliche Einheit mit dem Stahlrohr-Sessel, den Nelson ebenfalls für Herman Miller entwarf, einer Lampe von Flos und einer Nelson-Uhr.

Elsa Cameron, qui vient de Californie du Nord, a acquis sur un coup de cœur cette maison de 1908 dans le quartier de Castro à San Francisco à la fin de la grande période hippie du «Summer of Love». Le style est néo-victorien californien, avec un soupçon d'Arts and Crafts pour faire bonne mesure. Edifiée à l'origine pour le contremaître d'une fabrique de tuiles finlandaise locale, la petite maison est restée intacte. «Je suis à quelques pas du vieux cinéma de Castro, de tout plein de charmants cafés et de boutiques bio», raconte Elsa qui organise des expositions pour les galeries de l'aéroport de San Francisco. Elle a installé une nouvelle cuisine carrelée et une salle de bains à la place de celle de jadis confinée dans un appentis, et a revigoré toutes les pièces par son choix de couleurs. Dans cette maison amusante, tous les meubles proviennent de marchés aux puces, de ventes aux enchères, de brocantes, d'antiquaires, ou ont été trouvés dans la rue. L'approche de la propriétaire: beaucoup d'œuvres d'art, des formes très libres, pas de purisme de principe.

Elsa Cameron

Elsa Cameron acquired her Castro-district 1908 house in San Francisco just as the famous Summer of Love was dancing and singing its way into fall. "I suppose I bought it in the Autumn of Love," quipped Cameron, who grew up in Northern California. It's California neo-Victorian, with a bit of Arts and Crafts thrown in for good measure. Originally built for the foreman of the local Finnish brick factory, the house was tiny and unremodeled. "I'm within walking distance of the old Castro cinema, cozy coffee houses, and lots of health food markets," said Cameron, who curates and presents exhibits for the San Francisco airport galleries. She installed a new tiled kitchen and a new bathroom because there was only an outhouse and spruced up the rooms with color. In Elsa's funhouse, all the furniture is scavenged – either from flea markets, auctions, the side of the road, Mission junk shops, or antiques stores in quirky neighborhoods. Cameron's approach: lots of art, very free-form, non-purist.

Elsa Cameron kaufte ihr Haus im Castro District in San Francisco, als der berühmte »Summer of Love« tanzend und singend in den Herbst überging. »Ich habe im ›Herbst der Liebe‹ gekauft«, scherzt Cameron, die aus Nordkalifornien stammt. Das Haus im kalifornisch neo-viktorianischen Stil mit einem Touch von Arts and Crafts stammt aus dem Jahr 1908. Einstmals gebaut für den Vorarbeiter einer finnischen Ziegelei, blieb das Häuschen winzig und unverändert. »Um die Ecke liegen das alte Castro-Kino, Cafés und eine Menge Reformhäuser«, sagt Cameron, die den Galerien im Flughafen von San Francisco als Kuratorin vorsteht. Sie baute eine neue, gekachelte Küche und ein Badezimmer ein, das als würdiger Ersatz für das ehemalige Toilettenhäuschen im Garten dient. Die Zimmer wurden mit viel bunter Farbe aufgefrischt. In Elsas »Spielhaus« stammt die Einrichtung ausschließlich von Flohmärkten und Auktionen. Sie las sie am Straßenrand auf, durchkämmte Trödelläden und wühlte in bizarren Antikläden, denn ihr Motto ist: viel Kunst, jeder Stil und ja kein Purismus.

Previous pages: in the sunny kitchen. Cups and saucers are by California artists.
Above: Elsa placed vintage Navaho rugs on the floor as a graphic counterpoint to ruffled floral-print cushions and a Thonet sofa.
Right: in the summer parlor.
Facing page: An Eileen Gray "Transat" chair with taupe leather upholstery is juxtaposed with an old twig table.

Double page précédente: dans la cuisine ensoleillée. Les tasses et les assiettes sont signées d'artistes californiens.
Ci-dessus: Elsa a disposé des anciens tapis Navajo sur le sol, en contrepoint graphique des coussins à motifs floraux et volants et d'une banquette tout en courbes de Thonet.
A droite: dans le petit salon d'été.
Page de droite: Un fauteuil «Transat» d'Eileen Gray en cuir taupé est associé à une ancienne table de branchages.

Vorhergehende Doppelseite: in der sonnendurchfluteten Küche. Tassen und Unterteller haben kalifornische Künstler gefertigt.
Oben: Cameron verteilte Navajo-Teppiche auf dem Boden als optischen Gegenpol zu den gerüschten Kissen mit Blumenmotiven und dem kurvenreichen Thonet-Sofa.
Rechts: im Sommer-Salon.
Rechte Seite: Der »Transat«-Armlehnstuhl von Eileen Gray verliert an Schwere neben dem Reisigtisch eines lokalen Künstlers.

California Interiors   Elsa Cameron

Above: Cameron furnished the dining room with old wicker furniture which she painted white. Her serigraph "McDonald's Hamburgers Invading Japan" by Masami Teraoka hangs on the back wall.
Facing page: the bedroom. The Victorian turned-wood grille formerly graced her front porch. Among Elsa's collection: crêpe paper flowers from a festival in Oaxaca, "milagros" from New Mexico, Mexican folk art religious icons, a "Lipsticks" lithograph by Wayne Thiebaud, and an altar by Lauren Adams made of wood, paper, paint and ceramic.

Ci-dessus: Elsa a meublée la salle à manger de mobilier de rotin ancien peint en blanc. Sérigraphie «McDonald's Hamburgers Invading Japan» de Masami Teraoka sur le mur du fond.
Page de droite: la chambre. La grille victorienne ornait jadis le porche d'entrée. Parmi les trésors d'Elsa: des fleurs en papier crépon, souvenir d'une fête à Oaxaca, des ornements «milagros» du Nouveau-Mexique pour éloigner les maladies, des objets de culte populaires mexicains, une lithographie «Lipsticks» de Wayne Thiebaud, et un autel de Lauren Adams en bois, papier, peinture et céramique.

Oben: Cameron richtete das Eßzimmer mit alten Korbmöbeln ein, die sie weiß lackierte. Die Serigraphie »McDonald's Hamburgers Invading Japan« von Masami Teraoka hängt an der hinteren Wand.
Rechte Seite: das Schlafzimmer. Das viktorianische Holzgitter zierte früher die vordere Veranda. Zu Elsas Sammlung gehören: Kreppblumen vom Festival in Oaxaca, mexikanische Heiligenstatuen, die Lithographie »Lipsticks« von Wayne Thiebaud, ein Altar aus Holz, Papier, Farbe und Keramik von Lauren Adams sowie »milagros«, mexikanische religiöse Objekte, die vor Krankheit schützen sollen.

«C'est l'absence de perfection qui rend les antiquités et les trouvailles de marché aux puces si fascinantes», pense Fred Womack, associé de Patty Brunn dans la boutique d'antiquités Maison d'Etre au quartier de South Park, San Francisco. Leur magasin vend toute sorte d'«objets trouvés», dont des outils de jardin décoratifs, des tables de café, des miroirs, des sculptures décoratives, aussi bien que des bougeoirs chic, des chaises longues des années 50 et des livres sur le design. «Nous aimons particulièrement le mobilier de jardin, tout ce qui est quincaillerie curieuse, les peintures de paysages californiens, le mobilier de château, les statues en calcaire et les antiquités dans le goût parisien», ajoute Patty. «La rouille et la peinture écaillée, ou la patine des pièces anciennes, ont une âme. Ces vieux objets ont vécu», commente Fred, «et l'on ne peut pas trouver des antiquités ou même de vieilles reproductions dans la boutique de décoration du coin». Dans leur maison d'Oakland, un ancien atelier d'artiste, Patty et Fred ont mis en scène et orchestré plusieurs décennies d'heureuses trouvailles couvertes de poussière.

Patty Brunn and Fred Womack

"It's the lack of perfection that makes antiques and flea-market finds beautiful," said Fred Womack, partner with Patty Brunn in the Maison d'Etre antiques shop in San Francisco's South Park. Their store sells a variety of objets trouvés, including ornamental garden tools, café tables, mirrors and decorative sculptures, along with chic candles, 50s lawn chairs, and design books. "We especially love garden furniture, unusual hardware, California plein-air paintings, estate furniture, limestone statuary and Parisian-looking antiques," said Brunn. "Rust and chipped paint and patina on vintage pieces and antiques have soul. These old pieces have life. And you can't just get antiques and even old reproductions from your nearest design shop," added Womack. In their Oakland house, formerly an artist's studio, Brunn and Womack have orchestrated several decades of fortunate finds and dust-enhanced beauties.

»Flohmarktschätze sind deshalb so schön, weil sie nicht vollkommen sind«, sagt Fred Womack, der mit Patty Brunn den Antiquitätenladen Maison d'Etre im Viertel South Park in San Francisco besitzt. Der Shop verkauft eine Reihe von außergewöhnlichen Stücken, unter anderem dekorative Gartengeräte, Couchtische, Spiegel und wertvolle Skulpturen, aber auch feine Kerzen, Gartenstühle aus den 50er Jahren und Designbücher. »Wir lieben besonders Gartenmöbel, ungewöhnliche Gerätschaften, kalifornische Landschaftsmalereien, herrschaftliche Möbel, Skulpturen aus Kalkstein und Antiquitäten im Pariser Stil«, sagt Brunn. »Rost, Patina und abblätternde Farbe geben Antiquitäten eine Seele. Diese alten Stücke leben. Antiquitäten und originale Designstücke kann man nicht im nächsten Einrichtungsgeschäft finden«, erklärt Womack. In ihrem Haus in Oakland, einem ehemaligen Künstleratelier, horten Brunn und Womack spinnwebenumhüllte Fundstücke und Schönheiten aus mehreren Jahrzehnten.

Previous page: In a corner of their sky-lit dining room, a gilded vitrine contains old gilt frames, and a 40s floral painting.
Above: At the north end of the dining room stands an antique Parisian birdcage in the shape of a farmhouse. The yellow-painted table is the only new piece of furniture in the room.
Facing page: Lifetime collectors and self-admitted pack rats, Brunn and Womack are happy to cover every surface with prints, candlesticks, crystals, vases and books.

Page précédente: Dans un coin de leur salle à manger à éclairage zénithal, une vitrine dorée contient de vieux cadres et un tableau à motif floral des années 40.
Ci-dessus: Dans le coin nord de la salle à manger, une vieille cage à oiseau parisienne en forme de ferme. La table peinte en jaune est le seul meuble neuf de toute la pièce.
Page de droite: Collectionneurs de toujours et grands accumulateurs devant l'Eternel, Patty et Fred prennent plaisir à recouvrir la moindre surface d'estampes, de bougeoirs, de cristaux, de vases et de livres.

Vorhergehende Seite: In der Ecke des von oben beleuchteten Eßzimmers steht eine vergoldete Vitrine mit alten Rahmen und einem Blumengemälde aus den 40er Jahren.
Oben: Am Nordende des Speisezimmers steht ein alter Vogelbauer aus Paris in Form eines Bauernhauses. Der gelb gestrichene Tisch ist das einzige neue Möbelstück im Raum.
Rechte Seite: Als lebenslange Sammler und große Horter bedecken Brunn und Womack hemmungslos alle freien Flächen mit Drucken, Kerzenleuchtern, Kristallen, Vasen und Büchern.

Above left: Brunn and Womack make a family-friendly composition in the living room with their hodgepodge of flea-market and estate-sale furniture.
Above right: The baby plays in the living room, surrounded by architectural fragments, globes, Japanese prints, a rhinestone tiara, and a folding chair.
Right and facing page: Raspberry red, the juicy hue chosen for the staircase wall, splashes the living room with color. It's also the perfect foil for California plein-air paintings.

Ci-dessus, à gauche: Composition pour la famille dans le séjour, avec tout un mélange de mobilier trouvé aux marché aux puces ou dans des ventes publiques de grandes demeures.
Ci-dessus, à droite: Le bébé joue dans le séjour, entouré d'éléments architecturaux, de globes, de gravures japonaises, d'une tiare en strass et d'une chaise pliante.
A droite et page de droite: Le rouge framboise choisi pour le mur de la cage d'escalier impose sa tonalité juteuse dans le séjour. C'est un fond idéal pour les paysages californiens.

Oben links: Brunn und Womack gestalteten im Wohnzimmer ein familienfreundliches Sammelsurium aus Flohmarktmöbeln und Stücken aus Haushaltsauflösungen.
Oben rechts: Das Baby spielt im Wohnzimmer, umgeben von Architekturfragmenten, Globen, japanischen Drucken, einer Straßtiara und einem Klappstuhl.
Rechts und rechte Seite: Das satte Himbeerrot an der Wand zum Treppenaufgang gibt dem Wohnzimmer Farbe. Es ist ein idealer Fond für die kalifornischen Landschaftsgemälde.

California Interiors   Patty Brunn and Fred Womack

Above: The white-painted bedroom cabinet was improvised from metal garden furniture fragments.
Right: Brunn and Womack dream of flea markets in their French nickel-plated bed, dating from the 20s. The cobalt and clear glass chandelier is Italian.
Facing page: With ingenuity, white paint, and a nickel-plated basin, the couple, who share a fondness for chandeliers, transformed the plain bathroom into a room for lingering.

Ci-dessus: Dans la chambre, le cabinet peint en blanc a été improvisé à partir d'éléments de meubles de jardin métalliques.
A droite: Patty et Fred rêvent de toujours plus de marchés aux puces dans leur lit nickelé français qui date des années 20. Le lustre en verre clair et bleu cobalt est italien.
Page de droite: Beaucoup d'imagination, un peu de peinture blanche et une vasque nickelée, plus un goût marqué pour les lustres, ont transformé cette salle de bains un peu banale.

Oben: Das weißgestrichene Schränkchen im Schlafzimmer wurde aus den Metallteilen ausrangierter Gartenmöbel improvisiert.
Rechts: In ihrem nickelbeschichteten französischen Bett aus den 20er Jahren träumen Brunn und Womack von Flohmärkten. Der Kronleuchter aus Kobalt- und Klarglas stammt aus Italien.
Rechte Seite: Mit Fantasie, weißer Farbe und einem nickelbeschichteten Becken verwandelte das Ehepaar, das eine Leidenschaft für Kronleuchter hegt, das schlichte Bad in einen gemütlichen Raum.

Il a fallu à Scott Kalmbach, producteur de films indépendant, deux années d'incessantes errances dominicales pour trouver la maison de ses rêves. «Je recherchais une maison plus ou moins abandonnée, de hauts plafonds, beaucoup de possibilités et du charme à revendre», se souvient ce copropriétaire de Zonal, une boutique de meubles et d'antiquités de Polk Street à San Francisco. La maison, située à Cow Hollow et construite en 1896, était divisée en deux appartements. Sa rénovation est devenue l'objet exclusif des week-ends de Scott Kalmbach. En deux années de labeur forcé, il a réussi à transformer ce triste cottage victorien en maison de ville, avec salle de projection et bureau. En collaboration étroite avec un constructeur, Kalmbach s'est métamorphosé en démolisseur, apprenti-poseur de briques, peintre, couvreur et homme à tout faire. Il a meublé cette retraite dans laquelle se plaisent ses fidèles terre-neuve, Greta et Emma, de tables et de sièges américains anciens, et complété la mise en scène de souvenirs de cinéma et d'affiches de films.

Scott Kalmbach

It took two years of Sunday browsing for independent film producer, Scott Kalmbach, to find his fixer-upper dream house. "I was looking for a neglected house that had high ceilings, lots of possibilities, and tons of charm," recalled Kalmbach, who co-owns Zonal, a furniture and antiques store on Polk Street in San Francisco. His Cow Hollow house, built in 1896, was divided into two apartments. The renovation became Kalmbach's weekend project. It took him two more years of hands-on labor to turn the lackluster Victorian cottage into a city villa, complete with a miniature screening room and home office. Kalmbach, working closely with a master builder, metamorphosed into an apprentice bricklayer, a handyman, a painter, a demolition man, and a tile layer. Kalmbach, who shares the house with his trusty Newfoundlands, Greta and Emma, furnished his house with vintage American tables and chairs, and completed his production with film memorabilia, and dramatic movie posters.

Zwei Jahre lang durchkämmte der unabhängige Filmproduzent Scott Kalmbach Sonntag für Sonntag San Francisco auf der Suche nach seinem verfallenen Traumhaus. »Ich wollte eine heruntergekommene Absteige mit hohen Decken, vielen Möglichkeiten und einer Tonne Charme«, erinnert sich Kalmbach, unter anderem Mitbesitzer von Zonal, einem Möbel- und Antikladen in der Polk Street in San Francisco. Sein Haus im Viertel von Cow Hollow, Baujahr 1896, bestand aus zwei Wohneinheiten. Die Renovierung wurde Kalmbachs Wochenendbeschäftigung. In zweijähriger Eigenarbeit verwandelte er das düstere viktorianische Gebäude in eine City-Villa mit Filmvorführraum und Büro. Unter der Anleitung eines hervorragenden Handwerkers mutierte Kalmbach zum Maurergesellen, Malermeister und Mädchen für alles, schlug Wände heraus und verlegte Kacheln. Kalmbach, der das Haus mit seinen Neufundländern Greta und Emma teilt, möblierte die Zimmer mit alten amerikanischen Tischen und Stühlen und vervollständigte sein Werk mit cineastischen Memorabilien und dramatischen Filmplakaten.

Previous pages: The exterior of Scott Kalmbach's tiny Victorian cottage was painted cheerful indigo. The Thomas Church designed garden was renovated, and now includes a soothing fountain.
Above: Kalmbach designed his home office in a former bedroom. A faux coffered ceiling was improvised using inexpensive plywood squares and wood framing, all stained to look like mahogany. Kalmbach, since childhood an epic rummager and collector, has furnished his office with a vintage Pilot radio in a veneer case, an Eames chair, an old 16 millimeter camera, plus modern electronic equipment.

Double page précédente: L'extérieur du petit cottage victorien a été repeint d'un joyeux bleu indigo. Le jardin dessiné par Thomas Church a été repensé et s'est enrichi d'une fontaine au murmure reposant.
Ci-dessus: Scott Kalmbach a installé son bureau dans une ancienne chambre à coucher. Un plafond à faux caissons a été improvisé à par-

tir de panneaux de contreplaqué bon marché et de poutres, le tout teinté acajou. Enfant, Scott était déjà un chineur et un collectionneur maladif. Il a équipé son bureau d'une vieille radio Pilot en bois verni, d'un fauteuil Eames, d'une ancienne caméra 16 mm, et d'un ordinateur, bien entendu dernier cri.

Vorhergehende Doppelseite: Scott Kalmbachs winziges Cottage ist indigoblau gestrichen. In dem wieder hergerichteten Garten, der ehemals von Thomas Church angelegt worden war, sprudelt heute ein Brunnen.
Oben: Ein ehemaliges Schlafzimmer dient Kalmbach heute als Büro. Die Kassettendecke sieht aus wie Mahagoni, besteht aber aus Preßholzplatten und Holzrahmen. Im Büro stehen zwischen hypermodernem Equipment ein altes Pilot-Radio, ein Eames-Sessel und eine alte 16-Millimeter-Kamera.

Kalmbach discovered six old movie palace chairs outside a cinema that was closing. He had them upholstered with glamorous magenta velvet. The plywood walls and ceiling were given an imitation wood finish to create the authentic mood of an old movie house. Friends invited to his private screenings are treated to fresh popcorn, and encouraged to participate in highly opinionated and often volatile film critiques.

Scott Kalmbach a découvert six vieux fauteuils de cinéma devant une salle qui venait de fermer. Ils les a fait recouvrir d'un sensuel velours magenta. La peinture en faux-bois sur les murs et le plafond rappelle l'atmosphère d'un ancien cinéma. Les amis invités aux projections privées se voient offrir du pop-corn tout frais, et sont encouragés à manifester leurs critiques, souvent passionnées.

Die sechs Kinosessel fand Kalmbach vor einem pleite gegangenen Kino. Er ließ sie mit magentarot leuchtendem Samt beziehen. Die gemalte Holzimitation auf den mit Preßholz verkleideten Wänden und Decken läßt die alte Kinoatmosphäre wieder auferstehen. Die Freunde, die Kalmbach zu Privatvorführungen einlädt, werden mit Popcorn gefüttert und zu konstruktiven, lautstarken Filmkritiken angeregt.

To create a higher ceiling in the living room, Scott Kalmbach and his architect, Nic Bini, who designs interiors for Banana Republic, ripped out the old tattered ceiling, cut out the beams, and installed steel tension wires to support the roof. On the right: Kalmbach turned a former enclosed lightwell into an enlightened new stairwell, adding a new brick wall and a perforated steel stairway. A skylight with canvas shades lets the sunshine flood in. A pool table was set up in one corner of the L-shaped livingroom.

Pour rehausser le plafond du séjour, Scott Kalmbach et son architecte, Nic Bini, créateur des boutiques Banana Republic, ont mis à bas le plafond ancien délabré, et découpé les poutres qu'ils ont remplacées par des câbles d'acier tendus. A droite, un ancien puits de lumière a été transformé en une lumineuse cage d'escalier, délimitée par un mur neuf en briques et un escalier en acier perforé. Une verrière à store de toile laisse pénétrer le soleil. Un billard a été installé dans un des coins du séjour en forme de L.

Im Wohnzimmer legten Kalmbach und sein Architekt Nic Bini, der Interieurs für die Firma Banana Republic entwirft, die Decke frei, entfernten die Stützbalken und gaben dem Raum mit gespannten Drahtseilen eine neue Statik. Der Lichtschacht rechts wurde zu einem lichten Treppenaufgang mit Ziegelwänden und perforierter Stahltreppe umfunktioniert. Das Dachfenster mit Leinenrollo spendet das nötige Licht. In einer Ecke des L-förmigen Wohnzimmers steht ein Billardtisch.

The living room is the one room of the house which still feels Victorian – with a twist. The walls were painted olive green, with white moldings. His suede-and-nailhead sofa is from Pottery Barn. Kalmbach improvised his coffee table from an old fan paddle, formerly used in a steel factory to fan flames. In one corner, a "bookcase" disguises a door. The books were purchased for 25 cents each at a flea market. The floor is the original redwood planks, unearthed beneath a more recent floor covering.

Le séjour est la seule pièce de la maison qui ait conservé quelque chose du style victorien, revisité bien sûr. Les murs sont peints vert olive avec des moulures blanches. Le canapé en daim clouté vient de l'entreprise Pottery Barn. Scott a improvisé une table basse à partir d'une pale de ventilateur d'aciérie, qui servait jadis à oxygéner les

flammes. Dans un angle, une «bibliothèque» dissimule une porte. Les livres lui ont coûté 25 cents la pièce au marché aux puces. Le sol est le parquet d'origine en bois rouge, découvert sous un revêtement plus récent.

Das Wohnzimmer ist der einzige Raum des Hauses, der viktorianisch belassen blieb. Die olivgrünen Wände sind mit weißen Stuckblenden abgesetzt. Das Wildledersofa mit Nagelborten hat Kalmbach bei der Design-Kette Pottery Barn gekauft. Als Couchtisch dient der Flügel eines alten Ventilators, mit dem früher in einer Stahlfabrik die Flammen geschürt wurden. Hinter dem Bücherregal in der Ecke mit Flohmarktlektüre zu 25 Cents pro Buch versteckt sich eine Tür. Unter falschem Parkett fand Kalmbach die originalen Bohlen aus kalifornischem Redwood.

La jeune décoratrice de San Francisco Kelly Lasser a fait quelques dé-
tours – de la télévision au service du protocole de la ville – avant de se
consacrer à la décoration à temps plein. «Mon univers est passé du
tohu-bohu et de l'extinction d'incendies à la création d'environne-
ments apaisants et zen pour mes clients», explique-t-elle, «il est important de pouvoir trouver un lieu de retraite pour se protéger du tin-
tamarre extérieur.» Sa palette tend vers le monochrome, et ses tissus
retiennent plus l'attention pour leur richesse et leur texture que pour
leurs motifs. Sa vision esthétique marie les lignes tendues des modernistes du milieu du siècle comme Alvar Aalto, Charles Eames, Isamu
Noguchi, aux soies sensuelles de Donghia et de Gretchen Bellinger.
«J'aime particulièrement juxtaposer des meubles dessinés, produits
industriellement comme ceux de Aalto, à des paniers artisanaux, des
sculptures ethniques et des trouvailles du marché aux puces. Il faut
faire bouger le concept de ‹moderne›, et lui donner quelques impul-
sions pour qu'il ne se pétrifie pas. Les pièces même soignées ont besoin d'être réveillées par quelque chose d'exotique, ou de surprenant.»

Kelly Lasser

Young San Francisco interior designer Kelly Lasser took a few
twists and turns on her career path from television to city protocol
office before taking on decorating full time. "My world went from
hurly burly and putting out fires to creating soothing, Zen environ-
ments for my clients," she said. "It's important to have an escape,
a respite from all the noise outside." Her colors tend toward the
monochromatic. Fabrics have richness and texture rather than im-
posed patterns. Lasser's aesthetic combines the taut lines of mid-
century modern furniture by the likes of Alvar Aalto, Charles
Eames, Isamu Noguchi, with sensual silk fabrics by Donghia and
Gretchen Bellinger. "I especially like to juxtapose machine-made,
very precise furniture – like Aalto's – with hand-crafted baskets,
ethnic sculptures, and flea-market finds," she noted. "We have to
move the idea of 'modern' forward, give it a few quirks, never stay
frozen in time. Tailored rooms need the kick of something exotic,
something odd."

Die junge Interior-Designerin Kelly Lasser aus San Francisco fand erst
auf Umwegen – Karriere beim Fernsehen und Protokollantin im Bür-
germeisteramt – zu ihrer jetzigen Bestimmung. »Mein Leben war
früher immer auf der Überholspur«, sagt sie. »Heute schaffe ich Zen-
Welten für meine Kunden. Es ist wichtig, einen Ruhepol zur hektischen, lärmenden Außenwelt zu schaffen.« Ihre Farben sind meist
monochrom, die Stoffe überzeugen eher durch reiche Strukturen als
wilde Muster. Lassers Ästhetik basiert auf den klaren Linien der Moderne: Sie bevorzugt Möbel von Alvar Aalto, Charles Eames und
Isamu Noguchi, die mit sinnlicher Seide von Donghia und Gretchen
Bellinger bezogen sind. »Ich liebe es, die präzisen, industriell gefertigten Möbel von beispielsweise Aalto neben Flohmarktobjekte, handge-
flochtene Körbe und ethnologische Skulpturen zu stellen. Das Prinzip
der Moderne darf niemals stillstehen, es braucht immer neue Schübe.
Klassisch geschnittene Räume brauchen einen exotischen oder eigen-
willigen Kick.«

Previous page: The living room is a smoothly orchestrated mélange of taupes and chocolate tones, offset with Donghia's "Magic" silk on the cushions.
Facing page: In her bedroom and home office, San Francisco interior designer Kelly Lasser corralled a vintage Bruno Mathsson woven chair, an African Dogon ladder acquired in New Orleans, and a Charles Eames wire-base table.
Above: Lasser uses precise placement of furniture and accessories to make this living room feel restful, orderly.
Right: In her bedroom, a four-poster bed.

Page précédente: Le séjour est un mélange délicatement orchestré de tons taupe et chocolat, illuminés par les coussins en soie «Magic» de Donghia.
Page de gauche: Dans sa chambre-bureau, Kelly Lasser a rapproché une chauffeuse ancienne en lanières de toile de Bruno Mathsson, un escalier Dogon acheté à la Nouvelle-Orléans, et une table à piétement de fil de fer de Charles Eames.
Ci-dessus: L'implantation précise des meubles et des accessoires donne une impression d'ordre et de sérénité au séjour.
A droite: un lit à colonnes au centre de la chambre à coucher.

Vorhergehende Seite: Im Wohnzimmer ergänzen die Seidenkissen »Magic« von Donghia harmonisch die fein abgestufte Palette aus graubraunen und schokoladenbraunen Farbtönen.
Linke Seite: In dem Schlafzimmer, das gleichzeitig als Büro dient, kombinierte Kelly einen mit Gurten bespannten Stuhl von Bruno Mathsson und eine afrikanische Dogon-Leiter, die sie in New Orleans fand, mit einem Eames-Tisch, dessen Gestell aus Stahldraht besteht.
Oben: Lassers Credo ist die präzise Anordnung von Möbeln und Accessoires. Dadurch erhält das Wohnzimmer Ruhe und Ordnung.
Rechts: Im Schlafzimmer steht ein Bett mit vier Pfosten.

Above: Kelly Lasser, whose San Francisco design firm is called Shelter, combined in her home office a Japanese elmwood mizuya chest to conceal the stereo equipment, a black leather and walnut veneer Eames "Lounge Chair", and a sculptural lamp.
Facing page: Vintage steel hospital furniture is functional and hard-wearing, and looks modern in San Francisco residences from the 30s. Lasser juices it up with an orange steel chair and accessories by Rayon Vert, a fresh flowers and antiques gallery in Mission District.

Ci-dessus: Kelly Lasser, dont l'agence s'appelle «Shelter» (abri), a associé dans son bureau à la maison un «mizuya» en érable du Japon qui dissimule l'installation stéréo, le fauteuil «Lounge Chair» en cuir noir et contreplaqué vernis de Eames et une lampe sculpturale.
Page de droite: Fonctionnel et costaud, le mobilier d'hôpital ancien semble moderne dans une maison san-franciscaine des années 30. Kelly Lasser l'a réveillé en le rapprochant d'une chaise en acier laqué orange et des accessoires de Rayon Vert, une galerie d'antiquités-fleuriste dans le Mission District.

Oben: Kelly Lassers Designbüro in San Francisco heißt »Shelter« (Unterschlupf). In ihrem Büro sind die High-Tech-Geräte in einem japanischen Mizuya-Schrank aus Ulmenholz verborgen. Hier stehen auch der schwarze »Lounge Chair« von Eames aus gebogenem Schichtholz und eine originelle Lampe.
Rechte Seite: Die alten Stahlmöbel eines Krankenhauses sind unverwüstlich und sehen selbst in Häusern aus den 30er Jahren seltsam modern aus. Lasser belebt die Szenerie mit einem Stahlstuhl von Rayon Vert, einem Antik- und Blumenladen im Mission District.

Coastal Horizons

Pour échapper à l'univers people et paillettes de Los Angeles, le très acclamé photographe portraitiste Greg Gorman s'est enfui jusqu'à la côte sauvage de Mendocino. Là, au bord d'une falaise, il a découvert un hectare de terrain riche en possibilités, sur lequel se dressait une maison isolée, plus ou moins en ruine. «C'était comme une cabane à outils, en fait», se rappelle-t-il. «Nous avons entrepris une rénovation complète en commençant par les fondations.» En collaboration étroite avec l'entreprise Albion, Richard Fienburgi et ses talentueux compagnons, Gorman a recherché son inspiration du côté de Greene and Greene et a réalisé son rêve de retraite confortable dans la sensibilité Arts and Crafts. Construite pour résister aux vents violents de l'hiver – pour ne pas parler des tremblements de terre occasionnels – la petite maison de bois rouge s'est maintenant enrichie d'un sauna, d'un jacuzzi avec vue sur l'océan, et d'une cuisine d'où on peut observer les creux remplis d'abalones se vider et se remplir au rythme des marées.

Greg Gorman

When acclaimed Los Angeles portrait photographer Greg Gorman went looking for an escape from high-profile celebrities and glamor, he drove all the way to the rugged Mendocino coast. There on the edge of a cliff, Gorman discovered two acres of potential. A tumbledown house was perched on this prime site, nothing more. "It was like a toolshed, really," recalled Gorman. "We completely renovated it, starting with the foundation." Working closely with Albion contractor, Richard Fienburgi, and his talented crew, Gorman looked to Greene and Greene for inspiration, and dreamed up a cosy retreat with Arts and Crafts overtones. Built to withstand gale-force winter winds – not to mention the occasional earthquake – the redwood shingled house is now kitted out with a sauna, a seaview Jacuzzi, and a kitchen with views of abalone-filled tide pools.

Von Los Angeles bis an die rauhe Küste von Mendocino trieb es den Porträtfotografen Greg Gorman auf der Suche nach einem Zufluchtsort vor Prominenz und Schickeria. Am Rande einer Klippe fand Gorman einen halben Hektar vielversprechendes Land. Auf dem erstklassigen Grundstück stand ein verfallenes Haus und sonst gar nichts. »Es sah aus wie ein Werkzeugschuppen«, erinnert sich Gorman. »Das Ganze verlangte nach einer Totalüberholung inklusive eines neuen Fundaments.« Das Ergebnis ist heute ein verwunschener Ort mit Arts-and-Crafts-Elementen; eine gelungene Koproduktion des Bauunternehmers Richard Fienburgi aus Albion, der Interior-Designer der Firma Greene and Greene und natürlich von Gorman selbst. Solide genug, um die orkanartigen Winterstürme zu überstehen – nicht zu vergessen die gelegentlichen Erdbeben –, beheimatet das mit Redwood verkleidete Refugium eine Sauna, einen Jacuzzi mit Meeresblick und eine Küche, von der aus man auf die mit Meerohren gefüllten Felsbuchten schaut.

First page: Photographer Greg Gorman at his North Coast retreat. Gorman has amassed an impressive "batterie de cuisine" and often dazzles guests with virtuoso entertaining. Countertops are 19 mm burnished copper "planks".
Previous pages: Late afternoon sun glows on the rustic weathered timbers, hearty leather-upholstered furniture, and Mission-style chairs.
Above and facing page: Gorman's aesthetic: smooth river rocks, rough timbers, old copper, hand-crafted mica shades. Walls and custom cabinetry of old Douglas fir were cut with a bandsaw.
Following pages: Gorman's sunset finale. The house is 5 m from the cliff edge.

Première page: Le photographe Greg Gorman dans sa retraite de la North Coast. Il a rassemblé un impressionnant équipement de cuisine, et surprend souvent ses hôtes par ses talents de chef. Les plans de travail sont en lattes de cuivre patiné épaisses de 19 mm.
Double page précédente: Un soleil de fin d'après-midi illumine les poutres rustiques anciennes, les fauteuils de cuir et les chaises de style Mission, un style américain fonctionnel du tournant du siècle.
Ci-dessus et page de droite: Esthétique gormanienne: galets de rivière, bois équarri, cuivre patiné, plaques de mica. Les lambris et les meubles en pin de Douglas réalisés sur mesure ont été sciés à la scie à ruban.
Double page suivante: Grand final avec coucher de soleil vu de la maison accrochée à 5 m du bord de la falaise.

Eingangsseite: Der Fotograf Greg Gorman in seinem Haus an der kalifornischen Nordküste. Gorman besitzt eine beeindruckende »batterie de cuisine« und überrascht gerne Gäste mit seinen Kochkünsten. Die Arbeitsflächen bestehen aus 19 mm dicken, polierten Kupferplatten.
Vorhergehende Doppelseite: Das weiche Licht der späten Nachmittagssonne scheint auf verwitterte Balken, voluminöse Ledergarnituren und spartanische Stühle im Mission Style, einem funktional geprägten Einrichtungsstil im Amerika der Jahrhundertwende.
Oben und rechte Seite: Ästhetik à la Gorman: runde Flußsteine, rohe Holzbalken, altes Kupfer und handgemachte Lampenschirme aus Muskowit. Die Wandverkleidung und die maßgefertigten Schränke aus Douglasfichte wurden mit einer Bandsäge zugeschnitten.
Folgende Doppelseite: Sonnenuntergang à la Gorman. Das Haus steht 5 m vor dem Abgrund.

Big Sur, à trois heures de voiture au sud de San Francisco, est une côte d'accès difficile, étonnamment découpée, merveilleusement inspirée. Au printemps et en été, la brume de l'océan étend son aura psychédélique sur les champs émaillés de fleurs sauvages. En hiver, les vagues impétueuses s'écrasent en gerbes de mousse sur les rochers recouverts de varech, et les vents s'engouffrent dans des canyons oubliés. Ce paysage secret fut d'abord colonisé par des fermiers, rejoints au début du 20ᵉ siècle par des artistes et des rêveurs en tout genre, lorsque la première route côtière fut tracée. Plus tard vinrent des célébrités à la recherche d'une retraite, comme Henry Miller, Jack Kerouac, Orson Welles, et des colonies d'artistes et de musiciens. Les pierres qui servirent à construire la première route viennent de Rocky Point. C'est sur ce site de carrière que l'architecte de Carmel George Brook-Kothlow a choisi d'édifier une maison qui semble s'évanouir dans le paysage. Il a utilisé des poutres de bois rouge de récupération, qui avaient servi aux pont jetés sur les ravins et les gorges de Big Sur.

A House by George Brook-Kothlow

The Big Sur coast, three hours south of San Francisco, is a very remote, romantic and rugged setting. In spring and summer, mists paint a psychedelic haze over fields of wildflowers. In winter, towering waves crash and foam over coastal kelp beds, and winds screech through forlorn canyons. These hidden hills were first settled by ranchers, who were joined by artists and dreamers in the early 20th century when the first coastal highway was built. Later came seekers such as Henry Miller and Jack Kerouac, Orson Welles, and colorful bands of musicians and artists. Rocks for the first road were quarried at Rocky Point. It was on this stone-strewn site that Carmel architect George Brook-Kothlow chose to design a house which seems to disappear into the hillside. The architect selected recycled redwood trestle timbers, first milled to bridge Big Sur ravines and gorges.

Die Küste von Big Sur, drei Autostunden südlich von San Francisco, ist eine entlegene, romantische, wilde Gegend. Im Frühjahr und im Sommer wabern geradezu psychedelische Nebelschwaden über die blühenden Wildblumenwiesen. Im Winter spritzt die Gischt von mächtigen Brechern in die mit Tang gefüllten Buchten, und der Sturm heult in den einsamen Canyons. In diesen versteckten Hügeln siedelten ursprünglich Rancher. Als Anfang des 20. Jahrhunderts der erste Highway an der Küste gebaut wurde, fanden Künstler und Träumer den Weg hierher. Später kamen Suchende wie Henry Miller, Jack Kerouac und Orson Welles sowie eine bunte Truppe von Musikern und Künstlern. Die Steine für den Bau der ersten Straße wurden am Rocky Point gehauen, und George Brook-Kothlow beschloß, an genau dieser mit Steinen übersäten Stelle ein Haus zu errichten, das förmlich mit den Hügeln verschmelzen sollte. Der Architekt aus Carmel wählte dafür wiederverwendete Redwood-Balken, die einstmals in den Schluchten von Big Sur als Brückenhölzer gedient hatten.

Previous pages and above: Carmel-based architect, George Brook-Kothlow, whose own Nordic heritage inspires his architecture, likens the skeleton of his interiors to those in traditional Norwegian timber structures. The interior timbers of the house are redwood, with exposed bolts and washers. The interior is built as soundly as a bridge to stand up to storms and the occasional, inevitable earthquake.
Right: the simple, rather austere bathroom.
Facing page: This summer scene, with its southern vista to the cliffs and dark hillsides of Big Sur, is idyllic and clear. It's a perfect position for morning coffee, newspaper reading, and seal or whale watching.

Double page précédente et ci-dessus: Basé à Carmel, l'architecte George Brook-Kothlow évoque dans ses constructions les maisons de bois norvégiennes traditionnelles de ses origines. La charpente intérieure est en bois rouge à boulons et rondelles apparents. L'intérieur est construit aussi solidement qu'un pont, pour résister aux vents de l'hiver et aux tremblements de terre ou secousses occasionnelles.
A droite: Simple et assez austère, la salle de bains.
Page de droite: La terrasse est parfaitement située pour prendre son café du matin, lire le journal, ou regarder passer les baleines.

Vorhergehende Doppelseite und oben: Der Architekt George Brook-Kothlow aus Carmel, dessen nordische Herkunft seine Bauten inspiriert, gestaltete die Balkenkonstruktion im Innern des Hauses nach dem Vorbild traditioneller norwegischer Holzhäuser. Die Balken bestehen aus Redwood mit sichtbaren Muttern und Unterlegscheiben. Das Haus ist so solide wie eine Brücke gebaut, um Winterstürmen sowie den gelegentlichen Erschütterungen und Erdbeben zu trotzen.
Rechts: das einfache, eher strenge Badezimmer.
Rechte Seite: Im Süden sieht man die Klippen und dunklen Hügel von Big Sur – der ideale Ort für eine Tasse Kaffee am frühen Morgen, für Zeitungslektüre und für das Beobachten von Seehunden und Walen.

Prix Nobel et pacifiste, le Docteur Linus Pauling et son épouse, Ava,
se promenaient en 1956 en voiture sur l'Highway One, au sud de Big
Sur, lorsqu'ils aperçurent un panneau «A vendre» cloué à un portail.
Sans vraiment réfléchir, ils téléphonèrent au propriétaire de ce ranch
de 64 hectares et devinrent ainsi bientôt les heureux propriétaires de
l'un des plus spectaculaires emplacements de la côte californienne.
Leur fille, Linda Pauling Kamb, se souvient que l'argent nécessaire venait de son Prix Nobel. «Il ne restait qu'un bungalow et une grange,
et mes parents trouvèrent ce ranch très tranquille», explique
Madame Kamb, qui y passa sa lune de miel. En 1965, les Pauling
construisirent une maison en bois abritant quatre chambres à coucher. L'architecture s'inspirait d'une élégante maison de bois de la pé-
ninsule de Monterey que possédait la chanteuse Joan Baez, une amie
de la famille. «C'est très simple et sans prétention, et bien en accord
avec la nature», commente Madame Kamb. Les Pauling ont fait travailler des artisans locaux pour aménager l'intérieur tout en bois, et
confectionner les carrelages de la cuisine et de la salle de bains.

Linus Pauling

Nobel prize winner and peace activist Dr Linus Pauling and his
wife, Ava, were driving down Highway One, south of Big Sur, in
1956, when they saw a "For Sale" sign propped on a gate. On im-
pulse, they phoned the owner of the 640 000 sq.m. ranch and
soon became the fortunate owners of one of the most dramatic
properties on the California coast. Their daughter, Linda Pauling
Kamb, who spent her honeymoon there, recalled that funds to ac-
quire the homestead came from his first Nobel Prize."There were
just a cabin and a barn on the property then, and my mother and
father found the ranch very tranquil," she added. In 1965, the Paulings built a four-bedroom, board-and-batten house. The architecture was inspired by a handsome timber house on the Monterey
Peninsula owned by singer, Joan Baez, a friend of the family. "It's
very simple and unpretentious, and in tune with nature," said Mrs
Kamb. The Paulings engaged local craftspeople to craft the all-
wood interiors, and to make tiles for the kitchen and bathroom.

Südlich von Big Sur, im Jahr 1956: Nobelpreisträger und Friedensakti-
vist Dr. Linus Pauling und seine Frau Ava sehen ein »For Sale«-Schild
an einem Tor am Highway One. Sie rufen den Besitzer der 64 Hektar
großen Ranch an und werden kurz darauf glückliche Besitzer eines
der schönsten Grundstücke an der kalifornischen Küste. Sie bezahlen
es mit den Geldern, die Pauling für seinen ersten Nobelpreis erhalten
hatte. »Es gab lediglich eine Hütte und eine Scheune. Mein Vater
und meine Mutter fanden die Ranch ideal zum Ausspannen«, erzählt
Paulings Tochter, Linda Pauling Kamb, die hier ihre Flitterwochen
verbrachte. Im Jahr 1965 ließ der Nobelpreisträger dort ein Haus mit
vier Schlafzimmern aus groben Brettern bauen, inspiriert von der
hübschen Holzvilla der befreundeten Sängerin Joan Baez auf der
Halbinsel von Monterey. »Das Haus ist einfach und bescheiden, im
Einklang mit der Natur«, sagt Linda Kamb. Ortsansässige Handwerker bauten die Innenräume aus – natürlich ganz in Holz – und
fertigten die Kacheln für Küche und Badezimmer.

Facing page: Life at Big Sur was simple and rustic. The Paulings commissioned a local craftsman to hand-make the tiles for their kitchen, which overlooks the garden. The house is now enjoyed by the Paulings' children, grandchildren, and great-grandchildren.
Above, right and following pages: Papers, reference books, and journals are stacked on tables, shelves, the floor, even inside an old Norwegian stove. Some furniture was inherited from a friend in Norway. The glass and metal chandelier was purchased in Sweden. A stack of journals serve as a perch for a portrait of Ava Pauling.

Page de gauche: La vie à Big Sur était simple et rustique. Les Pauling demandèrent à un artisan du coin de fabriquer le carrelage de la cuisine qui donne sur le jardin. La maison fait maintenant le bonheur des enfants, petits-enfants et arrière-petits-enfants de Linus Pauling.
Ci-dessus, à droite et double page suivante: Articles, livres de référence et journaux sont restés empilés sur les tables, les étagères, le sol et même dans un vieux poêle norvégien. Certains meubles avaient été hérités d'un ami de Norvège. Le chandelier en verre et métal a été acheté en Suède. Une pile de journaux supporte un portrait d'Ava Pauling.

Linke Seite: Das Leben in Big Sur war einfach und ländlich. Die Paulings holten einen Handwerker aus dem Ort, der die Kacheln für die Küche fertigte. Heute verbringen hier ihre Kinder, Enkel und Urenkel wundervolle Zeiten.
Oben, rechts und folgende Doppelseite: Schriften, Nachschlagewerke und Zeitschriften stapeln sich überall, auf den Tischen, in den Regalen, auf dem Boden und sogar in einem alten norwegischen Kanonenofen. Einige Möbel hatten die Paulings von einem norwegischen Freund geerbt. Der Kerzenständer aus Glas und Metall stammt aus Schweden. Ein Zeitschriftenstapel dient als Sockel für ein Porträt von Ava Pauling.

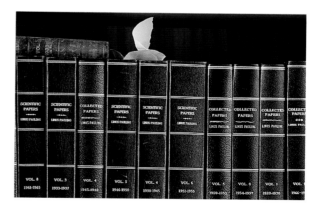

L'architecte de Big Sur, Mickey Muennig , a trouvé un terrain idéal de
12 hectares au-dessus de Partington Cove. Il s'est promené sur cet ancien pré à vaches pendant des mois avant de déterminer le site idéal
de sa petite maison. Pour la construction, il a acheté tout un stock de
poutres de bois rouge de 15 x 40 cm récupérées sur les anciens ponts
de la Central Coast Highway qui devaient être démolis pour être rem-
placés par des structures modernes en béton. «C'était un bois rouge
de première qualité, sans un seul nœud», se souvient Mickey qui a
remporté depuis un grand succès pour ses plans du Post Ranch Inn
écologique de Big Sur. Pleine d'ingéniosité, sa maison économique de
28 m² est en parpaings de béton enduits. «J'ai vécu dans des conditions minimalistes dans le plus bel endroit du monde», ajoute l'architecte qui utilise maintenant cette maison comme pavillon d'amis. «Je
ne pouvais pas posséder grand-chose ici, mais j'ai connu la force mou-
vante du vent, des centaines de couchers de soleil différents, la lumière de la lune lorsqu'elle devient fluorescente, et la sérénité.»

Mickey Muennig's Guest-house

High above Partington Cove, Big Sur architect Mickey Muennig
found 120 000 perfect square meters. Muennig walked the land for
months before choosing his ideal site for a small house, a former
pasture for local ranches. Muennig acquired a supply of 15 x 40 cm
redwood timber, salvaged from old Central Coast bridges that had
been demolished to make way for modern concrete structures. "It
was particularly fine first-growth redwood, with no knots," recalled
Muennig, who has since been acclaimed for his design for the
eco-friendly Post Ranch Inn at Big Sur. His cost-conscious 28 sq.m.
house was crafted with stucco-covered concrete blocks. "I lived
in minimal conditions in the most beautiful place in the world,"
said Muennig, who now uses the house as a guest-house. "I
couldn't have many possessions there, but I experienced every
wind gust, hundreds of different sunsets, fluorescent moonlight,
and quietness."

Hoch über der Bucht von Partington Cove in Big Sur fand Architekt
Mickey Muennig 12 perfekte Hektar Land. Monatelang schritt er die
Parzelle ab, bis er die perfekte Stelle für ein kleines Haus fand: einen
ehemaligen Weidegrund. Muennig erwarb einen Stapel Redwood-
Holz, 15 x 40 cm, Überreste von alten Brücken des Central Coast
Highway, die gegen moderne Betonkonstruktionen ausgetauscht wor-
den waren. »Es war erstklassiges Holz ohne Astlöcher«, erinnert sich
Muennig, der zwischenzeitlich für seinen ökologischen Entwurf des
Post Ranch Inn in Big Sur ausgezeichnet wurde. Das geniale und
kostenbewußte 28 m² große Haus besteht aus mörtelverputzten Be-
tonquadern. »Ich habe unter primitivsten Umständen am schönsten
Ort der Welt gelebt«, sagt Muennig, der das Gebäude nun als Gästehaus nutzt. »Hier kann man nicht viel besitzen. Dafür erlebe ich jeden Windhauch, Hunderte verschiedener Sonnenuntergänge, fluores-
zierenden Mondschein – und Stille«.

Mickey Muennig's ingenious "organic" house stands 3 km above
Highway One along a rocky, twisting road, 490 m above the Pacific
Ocean. The bed platform, suspended beneath the glass roof by steel
rods, is reached by a wooden ladder. Muennig slept on this platform –
with no shades – and admitted he likes to rise early, with the sun.
A small bare-bones kitchen is equipped with a gas refrigerator, a sink,
and a tiny stove. A stone fireplace with a steel chimney warms the
one-room house on foggy summer days and in winter. The house is
shaded by a stand of ancient eucalyptus trees. Next landfall: Hawaii.

L'ingénieuse maison «organique» de Mickey Muennig se trouve
à 3 km au-dessus de la Highway One, la route qui serpente entre
les rochers à 490 m au-dessus du Pacifique. Une échelle permet
d'accéder au lit suspendu au toit par des tringles d'acier. L'architecte
a dormi là – sans rideaux – mais admet qu'il aime se lever avec le
soleil. Une petite cuisine ouverte est équipée d'un réfrigérateur à gaz,
d'un évier et d'une petite cuisinière. Une cheminée en pierre à conduit
en acier chauffe la pièce unique par temps de brouillard en été, et en
hiver bien sûr. La maison est ombragée par un bosquet d'eucalyptus
anciens. La terre ferme la plus proche? Hawaii ...

Mickey Muennigs geniales »organisches« Haus steht 3 km oberhalb
des Highway One an einer steinigen, gewundenen Straße, rund
490 m über dem Pazifischen Ozean. Das Bett, das an Stahlseilen unter
dem Glasdach hängt, erreicht man über eine Holzleiter. Hier gibt es
keine Jalousien, und als überzeugter Frühaufsteher erwachte Muennig
jeden Morgen bei Sonnenaufgang. Die kleine Küche mit dem nackten
Boden ist mit einem gasbetriebenen Kühlschrank, einem Spülbecken
und einem winzigen Herd ausgestattet. Ein steinerner Kamin mit
einem Abzugsrohr aus Stahl wärmt das Ein-Zimmer-Haus an neb-
ligen Sommertagen und im Winter. Das nächste Festland: Hawaii.

Les vieux résidents de Big Sur, au centre du littoral pacifique californien, protègent avec vigueur et détermination la beauté forte et sauvage de ce paysage qui fait penser aux premiers jours de la Création.
Pour Henry Miller, qui y vécut longtemps, Big Sur est «la nature qui
se regarde en souriant dans le miroir de l'éternité». Producteur de
films et de télévision à Los Angeles, le propriétaire de cette maison
visita la région pour la première fois dans les années 70 et rêvait
depuis de s'y établir. Il y a trois ans, lui et sa femme demandèrent à
l'architecte de Big Sur, Mickey Muennig, de leur construire une maison sur un terrain retiré et engagèrent également le décorateur Craig
Wright, de Los Angeles. Selon la sourcilleuse réglementation locale,
la maison et le pavillon d'amis ne devaient pas être visibles de la
Highway I ou des autres résidences. Le pavillon est une construction
élégante et non sans audace. Son toit incurvé reproduit fidèlement
les contours du paysage de collines environnant.

A House in Big Sur

Longtime residents of Big Sur, on the central coast of California,
are fierce in their determination to protect the pure, powerful
beauty of the primeval landscape. Big Sur was "Nature smiling at
herself in the mirror of eternity", penned novelist Henry Miller, a
longtime resident. A Los Angeles television and movie producer
first visited the area 25 years ago and was determined to find a
place for himself there. Three years ago he and his wife engaged
Big Sur architect, Mickey Muennig, to build a house on a remote
piece of land. Los Angeles interior designer Craig Wright was
signed to design the interiors. It was understood that according
to strict local codes, the house and nearby guest-house would
not be visible from Highway One or neighboring residences. The
new guest-house is a sleek, bold structure. Its curving roof follows
faithfully the contours of the rugged hillsides.

Die alteingesessenen Bewohner von Big Sur an der kalifornischen Küste sind vehement entschlossen, die Reinheit und die kraftvolle Schönheit der urzeitlichen Landschaft zu schützen. Big Sur bedeutet »Die
Natur lächelt sich selbst an im Spiegel der Ewigkeit« – so schrieb
der Schriftsteller Henry Miller, der selber lange Jahre hier lebte. Der
Besitzer, ein Fernseh- und Filmproduzent aus Los Angeles, kam das
erste Mal vor 25 Jahren in diese Gegend. Schon damals wußte er, daß
er sich dort einmal niederlassen würde. Vor drei Jahren engagierten
er und seine Frau den Architekten Mickey Muennig aus Big Sur, um
auf einem entlegenen Stück Land ein Haus für sie zu bauen. Der
Interior-Designer Craig Wright aus Los Angeles wurde mit der Inneneinrichtung beauftragt. Ein strenges lokales Gesetz besagt, daß
weder Haus noch Gästehaus vom Highway One oder von den benachbarten Häusern eingesehen werden dürfen. Das neue Gästehaus
gibt sich schlank und kühn. Sein kurvenreiches Dach folgt den
Konturen der schroffen Hügellandschaft.

Previous pages: The guest-house, a 20-minute stroll from the main house, has plank-formed concrete walls and soaring arcs of glass. Doors in the bathroom slide open to invite nature indoors.

Facing page: Architect Mickey Muennig pieced the sitting room together like a jigsaw puzzle, giving it a snug coziness, along with cathedral-like lightness. Los Angeles interior designer Craig Wright selected chenilles and Kuba fabrics in soothing natural tones, and chose undemanding antiques and furnishings for comfort and style. The floor is patterned with a decorative and practical random-pattern criss-cross of slate tiles. Timbers, concrete and structural materials were left unadorned – the better to work with nature's beauty.

Above: In January and February most years, winter storms blast through Big Sur, lashing the hillsides and chilling hikers. Muennig's art has been to create a dwelling with the ancient feeling of a cave – with modern conveniences. The floors are dirt-defying slate, and the kitchen is hardy concrete and stainless steel. The stairway, right, leads down to the bedroom and bathroom.

Double page précédente: Le pavillon d'amis, à 20 minutes à pied de la maison, est en béton brut de décoffrage et vastes surfaces vitrées. Les portes de la salle de bains coulissent pour laisser entrer la nature.

Page de gauche: L'architecte Mickey Muennig a assemblé le séjour comme un puzzle, lui conférant un sens de confort intimiste, malgré les transparences dues aux immenses baies vitrées. Le décorateur de Los Angeles Craig Wright a sélectionné des étoffes en chenille et des tissus africains Kuba dans des tons naturels apaisants, ainsi que des antiquités et meubles point trop sérieux, juste pour le style et le confort. Le sol est recouvert d'ardoises à la fois décoratives et pra-

tiques. Les poutres, le béton et les matériaux structurels ont été laissés bruts, pour que la beauté de la nature garde toute sa force expressive.

Ci-dessus: En janvier et février, les tempêtes hivernales s'abattent sur Big Sur, balayant les collines et frigorifiant les promeneurs. L'art de Muennig a consisté à créer une maison qui donne un sentiment de protection. Une caverne, mais avec tout le confort moderne. Les plafonds de bois sont à la fois protecteurs et inspirants. Les sols sont en ardoise défiant toutes les salissures, et la cuisine en béton et acier inoxydable. L'escalier, à droite, permet de descendre vers la chambre et la salle de bains.

Vorhergehende Doppelseite: Das Gästehaus, das 20 Minuten zu Fuß vom Hauptgebäude entfernt liegt, besteht aus Sichtbetonwänden und hohen verglasten Bögen.

Linke Seite: Der Architekt Muennig setzte das Wohnzimmer wie ein Puzzle zusammen: Es ist gemütlich und gleichzeitig so lichtdurchflutet wie eine Kathedrale. Der Interior-Designer Craig Wright aus Los Angeles wählte Chenille und Kuba-Stoffe in beruhigenden, natürlichen Farbtönen. Nicht ganz echte Antiquitäten sorgen für Komfort und Stil. Den Boden schmücken Schieferplatten in einem dekorativen und praktischen Zufallsmuster. Holzbalken, Beton und strukturelle Baustoffe blieben unverziert.

Oben: Im Januar und Februar fegen oft heftige Winterstürme über die Hügel von Big Sur und die frierenden Wanderer. Muennig versteht sich auf die Kunst, ein urzeitliches Höhlengefühl aufkommen zu lassen, selbstverständlich mit allen modernen Bequemlichkeiten. Die Böden sind aus schmutzabweisendem Schiefer, die Küche aus robustem Beton und rostfreiem Stahl. Die Treppe rechts führt hinunter zum Schlaf- und Badezimmer.

Above: Craig Wright's color palette for the guest-house ranges from
sage to clay to fog and oak leaf. Simple woven rugs are set on the
concrete floors to temper the early morning chill.
Right: the bathroom. An English cabinet is used to store linens.
Facing page: Wright chose sturdy but silky chenille to upholster the
cushions of the chairs and the ottoman. Muennig sited the house
thoughtfully so that guests reading in bed could glance up and view
noble oaks and sprawling madrones.

Ci-dessus: La palette chromatique de Craig Wright va d'un vert sauge
à des tons d'argile en passant par un gris brouillard et le vert feuille de
chêne. De simples tapis de laine tissée sont posés sur le sol de béton
pour couper la froideur matinale.
A droite: la salle de bains. Une armoire anglaise sert à ranger le linge.
Page de droite: Craig a choisi un tissu chenillé, épais mais soyeux,
pour recouvrir les coussins des fauteuils et du pouf. L'architecte a im-
planté la maison avec soin, pour que les invités puissent bénéficier de
leur lit d'une vue sur les merveilleux vieux chênes et les «madrones»,
ou arbusiers californiens, envahissants.

Oben: Craig Wrights Farbpalette reicht von Salbeigrün und Ton bis
Nebelgrau und Eichengrün. Das elektronische Equipment ist in einem
lackierten Schrank neben dem Kamin verborgen. Gewebte Teppiche
auf den Betonböden schützen vor der morgendlichen Kälte.
Rechts: das Bad. Die Wäsche wird in einer englischen Vitrine aufbe-
wahrt.
Rechte Seite: Wright bezog die Kissen von Sessel und Hocker mit
haltbarem Seidenchenille. Muennig wählte den Standort des Hauses
mit Bedacht: Gäste können im Bett liegen und lesen und gleichzeitig
einen Blick auf stattliche Eichen und wuchernde »madrones«, die kalifornischen Erdbeerbäume, werfen.

Sur une butte recouverte d'arbustes à petites feuilles dures et persistantes du «chaparral», non loin de la Los Padres National Forest et dominant Pfeiffer Beach, se dresse une maison neuve qui semble très à l'aise dans ce paysage sauvage. Dans une région ou le bois jaune est exploité depuis 1880, l'architecte de Big Sur, Mickey Muennig, s'est créé une retraite permanente pour se protéger des chaleurs de la côte et s'abriter des tempêtes hivernales. Son plan composé de trois cylindres enchevêtrés, s'adapte habilement à la partie constructible du terrain. Des verrières piègent le soleil tout au long de la journée, et les portes principales en verre donnent sur un canyon. Connu pour ses originales maisons organiques, Mickey n'est pas de ces architectes à l'ego extraverti. A l'aide de parpaings de ciment recouverts de plâtre, de poutres de bois récupérées, et d'un sol en dalles de béton, il a créé une maison qui semble être là depuis des siècles.

Mickey Muennig in Big Sur

On a chaparral-covered knoll near the Los Padres National Forest, high above Pfeiffer Beach, stands a new house that's very much at home in the wild landscape. In a region where tanbark timber was first felled about 1880, Big Sur architect Mickey Muennig planned for himself a year-round retreat that would be a cool refuge in the hot coastal summers, and a cosy shelter during winter storms. From the start he configured a site-specific floor plan based on three interlocking cylinders to provide maximum use of the buildable land. Skylights trap day-long sun, and large glass front doors afford views over a canyon. Muennig has made a name for himself as an architect of highly original organic houses and frowns on man-made grandeur. Using concrete blocks covered in stucco, recycled redwood timbers, and a concrete slab floor, Muennig crafted a house that appears to have stood sentry on the untamed coastal land for centuries.

In der Nähe des Los Padres National Forest, hoch über dem Pfeiffer Beach, steht auf einem Hügel, der mit dem dichten Buschwerk des »chaparral« bedeckt ist, ein Haus, das sich harmonisch in die wilde Landschaft einfügt. Hier in dieser Region, wo seit etwa 1880 Gerbereichen gefällt werden, plante der Architekt Mickey Muennig aus Big Sur sein ganzjähriges Domizil. Es sollte während der heißen Monate an der Küste ein kühles Refugium und andererseits ein gemütlicher Unterschlupf während der Winterstürme sein. Der Grundriß paßt sich der Umgebung an und basiert auf drei miteinander verbundenen Zylindern, um das bebaubare Land optimal auszunutzen. Dachfenster lassen den ganzen Tag das Sonnenlicht ein, und durch die großen Eingangstüren aus Glas blickt man auf einen nahen Canyon. Muennig machte sich einen Namen als Architekt von höchst originellen ökologischen Häusern und verabscheut künstliche Erhabenheit. Für das Haus verwendete er mit Mörtel verputzte Betonblöcke und wiederverwendetes Redwood, die Böden goß er aus Beton. Dadurch wirkt das Haus, als wache es schon seit Jahrhunderten über das Land.

The Big Sur house that architect Mickey Muennig designed for himself is 150 sq.m., but the open plan makes it appear more spacious.
Graceful in concept, and with refined craftsmanship, it is still very
much part of the dramatic coastal topography. Natural materials
were used throughout the interiors for summer comfort and winter
warmth. The concrete floor is installed with radiant heating. Glass
doors in each room open to a sheltered terrace and views across a
swale and rolling hills to the rocky Big Sur coastline. The soil-clad roof
makes the house fire-proof and has proved to be a fine insulator.

La maison que l'architecte Mickey Muennig s'est construit à Big Sur,
semble beaucoup plus spacieuse que ses 150 m². Pleine de grâce et de
raffinement, elle est parfaitement intégrée à la topographie spectaculaire de la côte. Les matériaux naturels ont été privilégiés au maximum parce qu'ils apportent fraîcheur en été et chaleur en hiver. Le
sol en béton est équipé d'un chauffage radiant. Dans chaque pièce,
des portes en verre donnent sur une terrasse abritée, une dépression
de terrain ou le moutonnement des collines jusqu'aux falaises ro-
cheuses de Big Sur et l'océan. Le toit recouvert de terre ignifuge la
maison et fournit une isolation thermique étonnamment efficace.

Das Haus in Big Sur, das der Architekt Mickey Muennig für sich entwarf, hat rund 150 m² Wohnfläche. Durch den großzügigen Grundriß
wirkt es wesentlich geräumiger. Dank seiner Anmut und der hervorragenden Verarbeitung fügt es sich perfekt in die Küstenlandschaft ein.
Das mit Gras bewachsene Dach isoliert das Haus und macht es
gleichzeitig feuerfest. In den Innenräumen wurden ausschließlich
natürliche Materialien verwendet, die im Sommer für Komfort und
im Winter für Wärme sorgen. Im Betonboden installierte Muennig
eine Fußbodenheizung. In jedem Zimmer führen Glastüren auf eine
geschützte Terrasse mit Blick über sanfte Hügel bis zur Felsküste.

The center of the house, illuminated by four retractable glass-panel skylights, has a large courtyard planted with banana, guava, papaya and palm trees. The banana trees bear fruit in the summer, reports Muennig. The central support posts of salvaged redwood trunks were turned on a lathe in keeping with the curvy aesthetics. Above Muennig's desk is an arched open "bay" which receives light from the sky-light.

La partie centrale de la maison est illuminée par quatre verrières ré-tractables. Elle est occupée par une sorte de cour plantée de goyaviers, de papayers, de palmiers et de bananiers qui donnent des fruits en été. Les piliers centraux de soutènement sont des troncs de bois rouge passés au tour pour les harmoniser à l'esthétique curviligne de la maison. Près de la table à dessin de l'architecte, une «baie» en demi-lune capte la lumière des verrières.

In der Mitte des Hauses befindet sich ein großer Innenhof, der Licht durch vier ausfahrbare Dachfenster erhält und in dem Bananen, Gua-ven, Papayas und Palmen wachsen. Die Bananenstauden tragen im Sommer Früchte, sagt Muennig. Die zentralen Stützen bestehen aus wiederverwendeten Redwood-Stämmen und wurden in einer ge-schwungenen Linie aufgestellt, um die Kurvenästhetik des Hauses aufzunehmen. Über Muennigs Reißbrett läßt ein offener Rundbogen über ein Dachfenster Licht herein.

Right: Muennig's bedroom has a fan-shaped recycled redwood ceiling and a sculptural headboard of planed redwood.
Below: The arched opening into the lightwell offers diffused sunlight and an abstract alliteration of the sunsets Muennig sees every night from his front terrace. The sweep of redwood lathe cabinet tops are covered with 3 mm thick tan-colored linoleum, formerly used for battleships, reported Muennig. The lozenge-shaped butcher-block island, which stands on a steel support, is ideal for breakfast for two.

A droite: La chambre de Mickey Muennig possède un plafond de bois rouge en forme d'hélice, et un fond de lit sculptural dans le même matériau.
Ci-dessous: L'ouverture demi-circulaire donne sur le puits de lumière et laisse entrer une lumière naturelle diffuse, tout en rappelant par sa forme les couchers de soleil que l'architecte observe de sa terrasse. Le plan de travail du meuble de cuisine en bois rouge doucement arqué est recouvert d'un linoléum jaune de 3 mm d'épaisseur, utilisé jadis sur les navires de guerre. L'îlot en forme de losange, soutenu par un piétement en acier, forme une table parfaite pour un petit déjeuner en tête à tête.

Rechts: Die Decke in Muennigs Schlafzimmer besteht aus fächerför-mig angeordnetem, wiederverwendetem Redwood, das Kopfende des Bettes aus glatt gehobeltem Redwood.
Unten: Der Rundbogen öffnet sich zu einem Lichthof und läßt diffu-ses Sonnenlicht ein. Er erinnert an die Sonnenuntergänge, die Muen-nig jeden Abend von seiner vorderen Terrasse aus genießt. Die in einer geschwungenen Linie angeordneten Küchenschränke sind mit Red-wood verkleidet und haben eine 3 mm dicke Auflage aus hellbraunem Linoleum, das früher auf Schlachtschiffen verwendet wurde, erzählt Muennig. Der bonbonförmige Fleischerblock ruht auf einem Stahl-sockel – ein perfekter Platz für ein Frühstück zu zweit.

Ensommeillée au bord de la baie, Sausalito, petite ville centenaire de 7 000 habitants, jouit d'une réputation de colonie d'artistes. «La vie s'y déroule comme de longues vacances – sans les valises», commente l'écrivain new-yorkais Cynthia Franco, qui vit sur son bateau, l'Archangel, depuis 15 ans. Sausalito est synonyme de bateaux aménagés et celui de Cynthia est l'un des plus beaux. Construit par des charpentiers hippies dans les années 60, il flotte en toute sécurité dans un bassin en béton, et sa grande fenêtre-verrière donne sur un paisible lagon. D'aimables phoques viennent lui rendre visite lorsqu'elle lit son journal matinal sur sa terrasse. «Les bateaux ont une âme», ajoute-t-elle. «C'est un style de vie qui attire certaines personnes: designers, sculpteurs, inventeurs, juristes et artistes, architectes navals et bourlingueurs.» Cynthia qui partage sa vie avec Jake, un pointer allemand à poil ras, fait remarquer que chaque propriétaire doit entretenir son bateau. Mais la vie sur l'eau est relaxante. Après neuf heures du soir, le silence tombe sur le port.

Cynthia Franco

Sausalito, a sleepy, centuries-old town of just 7 000 people, has the lingering aura of an artists' colony. "Life in Sausalito is like a vacation every day – without the packing," said writer Cynthia Franco, a former New Yorker who has lived on her houseboat, The Archangel, for 15 years. Sausalito is synonymous with houseboats and Franco's is one of the finest. Built by hippie carpenters in the 60s, it floats securely on a concrete barge and boasts a large bay window overlooking a quiet lagoon. Friendly seals often bob about as she reads the morning newspaper on her terrace. "Houseboats have soul," she said. "It's a way of life that attracts a range of people – designers, sculptors, inventors, lawyers, and artists, master boat builders and world-class sailors." Franco, who shares her life with Jake, a German short-haired pointer, noted that each houseboat dweller has the responsibility of keeping their vessel ship-shape. But life on the water is relaxing. After 9pm, silence falls over the peaceful harbor.

Sausalito ist ein verschlafenes Städtchen und gerade mal 100 Jahre alt. Das 7 000-Seelen-Nest ist eine verträumte Künstlerkolonie. »Leben in Sausalito ist wie jeden Tag Ferien zu haben – nur das Kofferpacken kann man sich sparen«, behauptet die Schriftstellerin Cynthia Franco. Seit 15 Jahren lebt die gebürtige New Yorkerin auf ihrem Hausboot »Archangel«. Halb Sausalito besteht aus Hausbooten, und das von Cynthia ist eines der schönsten. Die »Archangel« wurde in den 60er Jahren von ein paar Hippies mit Schreinererfahrung gebaut, ein stabiles Boot, das auf einer Betonbasis verankert ist. Durch ein großes Fenster hat man einen fantastischen Blick über die stille Bucht. Morgens, bei Frühstück und Zeitungslektüre auf der Terrasse, wird Cynthia von Seehunden begrüßt. »Hausboote haben eine Seele«, sagt sie. »Es ist eine ganz eigene Lebensweise, die eine Reihe interessanter Leute anzieht: Designer, Bildhauer, Erfinder, Anwälte und Künstler, aber auch Schiffsbauer und Weltklasse-Segler.« Doch auch für Hausboote gibt es Regeln, sagt Cynthia, die das Hausboot mit Vorstehhund Jake teilt: Man muß die schwimmende Behausung jederzeit flott machen können. Das Leben auf dem Wasser ist friedlich, nach 21 Uhr kehrt am Hafen Ruhe ein.

Above: Franco's sofa, covered in natural cotton cloth, is a favorite place for reading in the sun. Possessions are kept at a modest minimum, and it's best if they don't mind the sea air.
Facing page: Cynthia Franco dines sitting on a Mission-style chair, and at a fold-down Arts and Crafts table, which also serves as a desk. "Everything has to perform two or three tasks and collapse, fold-up or stack," said Franco.
Following pages: Cynthia Franco's houseboat retains its hippie-built nautical charm and character.

Ci-dessus: Le canapé de Cynthia, recouvert de toile de coton naturel, est son siège préféré pour lire au soleil. Les objets sont limités au maximum et il vaut mieux qu'ils résistent à l'air marin.
Page de droite: Cynthia dîne assise sur une chaise de style Mission à une table pliante Arts and Crafts, qui lui sert également de bureau. «Tout doit remplir deux ou trois fonctions, et se plier, s'empiler... ou disparaître.»
Double page suivante: le bateau a conservé son charme hippie.

Oben: Das Sofa mit naturfarbenem Baumwollbezug ist Cynthias Lieblingsleseplatz in der Sonne. Ihre Besitztümer sind auf ein Minimum beschränkt und müssen gegen die salzige Luft resistent sein.
Rechte Seite: Cynthia speist auf einem Mission-Style-Stuhl an einem Arts-and-Crafts-Klapptisch, der auch als Schreibtisch dient. »Jeder Gegenstand muß mindestens zwei Funktionen haben, zusammenklappbar oder stapelbar sein«, sagt Cynthia Franco.
Folgende Doppelseite: Cynthias Hausboot hat seinen Hippie-Charme bewahrt.

Les amis qui rendent visite à Sausalito à Suzanne Simpson et à son mari, l'expert-comptable Lew Litzky s'attendent à être reçus royalement. Tout commence par la traversée spectaculaire du Golden Gate Bridge, suivie d'une descente vertigineuse vers le port où est ancré leur houseboat. Acheté il y a 15 ans, ce bateau de cinq niveaux reposait sur une quille en béton solide et massive, mais ses 110 m² habitables avaient besoin d'une sérieuse rénovation. Après deux mois de chantier, Suzanne et l'architecte d'intérieur Brent M. Smith ont réussi à faire aboutir leur rêve. C'est une sorte de fantaisie hybride néo-mexico-vénitienne, enrichie d'art populaire d'Oaxaca, de murs de plâtre rose anti-stress, de carrelages artisanaux, de colonnes classiques et même d'un poêle en fonte pour l'hiver. Suzanne Simpson a agrandi sa cuisine d'un bow-window-serre pour laisser entrer davantage de lumière. Et lorsqu'ils sont lassés de la vie en bordure de la baie, ils partent pour les collines, pédalent dans les hautes terres du comté de Marin, ou font de la marche à Muir Beach.

Suzanne Simpson and Lew Litzky

Friends who visit artist Suzanne Simpson and her husband, accountant Lew Litzky, in Sausalito know they are in for a treat. First there is the jaunt over the Golden Gate Bridge, then there is the hop and skip down a dock to their houseboat. When Simpson and Litzky acquired their five-level houseboat 15 years ago, it was on a solid concrete hull but the 110 sq.m. house was in need of attention. After a two-month restoration, Simpson and interior designer Brent M. Smith came up with a fantasy. It's a Neo-Mexico-meets-Venice trip, complete with Oaxacan folk art, soothing hand-plastered pink walls, hand-crafted tiles, classical columns, an old iron stove for winter warmth. Simpson added a greenhouse window in the kitchen to draw in more light. And when they tire of shore life, the couple takes to the hills, biking on the Marin headlands and hiking along the Muir Beach trails. They never miss the city.

Freunde, die die Künstlerin Suzanne Simpson und ihren Mann, den Wirtschaftsprüfer Lew Litzky, in Sausalito besuchen, können sicher sein, daß ihnen ein Höchstmaß an Lebensart geboten wird. Es fängt an mit der Fahrt über die Golden Gate Bridge. Dann folgt der Sprung von einem Bootssteg direkt auf das 110 m² große Hausboot. Das fünfstöckige Wohnschiff, das Simpson und Litzky vor 15 Jahren kauften, war eine marode Behausung auf einem soliden Betonfundament. Nach zwei Monaten intensiver Renovierung entstand allmählich das Fantasialand, von dem Suzanne Simpson und Interior-Designer Brent M. Smith immer geträumt hatten. Das baufällige Boot von einst ist jetzt ein neomexikanischer Trip mit Abstecher nach Venedig, komplett mit Folk Art aus Oaxaca, handverputzten rosa Wänden, handgefertigten Kacheln, klassizistischen Säulen und einem alten Kanonenofen, der im Winter Wärme spendet. Suzanne Simpson ließ in der Küche ein Wintergartenfenster einbauen, um mehr Licht hereinzulassen. Wenn dem Ehepaar das Leben an der Küste zu eng wird, zieht es in die Berge. Sie radeln auf der Ebene der Marin Headlands oder wandern am Muir Beach. Die Stadt aber vermissen sie nie.

Un cottage de pêcheur n'était pas exactement ce que recherchaient le décorateur Stephen Shubel et son compagnon, l'artiste Woody Biggs. Ils avaient longtemps aimé leur bel appartement de Berkeley et espéraient trouver une élégante maison de grandes proportions à rénover. Un ami les persuada d'emménager dans la calme petite cité de Sausalito, en bordure de la baie. Là, au flanc d'une colline escarpée, ils découvrirent ce ravissant petit bungalow de bois construit juste après le tremblement de terre de 1906 qui avait effacé la plus grande partie de la ville. Sans fondation et un peu bancale, la maison n'en possédait pas moins un certain charme suranné et beaucoup d'authenticité. Stephen et Woody l'ont assise sur une base plus solide, ils ont refait l'électricité, installé une nouvelle cuisine et ajouté un atelier de peinture. Les cloisons de bois et les sols en planches ont été laissés tels quels et soulignés de rayures passées à la peinture noire de bateau. Les plafonds et les murs ont été peints en blanc pour éclairer les pièces, et les fenêtres en noir pour créer un effet graphique.

Stephen Shubel and Woody Biggs

A fisherman's cottage was not exactly what interior designer Stephen Shubel and his partner, artist Woody Biggs, were looking for in a new residence. They had enjoyed a sophisticated apartment in Berkeley for many years, and hoped to find a handsome house with grand proportions to renovate. A friend persuaded them to cross San Francisco Bay and to move to the quiet bay-view town of Sausalito. There, on a steep hillside, they found a charming little shingled bungalow built just after the 1906 earthquake which leveled San Francisco. Foundationless and a little lop-sided, the house nevertheless had a certain timeworn charm and authenticity. Shubel and Biggs underpinned it with a new solid footing, rewired the house, installed a new kitchen, and added a painting studio. Wood paneling and plank floors were left intact and striped with black deck paint. Ceilings and walls were painted white to lighten the rooms, and windows were outlined in graphic black paint.

An ein Fischerhäuschen hatten der Interior-Designer Stephen Shubel und der Künstler Woody Biggs nicht gedacht, als sie sich auf die Suche nach einer neuen Bleibe machten. Jahrelang wohnten die beiden in einem schicken Apartment im Stadtteil Berkeley in San Francisco. Eigentlich träumten sie von einem großzügigen Haus, das sie gemeinsam herrichten wollten. Ein Freund überredete sie, sich in dem ruhigen Küstenstädtchen Sausalito jenseits der Bucht von San Francisco umzusehen. Dort fanden sie einen kleinen Bungalow, der 1906 errichtet worden war, nachdem das tragische Erdbeben San Francisco zerstärt hatte. Das Haus besaß kein Fundament und war ein wenig windschief. Aber der bröckelnde Charme und die Ursprünglichkeit überzeugten Shubel und Biggs. Als erstes stellten sie das Gebäude auf ein solides Fundament. Dann wurden neue Elektroleitungen verlegt, eine Küche gebaut und ein Atelier eingerichtet. Sie beließen die Holzpaneele und Plankenböden, die sie mit schwarzer Schiffsfarbe lackierten. Decken und Wände sind weiß, schwarzgestrichene Rahmen betonen die Fenster.

Stephen Shubel, Woody Biggs and their dog, Sophie, share a 93 sq.m. Sausalito fisherman's cottage that feels like it ran aground somewhere much more cosmopolitan. Shubel travels to Paris and the South of France two or three times a year, and his flea-market forays have yielded a treasure chest of gilt-framed mezzotints, water-gilded mirrors, along with a gleaming clutter of old hotel silver. The monochromatic white-with-stripes color scheme is splashed with chartreuse silk trimmed with silk cord. Another source of stripes: ebony lacquered stairs with glossy white risers.

Stephen Shubel, Woody Biggs et leur chienne, Sophie, partagent un cottage de pêcheur de 93 m², qui n'est pas dénué d'un certain parfum cosmopolite. Stephen se rend à Paris et dans le sud de la France deux ou trois fois par an, et ses trouvailles aux Puces alimentent un trésor de mezzo-tinto sous cadres dorés, de miroirs dorés et de tout un assortiment de vieille argenterie d'hôtel. La coloration essentiellement blanche à rayures est égayée de soie chartreuse à passementerie de soie. Autre occasion de rayures: des escaliers laqués noir ébène à contremarches blanc brillant.

Stephen Shubel, Woody Biggs und ihre Hündin Sophie leben in Sausalito in einem 93 m² großen Fischerhaus mit kosmopolitischem Charme. Shubel reist mehrmals im Jahr nach Paris und Südfrankreich. Seine Flohmarktfunde sind ein Schatz an goldgerahmten Mezzotinto-Stichen, vergoldeten Spiegeln und schimmerndem alten Hotelsilber. Die Grundfarbe im Haus ist Weiß. Chartreusefarbene Streifen und Seidenkordeln geben Schwung. Das Streifenschema setzt sich in der ebenholzschwarz und strahlend weiß lackierten Treppe fort.

Facing page and above: Stephen Shubel is a master at displaying his "Marché aux Puces" purchases, and his tableaux are a mélange of Parisian etchings, Provençal gilt-framed mirrors, terracotta busts, paper clocks, Irish mezzotints, and pure white Italian ceramics. What holds them together: a certain time-worn allure. Chips and nicks are welcome.
Right: The galley kitchen, with its boldly striped hardwood floor, has a handsome old armoire.

Page de gauche et ci-dessus: Stephen Shubel maîtrise l'art de mettre en valeur ses achats au marché aux puces, et ses mises en scène marient gravures parisiennes, miroirs provençaux à cadre doré, bustes en terre cuite, horloges en papier, mezzo-tinto irlandais et céramiques italiennes d'un blanc éclatant. Leur aspect légèrement fatigué les réunit. Ebréchures et fêlures sont les bienvenues.
A droite: La cuisine-couloir, au sol en bois peint non sans audace, est équipée d'une belle armoire d'époque.

Linke Seite und oben: Stephen Shubel versteht es meisterhaft, seine Flohmarktfunde auszustellen. Hier hat er gekonnt Radierungen aus Paris, provenzalische goldgerahmte Spiegel, Terrakottabüsten, Uhren aus Pappmaché, irische Mezzotinto-Stiche und reinweiße italienische Keramik gemischt. Eines haben die Fundstücke gemeinsam: eine gewisse abgenutzte Schönheit. Und Nippes ist jederzeit willkommen.
Rechts: In der Kombüse mit dem kühn gestreiften Hartholzboden steht ein hübscher alter Vitrinenschrank.

What every gentleman needs: a full-length mirror, a capacious Victorian bath, hooks and hangers for ties and shirts, and a sturdy tray for eau de Cologne, brushes, cuff links boxes, and vintage porcelain. The old floor was rejuvenated with black deck paint, bedroom walls were lightened with creamy white paint, and the bathroom was treated to cheerful cream. Golden fabric draperies lined with fine black and white cotton add dimension and graciousness to the bedroom and dressing room.

Tout ce dont peut rêver un gentleman: un miroir toute hauteur, une profonde baignoire victorienne et des patères pour les cravates et les chemises, un plateau sur tréteau pour l'eau de Cologne, les brosses à cheveux, les boîtes de boutons de manchette et les porcelaines anciennes. Le vieux parquet a été recouvert de noir de bateau, les murs des chambres éclaircis grâce à une peinture d'un blanc crémeux et la salle de bains traitée en crème chaleureux. Des tentures de toile dorée doublée de fin coton blanc et noir donnent grâce et un air d'intimité à la chambre et au dressing-room.

Alles, was ein Gentleman braucht: einen großen Spiegel, ein großzügig geschnittenes viktorianisches Bad, Haken und Kleiderbügel für Krawatten und Hemden, einen soliden Tablettisch für Eau de Cologne, Bürsten, Kästchen für Manschettenknöpfe und antikes Porzellan. Der alte Boden wurde mit schwarzer Schiffsfarbe gestrichen, das Schlafzimmer und das Bad erstrahlen in freundlichem Cremeweiß. Goldfarbene Leinenvorhänge mit feinsten schwarzweißen Baumwollbordüren verleihen dem Schlaf- und Ankleidezimmer Stil und Anmut.

Quelques interventions simples ont permis au décorateur Stephen Brady de donner à la maison de plage qu'il loue à Stinson une atmosphère à la fois confortable, calme et décontractée. «Les maisons de plage peuvent être aussi chics et stylées que bien des résidences de ville, mais doivent savoir rester plus décontractées», précise Stephen, vice-président responsable de la création visuelle pour l'entreprise de mode The Limited. «Le style estival est tout d'aisance et de simplicité, mais cela ne veut pas dire qu'il faille laisser tout effort de style à la porte.» Lorsqu'il s'est installé à Stinson Beach, il a opté pour une palette de couleurs neutres et de blanc, avec quelques nuances de bleu, pour évoquer la fraîcheur de l'océan. De vastes fauteuils recouverts de denim, de vieux livres, quelques antiquités ramenées de Paris, des panier de coquillages et d'anciennes chaises françaises donnent caractère et matière à cette maison cachée au milieu des dunes. Dans cette petite ville en bordure de l'océan, à une heure à peine au nord de San Francisco, le style de vie estival veut que l'on cueille ses fleurs au petit matin avant de les disposer avec art dans de vieux pichets français ...

Stephen Brady

With a few simple design moves, interior designer Stephen Brady gave his rented Stinson Beach house a mood that's casual, cool, and calm. "Beach houses can be as chic and style-conscious as places in the city – except they must be more relaxed," said Stephen Brady, the vice-president for visual design development for The Limited. "Summer style is all about ease and simplicity. But that doesn't mean leaving style at the door." When Brady moved to Stinson Beach, he started with a palette of neutral colors splashed with white, plus tones of blue for its seaside freshness. Large denim-covered club chairs, old books, Parisian antiques, baskets of shells, and vintage French café chairs add character and texture to Brady's house, which is hidden among the dunes. Summer style at this oceanside town just an hour north of San Francisco involves picking fresh flowers in the early morning and arranging them simply in vintage French pitchers.

Mit ein paar einfachen Einrichtungstricks verwandelte der Interior-Designer Stephen Brady sein gemietetes Haus am Stinson Beach in ein einfaches, kühles und beruhigendes Refugium. »Strandhäuser dürfen genauso schick und stilvoll sein wie Apartments in der Stadt. Wichtig ist nur, daß man entspannen kann«, sagt Stephen Brady, Vizepräsident für visuelles Design bei der Modefirma The Limited. »Leichtigkeit und Einfachheit, das ist der Stil des Sommers. Das heißt aber nicht, daß Eleganz außen vor bleiben muß.« Als Brady das Haus am Stinson Beach bezog, brachte er eine Palette neutraler Farben ein, viel Weiß und verschiedene Blautöne, die das Meer widerspiegeln. Riesige Clubsessel mit Jeansbezug, alte Bücher, Antiquitäten aus Paris, Körbe voller Muscheln und alte französische Stühle verleihen dem Haus in den Dünen Charakter und Stil. Hier, in diesem kleinen Küstenstädtchen eine Stunde nördlich von San Francisco werden die Blumen früh am Morgen gepflückt und in alten französischen Karaffen arrangiert.

On weekends, Brady's goal is to provide a place of comfort and fun for friends. "They can relax and chat, head off to the beach, or wrap themselves in a cashmere throw and read the Sunday paper. They can put their feet up on the coffee table," explains the interior designer. A bar with beach views is there for the guests' enjoyment.

Pendant les week-ends, la maison de plage de Brady joue le rôle de havre pour ses amis. «Ils peuvent se détendre, bavarder, aller à la plage, ou s'envelopper dans une couverture de cachemire pour lire le journal du dimanche. Ils peuvent même poser leurs pieds sur la table basse», explique le décorateur. Un bar, avec vue sur la baie, est à la disposition des invités.

An den Wochenenden erholen und amüsieren sich Bradys Freunde in dem Strandhaus . »Bei mir können sie sich entspannen, quatschen, am Strand bummeln, sich in eine Kaschmirdecke hüllen, die Sonntagszeitung lesen und die Füße auf den Couchtisch legen«, erklärt der Interior-Designer. Die Bar mit Strandblick ist für alle und immer geöffnet.

Above: Stephen Brady's living room is a cool breeze, with white walls, colorful paintings, blue-striped ticking cushions, easy chairs. "In summer, you should take fabrics down a few notches," said the designer. "Heavy-weight cotton denims, ticking and linens are more appropriate. They feel great against bare skin – and you can throw them in the washing machine."
Right: On summer evenings, Brady enjoys sitting on the terrace.
Facing page: Stephen Brady gathered favorite flotsam and jetsam around the front door. The ladder leads to his attic study overlooking the beach.

Ci-dessus: La salle de séjour évoque une brise fraîche, avec ses murs blancs, ses tableaux colorés, ses coussins de coutil à rayures bleues et des chaises longues. «En été, vous devez alléger les tissus», conseille le décorateur. «Les denims de coton lourds, les coutils et les lins sont plus appropriés. Ils sont agréables à la peau, et vous pouvez les passer à la machine à laver.»
A droite: Brady aime passer les soirées d'été sur la terrasse.
Page de droite: Stephen Brady a réuni quelques trouvailles bien aimées de récupération autour de la porte d'entrée. L'échelle conduit au bureau installé dans le grenier qui donne sur la plage.

Oben: Stephen Bradys Wohnzimmer ist so frisch wie eine Meeresbrise: weiße Wände, farbenfrohe Gemälde, blaugestreifte Drillichkissen, gemütliche Sessel. »Im Sommer muß man bei der Wahl der Stoffe bescheiden werden«, rät Brady. »Schwere Jeansstoffe, Drillich und Leinen sind angemessen. Sie fühlen sich auf nackter Haut gut an, und man kann sie einfach in die Waschmaschine werfen.«
Rechts: Sommerabende genießt Brady auf der Terrasse.
Rechte Seite: Neben der Eingangstür stapelt Brady allerlei »Strandgut«. Die Leiter führt zu seinem Arbeitszimmer, von dem aus man das Meer überblickt.

Right: Sea-theme collections on a concrete fireplace mantel include coral, an old tortoiseshell, and Chinese porcelain.
Below: Brady is a thoughtful, relaxed host. Living at the beach means a big table set for four or ten. The dining room is furnished with a large table and folding chairs to make entertaining and relaxing memorable indeed. Brady likes a generous table – for dining, drawing, working, or gathering. The café chairs – brought over from France – easily move outdoors when weather permits. An old hamper near the door stores beach towels. It's also an impromptu stage for beach finds.

A droite: Les collections à thème marin sur le manteau de la cheminée réunissent coraux, carapaces de tortues et porcelaines de Chine.
Ci-dessous: Stephen est un hôte accompli mais décontracté. Vivre au bord de l'eau attire les invités et une table de dix couverts n'est pas rare chez lui. La salle à manger est meublée d'une grande table cernée de chaises pliantes. L'hôte aime les tables de proportions généreuses pour dîner, dessiner, travailler, ou se retrouver entre amis. Les chaises, achetées en France, passent dehors lorsque le temps le permet. Près des portes, un vieux panier d'osier reçoit les serviettes de plage. C'est également là que sont rangées les trouvailles faites sur la plage.

Rechts: Auf dem Kaminsims aus Beton steht Sammelsurium zum Thema »Meer«: Korallen, ein alter Schildkrötenpanzer und chinesisches Porzellan.
Unten: Brady ist ein aufmerksamer und entspannter Gastgeber. Leben am Strand ist für ihn Synonym für einen großen Tisch für vier bis zehn Personen. Im Eßzimmer stehen ein großer, gemütlicher Tisch und Klappstühle, um Einladungen unkompliziert und erinnerungswürdig zu machen. Brady liebt großflächige Tische. An ihnen ißt, zeichnet, werkelt und sammelt er. Die Stühle, Mitbringsel aus Frankreich, lassen sich bei schönem Wetter schnell nach draußen transportieren. In dem alten Wäschekorb neben der Tür liegen Strandhandtücher. Dort kann man auch mal schnell Fundsachen vom Strand ablegen.

Rigid styles of decor are an anathema to Brady, who believes that rooms which mix antiques with new household goods are the most successful. Restaurant-ware, stacks of favorite books, oil paintings, and ceramics that traveled with him from the city make the interiors look as if he's lived there for years. "The architecture speaks of no particular time or place. The walls and woodwork are painted white, a great background for summer style. You can bend the decor in any direction." Paintings, coral, a folk-art cross, and old linens offer their own tribute to seaside living.

Tout décor unifié et figé déplaît souverainement à Stephen. Il préfère marier objets anciens et nouveaux. De la vaisselle de restaurant, des piles de livres bien aimés, des tableaux, et des céramiques rapportées de la ville donnent l'impression que cette pièce existe depuis toujours. «L'architecture ne raconte rien de particulier. Les murs et les boiseries sont peints en blanc, un fond qui convient au style d'été. Vous pouvez ainsi orienter votre décor dans la direction que vous désirez.» Des peintures, des coraux, une croix de l'art populaire et des draps anciens apportent leur tribut à ce style de vie particulier en bordure de l'océan.

Brady glaubt nicht an Dekor auf Knopfdruck. Er weiß, daß eine Mischung aus Alt und Neu das beste Einrichtungskonzept ist. Mit Restaurantgeschirr und Lieblingsbüchern, Ölgemälden und Keramik, die er aus der Stadt mitgebracht hat, wirkt das Haus wie seit Jahren bewohnt. »Die Architektur verrät nichts über Alter und Standort. Die Wände und Holzelemente sind weiß gestrichen und ein idealer Hintergrund für den Sommerstil. Vor Weiß kann man alles stellen.« Die Gemälde und Korallen, ein Folk-Art-Kreuz und altes Leinen – sie sind Sinnbilder für das einfache Leben am Strand.

Susie Tompkins Buell, cofondatrice d'Esprit et aujourd'hui très impliquée dans la politique, a vécu une enfance idyllique dans une petite ville côtière, au nord de San Francisco. Là, dans les années 50 et 60, elle aimait se promener avec ses amis sur les immenses plages, longtemps après le coucher du soleil. Trente ans plus tard, elle a acquis un superbe terrain sauvage près de sa ville natale, avec vue directe sur le fameux Mount Tamalpais. Tout près, se trouve une réserve de hérons bleus. «J'ai toujours apprécié la tranquillité de cette partie de la côte et souhaité protéger ce paysage», ajoute-t-elle. Elle avait rêvé d'une ferme modernisée, construite en humbles matériaux, où elle, son mari Mark et ses enfants puissent se réunir pendant les week-ends d'été. Cette maison facile à vivre, implantée dans un creux suspendu au-dessus des marais, est aujourd'hui entourée de jardins où poussent herbes aromatiques et légumes. Susie, sa famille et leurs nombreux amis marchent, se promènent ou font du vélo le long de la plage. Les beaux jours de l'enfance sont de retour.

Susie and Mark Buell

Susie Tompkins Buell, Esprit co-founder and now a political activist, spent her idyllic childhood in a small coastal town north of San Francisco. There in the 50s and 60s, she recalls, she would roam far and wide with her friends, lingering on the wide beaches long after twilight. Thirty years later, she acquired a prize piece of undeveloped property near the town, with a front-on lookout to fabled Mount Tamalpais. Nearby is a blue heron sanctuary. "I've always loved that quiet part of the coast and wanted to protect this hillside," said Buell. She planned an updated farmhouse, built of humble materials, where she and her husband Mark and their children could gather on summer weekends. The easy-going house, set in a swale above the marshlands, is now surrounded by gardens where fresh herbs and vegetables are nurtured. "We lead a natural, outdoor life here," said Susie. She and her family cycle, hike, wander along the beach, huddle with friends – and childhood does not seem so far away.

Susie Tompkins Buell, Mitbegründerin der Modefirma Esprit und heute engagierte politische Aktivistin, verbrachte ihre idyllische Kindheit in einem kleinen Küstenstädtchen nördlich von San Francisco. In den 50er und 60er Jahren unternahm sie mit ihren Freunden lange Ausflüge an den breiten Stränden, oft bis weit nach Einbruch der Dunkelheit. Und 30 Jahre später kaufte sie ganz in der Nähe des Städtchens ein erstklassiges Stück unerschlossenes Land, das einen fantastischen Blick auf den berühmten Mount Tamalpais bot. Nicht weit vom Grundstück entfernt befindet sich ein Schutzgebiet für Blaureiher. »Diesen stillen Küstenabschnitt habe ich schon immer geliebt«, sagt Buell. »Und dieser Berghang sollte unberührt bleiben.« Sie entwarf aus einfachen Materialien ein modernes Farmhaus, in dem sie, ihr Mann Mark und die Kinder die Sommerwochenenden verbringen konnten. Das bescheidene Gebäude liegt auf einer Anhöhe über dem Marschland und ist von einem Kräuter- und Gemüsegarten umgeben. »Hier führen wir ein naturverbundenes Leben im Freien«, sagt Susie. Sie fahren Fahrrad, wandern, machen lange Strandspaziergänge und trommeln ihre Freunde zusammen – hier leben sie ein Stück vergangene Kindheit.

Facing page: Susie and Mark Buell enjoy an autumn afternoon above the quiet tidal lagoon; their U-shaped house encloses broad verandahs and a sunny terrace.
Above and right: Susie and her family lead a natural, outdoor life. The chairs were crafted from recycled local wood.

Page de gauche: Susie et Mark Buell adorent les après-midi d'automne au bord du lagon calme. Leur maison en forme de U comporte de profondes vérandas et une terrasse ensoleillée.
Ci-dessus et à droite: Susie et sa famille mènent une vie naturelle en plein air. Les fauteuils ont été fabriqués en bois du pays recyclé.

Linke Seite: Susie und Mark Buell verbringen einen herbstlichen Nachmittag oberhalb der ruhigen Bucht; breite Verandas und eine Sonnenterrasse umgeben das U-förmige Haus.
Oben und rechts: Susie und ihre Familie lieben das naturverbundene Leben. Die Stühle wurden aus wiederverwendetem Holz gezimmert.

Above: 50s chairs and a velvet-upholstered banquette invite the family to relax around the winter fire. Susie's Jack Russell, Gracie, takes in the view.
Right and facing page: The living room, with its plank-formed concrete fireplace, has the noble proportions of a traditional barn, complete with beams and trusses. Susie's 50s style: hand-crafted Afghans, mustard and avocado velvet cushions, Paris flea-market finds.

Ci-dessus: Des fauteuils des années 50 et une banquette recouverte de velours invitent à se relaxer autour d'une flambée hivernale. Le jack-russell de Susie, Gracie, a trouvé son coin.
A droite et page de droite: Le séjour à cheminée en béton brut de décoffrage, affiche les nobles proportions d'une grande demeure traditionnelle, y compris celles des poutres et des chevrons. Le style de Susie des années 50: tapis afghans, coussins de velours moutarde et avocat, trouvailles faites au marché aux puces de Paris.

Oben: Armlehnstühle aus den 50er Jahren und eine samtgepolsterte Eckbank laden im Winter zum Entspannen am Kamin ein. Susies Jack-Russell-Terrier Gracie nimmt hier gerne Platz.
Rechts und rechte Seite: Das Wohnzimmer mit dem Kamin in Sichtbetonoptik hat die harmonischen Proportionen einer traditionellen Scheune, komplett mit Balken und Verstrebungen. Susies Interpretation der 50er Jahre: handgewebte Afghanen, Samtkissen in Senfgelb und Avocadogrün sowie Accessoires vom Pariser Flohmarkt.

Above: Susie's dear friend, renowned Chez Panisse chef Alice Waters, often cooks in the sky-lit kitchen. Vegetables are gathered at the farmer's market. Broad wooden counters and a large walk-in pantry were built for crowds of hungry beachgoers and hikers.
Right: Mark Buell hand-carved the birch napkin rings for a recent Thanksgiving dinner.
Facing page: Ripe persimmons and autumn leaves paint an impression of late autumn on the northern California coast.

Ci-dessus: Un des grands amis de Susie, Alice Waters, le chef réputé de Chez Panisse opère souvent dans cette pièce à éclairage zénithal. Les légumes proviennent du marché local. Les grands comptoirs de bois et un vaste office ont été construits pour répondre aux fringales des nombreux visiteurs.
A droite: Mark Buell a sculpté lui-même ces ronds de serviette à l'occasion d'un récent dîner de Thanksgiving.
Page de droite: Plaquemines, fruits typiques de ces contrées, et feuillage couleur de rouille laissent une impression de fin d'automne sur la côte du nord de la Californie.

Oben: Alice Waters, Küchenchefin des renommierten Restaurants Chez Panisse, ist eine von Susies besten Freundinnen. Sie kocht häufig in der Küche mit Oberlicht. Das Gemüse kommt vom Wochenmarkt. Die breiten Arbeitsflächen aus Holz und die begehbare Speisekammer wurden für Horden hungriger Sonnenanbeter und Wanderer gebaut.
Rechts: Mark Buell schnitzte die Serviettenringe aus Birkenholz für ein Thanksgiving-Dinner.
Rechte Seite: Farbspiel mit verfärbten Blättern und reifen Persimonen, einer nordamerikanischen Dattelpflaume – Impressionen aus dem nordkalifornischen Spätherbst.

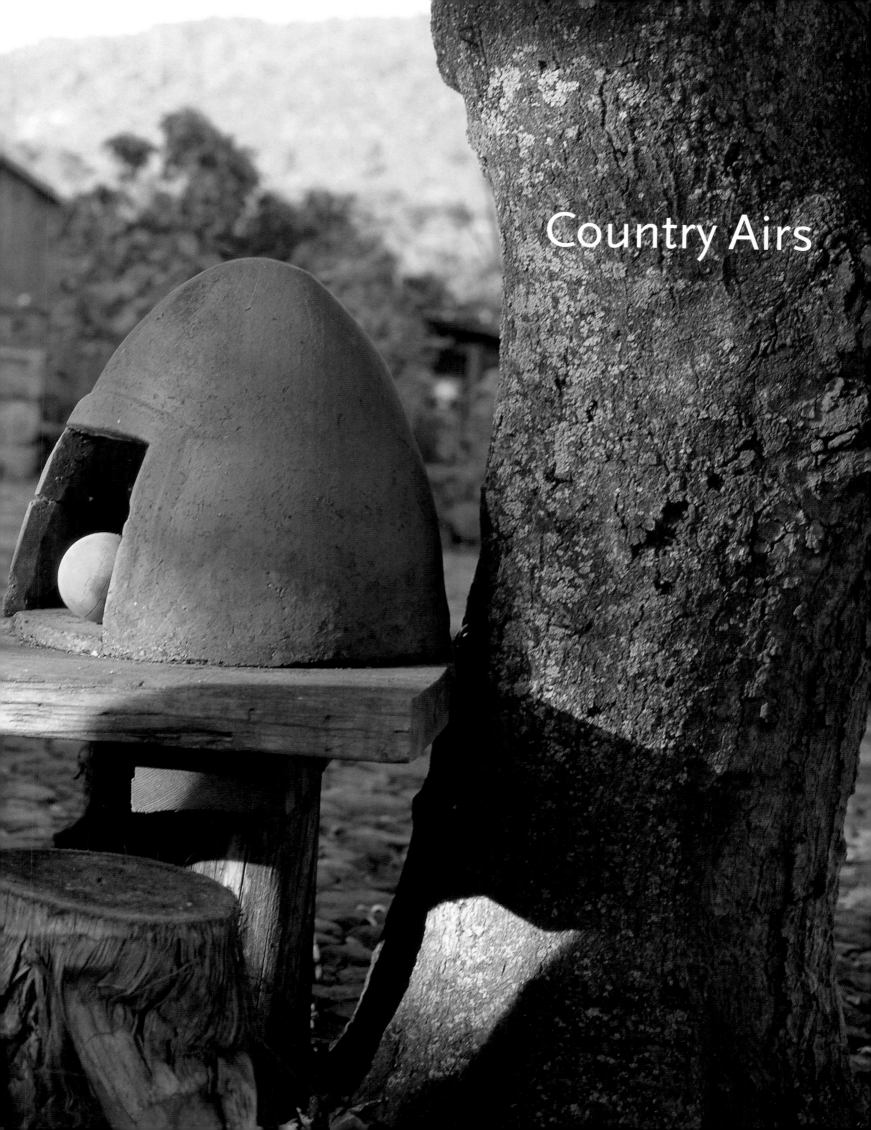

Country Airs

En acquérant cette ferme de la région de Sonoma il y a une douzaine d'années, le décorateur Ron Mann et son épouse, Louise La Palme Mann, créatrice textile, attendaient beaucoup de la vie à la campagne. Louise planta derechef un superbe jardin de fines herbes et de salades. «Lorsque les laitues et la roquette furent à point, des oiseaux et des daims affamés se précipitèrent pour nous ôter notre repas de la bouche», se rappelle Louise. Voulant s'intégrer à la vie sauvage locale, serpents à sonnettes inclus, ils partirent donc à la recherche de plantes qui laissent les daims indifférents. «Nous avons fini par découvrir une lavande à Majorque et décidé de la tenter chez nous», poursuit Louise. Ils acclimatèrent 1 000 plants de Lavandula Intermedia 'Provence' et de Lavandula 'Grosso', et installèrent un système d'arrosage. L'été suivant, leurs champs n'étaient plus qu'un nuage de bleu et de vert. Avec Jeronimo Perez, maître maçon, ils ont aussi transformé un bout de terrain poussiéreux en élégant jardin à terrasses de pierre. A partir de pierres volcaniques, ils ont monté des murs de pierre sèche et une terrasse pour dîner sous les vieux chênes.

Louise and Ron Mann

When interior designer Ron Mann, and his wife, Louise La Palme Mann, a fabric designer, acquired their Sonoma farm twelve years ago, they had high hopes of living off the land. Louise planted a luscious garden of herbs and salad greens. "When the lettuces and arugala were ready for harvesting, voracious birds and deer munched our planned lunch," recalled Louise. They wanted to get along with the local wildlife, which includes rattlesnakes, so they went hunting for plants that deer wouldn't savor. "We discovered lavender in Majorca and decided to experiment," Louise said. They planted a thousand plants of Lavandula Intermedia 'Provence' and Lavandula 'Grosso', and set up a watering system. The following summer, their fields were a cloud of blue and green. With Jeronimo Perez, an expert stonemason, the Manns transformed their dusty garden into elegant stone terraces. Volcanic rocks from their property were shaped into dry-stacked walls, and a new stone dining terrace appeared beneath their ancient native oaks.

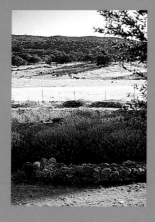

Vor zwölf Jahren kauften der Interior-Designer Ron Mann und seine Frau, die Stoffdesignerin Louise La Palme Mann, eine Farm in Sonoma. Sie träumten davon, sich von dem neu erworbenen Land zu ernähren. Louise legte einen üppigen Gemüsegarten an. »Als der Salat und die Arugula-Pflanzen geerntet werden konnten, hatten gierige Vögel und Rehe sie schon längst vernichtet«, sagt Louise. Sie mußten sich irgendwie mit der ortsansässigen Tierwelt – unter anderem auch Klapperschlangen – arrangieren. Also verlegten sie sich auf reh- und vogelresistente Pflanzen. »In Mallorca entdeckten wir Lavendel und beschlossen, mit dieser robusten Pflanze zu experimentieren«, erzählt Louise. Sie setzten Tausende Schößlinge von Lavendula Intermedia ›Provence‹ und Lavendula ›Grosso‹ und installierten ein Bewässerungssystem. Im darauffolgenden Sommer saßen sie in einem dichten Feld aus Blau und Grün. Der Steinmetz Jeronimo Perez verwandelte den staubigen Garten der Manns in elegante Terrassen aus Stein. Das Vulkangestein für die Trockenmauern stammt von dem Grundstück. Unter den alten Eichen läßt sich auf der neuen Steinterrasse herrlich im Freien essen.

Above: Ron Mann designed the "Tab" sofa, which is upholstered in chrome yellow cloth by Louise Mann. The steel and fir tables and blown Majorcan-glass vessel are all by Ron Mann.
Right: view of the barn.
Facing page: Dream on: Ron Mann unearthed the 19th-century Mexican military officer's campaign bed, all brass, in a hill town near Mexico City. It's covered in washed charmeuse silk pillows of acid green, a bi-colored denim bedcover, and cotton sheets. Bark draped from the rafters is eucalyptus, from the farm's own trees.

Ci-dessus: Ron Mann a dessiné le canapé «Tab» recouvert d'une toile jaune de chrome de Louise. Les tables en pin et acier et les verreries majorquines soufflées sont toutes de Ron Mann.
A droite: vue de la grange.
Page de droite: Un rêve ... Ron a découvert ce lit d'officier mexicain du 19e siècle, tout en cuivre jaune, dans un village près de Mexico. Il est recouvert de coussins en soie lavée vert acide, d'une couverture bicolore en denim, et de draps de coton. Suspendues aux poutres, des écorces d'eucalyptus ramassées sur le domaine.

Oben: Ron Mann entwarf das »Tab«-Sofa, das mit chromgelbem Leinen von Louise Mann bezogen ist. Er gestaltete auch die Tische aus Stahl und Fichtenholz. Die mundgeblasenen Glasgefäße fertigte er auf Mallorca an.
Rechts: Blick auf den Geräteschuppen.
Rechte Seite: Das Messingbett aus dem 19. Jahrhundert war einst das Feldbett eines Offiziers der mexikanischen Armee. Ron Mann entdeckte es in einem Bergdorf in der Nähe von Mexico City. Als Auflagen dienen Kissen mit einem Bezug aus säuregrüner Waschseide, ein zweifarbiger Denimüberwurf und Baumwollwäsche. Von den Dachsparren hängt Eukalyptusrinde von farmeigenen Bäumen.

Tous deux artistes et vivant en Californie du Sud, Jean Lowe et Kim MacConnel ne se sentent aucunement liés par les conventions, que ce soit dans leur art subtilement subversif ou leur architecture. Quand ils décidèrent de se faire construire une maison, ils furent donc très réceptifs aux solutions de l'architecte de San Diego, Ted Smith, qui se révélèrent habiles, simples et économiques. Il leur proposa de travailler sur une trame de 3,65 x 8,55 m et des plafonds de 3,95 m de haut, concept facile à mettre en œuvre qu'il avait imaginé pour des logements économiques. La maison serait implantée au fond du terrain, pour mieux utiliser l'espace et réduire les coûts de construction. Quatre grandes pièces courraient derrière la façade de 34 m de long. Kim apprécie particulièrement ce système d'enfilade. Pour signaler cette construction basse et allongée, et aussi répondre au rêve de Jean d'un «château en Espagne», Smith a édifié une salle de bains tout en hauteur recouverte de tôle ondulée.

Jean Lowe and Kim MacConnel

Southern California artists Jean Lowe and Kim MacConnel don't feel bound by convention either in their subtly subversive art or in their architecture. So when the time came to build their own house, they approached San Diego architect Ted Smith with open minds. Smith's solutions were artful, simple, and cost-effective. He proposed working on a 3.65 x 8.55 m grid with 3.95 m ceilings. This basic and easy-to-construct concept was one he had developed previously for low-cost housing projects. Four straightforward rooms would be stretched across the 34 m house. It would stand at the back of the property, saving open space and construction costs. MacConnel said he particularly likes the way one room opens directly onto another. To punctuate the attenuated building – and fulfill Lowe's dream of a "Spanish castle", Smith built a tall bathroom at one end and sheathed it in corrugated steel.

Die südkalifornischen Künstler Jean Lowe und Kim MacConnel halten sich nicht an Konventionen, weder bei ihrer leicht subversiven Kunst noch bei ihrem Haus. Folglich legten sie dem Architekten Ted Smith aus San Diego keinerlei Restriktionen auf. Smith fand kunstvolle, einfache und preiswerte Lösungen. Er schlug vor, auf der Basis eines Grundrisses von 3,65 x 8,55 m und mit 3,95 m hohen Decken zu arbeiten. Dieses einfach zu realisierende Konzept hatte er einmal für Niedrigpreishäuser entwickelt. Das Haus sollte außerdem in der hintersten Ecke des Grundstücks stehen, um Platz und Geld zu sparen. Hinter der Fassade von 34 m Länge verbergen sich vier direkt nebeneinander liegende Räume. MacConnel gefällt besonders, daß die Räume direkt ineinanderübergehen. Um das langgestreckte Gebäude zu akzentuieren und gleichzeitig Lowes Traum eines »Luftschlosses« zu erfüllen, setzte Smith einen Badezimmerturm an ein Ende und verkleidete ihn mit gewelltem Stahl.

Previous pages: Jean Lowe and Kim MacConnel at their home near Escondido Creek by architect Ted Smith. The exterior of the house, which stands on two acres at the edge of a flood plain in San Diego County, is a patchwork of steel-reinforced masonry blocks and indigenous rocks. The secluded house is surrounded by a drought-resistant garden of lavender and native plants. Rooms also open directly onto patios and the garden.
Above: The kitchen's bare concrete block walls are enlivened with brightly painted cabinets and shelves, and Lowe and MacConnel's art works. The narrow proportions enhance their quick access to the great outdoors. Large steel-framed doors on each side offer cross ventilation in hot summers.

Double page précédente: Jean Lowe et Kim MacConnel dans leur maison d'Escondido Creek dessinée par l'architecte Ted Smith. L'extérieur de cette maison édifiée sur un terrain d'un hectare en bordure d'une plaine inondable du comté de San Diego, est un quilt de parpaings de maçonnerie, renforcés par une armature d'acier et de pierres locales. Retirée, la maison est entourée d'un jardin de lavandes et de plantes locales qui ne craignent pas la sécheresse. Les chambres ouvrent directement sur les patios et le jardin.
Ci-dessus: Les murs en parpaings de béton bruts sont animés de meubles et d'étagères peints de couleurs vives, et d'œuvres des deux artistes. Les proportions étroites mettent en valeur le lien direct avec la nature. Sur chaque façade, de grandes portes à cadre métallique assurent une ventilation naturelle pendant les chaleurs de l'été.

Vorhergehende Doppelseite: Jean Lowe und Kim MacConnel in ihrem von Ted Smith entworfenen Haus in der Nähe von Escondido Creek. Das Haus, das auf einem Hektar in der Nähe eines Hochwassergebietes im San Diego County steht, gleicht außen einem Patchwork aus stahlverstärktem Mauerwerk und Felsbrocken aus der Gegend. Das abseits gelegene Refugium ist von einem Garten mit Lavendel und einheimischen Pflanzen umgeben, die jeder Trockenperiode trotzen. Jedes Zimmer geht direkt auf den Garten oder einen Patio.
Oben: Die blanken Küchenwände aus Betonblöcken werden durch farbenfrohe Schränke und Regale belebt. Hier hängen auch Werke von Lowe und MacConnel. Die engen Proportionen gestatten den schnellen Zugang nach draußen. Während der heißen Sommermonate sorgen große stahlgerahmte Türen auf jeder Seite für die nötige Belüftung.

Right: *Painted volumes by Jean Lowe and works in progress make for happy clutter in the studio. The artists are represented by the Holly Solomon Gallery, New York.*
Below: *In Lowe and MacConnel's funhouse, art works come and go. "We really love to be surrounded by hot colors," said MacConnel and his wife, who were inspired in their color palette by visits to nearby Mexico, India and Spain. They purchased their paints in Tijuana, Mexico, just across the border from San Diego.*
Following pages: *the living room with hand-painted furniture and impromptu art works made with found objects.*

A droite: *Des volumes peints par Jean Lowe et des œuvres en gestation créent un heureux désordre dans l'atelier. Les deux artistes sont représentés par la galerie Holly Solomon, à New York.*
Ci-dessous: *Dans cette maison si vivante, les œuvres d'art vont et viennent. «Nous aimons réellement nous sentir entourés de couleurs chaudes», précisent Kim et Jean dont le chromatisme s'inspire de leurs voyages au Mexique tout proche, en Inde et en Espagne. Ils ont acheté des peintures à Tijuana, de l'autre côté de la frontière de San Diego.*
Double page suivante: *Le séjour est décoré de meubles peints à la main et d'œuvres d'art confectionnées à partir d'objets trouvés.*

Rechts: *Von Jean Lowe bemalte Bücher und unvollendete Werken sorgen im Studio für ein fröhliches Durcheinander. Beide Künstler werden von der Holly Solomon Gallery in New York vertreten.*
Unten: *In der unkonventionellen Wohnstätte von Lowe und MacConnel kommen und gehen die Kunstwerke. »Wir brauchen knallige Farben um uns herum«, sagen MacConnel und seine Frau, die sich für ihre Farbpalette im benachbarten Mexiko, in Indien und Spanien inspirieren lassen. Ihre Farben kaufen sie in Tijuana, einer kleinen Stadt gleich hinter der Grenze bei San Diego.*
Folgende Doppelseite: *das Wohnzimmer mit handbemalten Möbeln und improvisierter Kunst aus Fundstücken.*

Lowe and MacConnel's cheerful color scheme was inspired by trips south of the border into Mexico. Just as in village houses, the faux dado was hand-rolled, with Lowe and MacConnell hazarding a guess at the height. The resulting inexactitude and odd color proportions in the bedroom and living room add to the rooms' charm. The plan is not to "match" or create sedate perfection, but rather to send patterns and colors careening and caroming around the house, exciting the eye and the senses. A paved open patio separates the living areas and the bedroom.

La chaleureuse palette de Jean et de Kim leur a été inspirée par leurs voyages de l'autre côté de la frontière. Comme dans une maison de village, le faux lambris a été peint au rouleau en espérant que la hauteur serait la bonne. Le flou des proportions et les couleurs étranges donnent beaucoup de charme à la chambre et au séjour. L'idée n'est pas d'accéder à une perfection immuable, mais plutôt de créer des motifs et des couleurs qui se glissent et se bousculent dans la maison pour exciter le regard et les sens. Un patio ouvert et pavé sépare les pièces de séjour de la chambre.

Die Inspiration zu den fröhlichen Farben in Lowes und MacConnels Domizil stammt von Reisen nach Mexiko. Wie in den mexikanischen Dorfhäusern wurden die falschen Paneele mit der Hand gemalt, wobei deren Höhe von Lowe und MacConnel geschätzt wurde. Die daraus resultierenden schiefen Linien und die skurrilen Farbzusammenstellungen tragen unbedingt zum Charme im Wohn- und Schlafzimmer bei. Lowe und MacConnel wollten nichts »Passendes« oder Perfektes schaffen, sondern die Muster und Farben zum Tanzen bringen, um Auge und Sinne zu stimulieren. Ein gepflasterter Innenhof trennt den Wohn- vom Schlafbereich.

Above: 2.75 m tall arched doors which open directly on the outdoors give the long, narrow rooms a feeling of space and light. Tall twin armoires painted by Jean at the end of the bedroom also give the interior architecture more oomph. Entry to the steel-clad bathrooms is between the "faux-bois" armoires.
Right: Architect Ted Smith chose concrete blocks to give the house a sense of stability and permanence. The stock-colored blocks are also extremely budget-friendly, at 1 dollar per block.

Ci-dessus: De hautes portes arrondies de 2,75 m de haut ouvrent directement sur la nature et donnent un sentiment d'espace et de lumière même dans ces pièces longues et étroites. Les deux armoires jumelles peintes par Jean au bout de la chambre ajoutent un peu d'allant à l'architecture. L'entrée vers les salles de bains aux murs plaqués d'acier se trouve entre les armoires en faux-bois.
A droite: Ted Smith, l'architecte, a choisi des parpaings de ciment colorés pour donner à la maison un air de stabilité et de permanence. Ils sont par ailleurs très bon marché: 1 dollar la pièce!

Oben: Die 2,75 m hohen Rundbogentüren, die direkt ins Freie führen, geben den langen, schmalen Räumen Volumen und Licht. Das Schlafzimmer wird zusätzlich mit zwei von Jean bemalten Schränken aufgelockert. Zwischen den beiden mit Holzimitation bemalten Schränken befindet sich der Eingang zu den stahlverkleideten Badezimmern.
Rechts: Der Architekt Ted Smith wählte vorgefärbte Betonblöcke, um dem Haus Stabilität und Dauerhaftigkeit zu verleihen. Sie sind zudem extrem günstig und kosten nur 1 Dollar pro Stück.

Les maisons négligées, plus ou moins décaties, cachées dans les rues des banlieues de petites villes californiennes comme Mill Valley demandent souvent beaucoup de courage à leurs sauveteurs. Des acheteurs audacieux et visionnaires comme Dale et Philip Going ont su voir par-delà la poussière, la saleté et les recoins, et imaginer des intérieurs ensoleillés, chaleureux, emplis de musique et de poésie. «Certaines maisons de prix raisonnable dans des lieux séduisants ont souvent été négligées ou même laissées retourner à la terre» raconte Philip Going, constructeur. «La nôtre tombait en morceaux et allait se transformer en compost sous nos yeux.» Les Going ont interprété avec beaucoup de sensibilité l'esprit de cette maison Arts and Crafts de 1903 et sa situation agréable dans les arbres, juste au nord de San Francisco. Ils ont mis en valeur le meilleur de l'architecture de cet humble logement de meunier, et lui ont insufflé grâce et lumière au moyen de fenêtres métalliques anciennes à petits carreaux, tout en conservant les poutres d'origine sciées à la main.

Dale and Philip Going

Overlooked, neglected, and tumbledown houses in hidden streets on the outskirts of old California towns like Mill Valley often require valiant rescue missions. Brave and visionary buyers like Dale and Philip Going see beyond the grime and dust and poky corners, and imagine sunny interiors glowing with warmth, music and poetry. "Houses at reasonable prices in attractive locations have often been abandoned or simply left to go to seed," said Philip Going, a building contractor. "Ours was falling apart and turning into compost before our eyes." The Goings translated their ideas with great sensitivity both to the spirit of the original 1903 Arts and Crafts house and to their leafy location just north of San Francisco. They enhanced the best architectural features of its earlier incarnation as a humble millworker's house and bestowed new grace and light with vintage steel casement windows, while keeping the original hand-sawn timbers and handsome hardwood floors.

Vergessene, vernachlässigte und verfallene Häuser in Nebenstraßen alter kalifornischer Ortschaften wie Mill Valley verlangen viel Mut für ihre Instandsetzung und Renovierung. Unerschrockene Visionäre wie Dale und Philip Going sehen weit über Schmutz, Staub und Enge hinaus und können sich auch im allerschlimmsten Fall ein sonnen- und musikdurchflutetes Heim vorstellen. »Häuser zu akzeptablen Preisen in guten Gegenden sind oft heruntergekommen und von der Natur bereits vereinnahmt worden«, sagt Bauunternehmer Philip Going. »Das Haus, das wir im Auge hatten, fiel bereits zusammen und verwandelte sich vor unseren Augen zu Staub«. Sehr subtil und behutsam brachten die Goings ihre Ideen in das Arts-and-Crafts-Haus aus dem Jahr 1903 nördlich von San Francisco ein. Ursprünglich die bescheidene Bleibe eines Sägewerkarbeiters, offenbarte das Gebäude erstaunliche architektonische Details. Anmut und Licht kamen mit den antiken bleigefaßten Fenstern. Die originalen handgesägten Bohlen und den Hartholzboden beließ das Paar.

Previous pages and facing page: *Poet Dale Going is also a hand-printer of poetry books. In her tiny studio, overlooking the garden, she creates works-on-paper of grace and charm with her hand-cranked old press.*
Above and right: *Hidden behind a tangle of roses and clematis on a 12 x 56 m lot, the Goings' house is surrounded by mature plum, cherry and peach trees. It had been constructed by a millworker from redwood hand-milled at the Mill Valley Lumber Co. There was at first no foundation – the house was sitting on rocks.*

Double page précédente et page de gauche: *Dans son petit atelier qui donne sur le jardin, la poétesse Dale Going imprime à l'aide d'une vieille presse à main des livres de poésie et crée des œuvres sur papier imbues de charme.*
Ci-dessus et à droite: *Dissimulée derrière un fouillis de roses et de clématites sur un terrain de 12 x 56 m, la maison des Going est cernée de vieux pruniers, cerisiers et pêchers. Sans fondations, juste posée sur le rocher, elle avait été construite pour un meunier, dans un bois rouge façonné à la main par la Mill Valley Lumber Co.*

Vorhergehende Doppelseite und linke Seite: *Die Dichterin Dale Going druckt auch Gedichtbände auf ihrer alten Handpresse. Die Werke voller Anmut und Charme entstehen in ihrem winzigen Atelier, das auf den Garten hinausgeht.*
Oben und rechts: *Das Haus steht auf einem Grundstück, das kaum 12 x 56 m mißt. Es liegt verborgen hinter einer Wand aus Rosenbüschen und Klematis und ist umgeben von alten Pflaumen-, Kirsch- und Pfirsichbäumen. Ein Arbeiter des Sägewerks Mill Valley Lumber Co. hatte es für sich aus handgesägtem Redwood gebaut. Damals hatte das Haus nicht einmal ein Fundament, sondern war direkt auf den Felsen gesetzt worden.*

"Our house was formerly a warren of tiny dark rooms in dismal repair," recalled Dale Going. The couple painstakingly stripped off decades of wallpaper, cleaned and bleached the floors, and gave the interior a refreshing coat of bright white paint. The Goings furnished the new white-walled rooms with antiques, paintings and vintage accessories found in California antiques shops and upstate New York junk shops.

«Au départ, notre maison était une succession de petites pièces sombres en très mauvais état», se souvient Dale Going. Le couple a arraché à grand peine des décennies de papier peint, nettoyé et blanchi les sols, et repeint tout l'intérieur d'un blanc lumineux et rafraîchissant. Il l'a meublé d'antiquités, de tableaux et d'objets anciens trouvés chez les antiquaires californiens et des brocanteurs de l'Etat de New York.

»Unser Haus bestand aus einem Wirrwarr von winzigen, düsteren Kammern, die völlig heruntergekommen waren«, erinnert sich Dale Going. In minutiöser Kleinarbeit entfernte das Paar Schichten jahrzehntealter Tapeten, säuberte und bleichte die Böden und strich die Innenwände strahlend weiß. Die Goings richteten die aufgehellten Räume mit Antiquitäten, Gemälden und Accessoires ein, die sie in kalifornischen Antikläden und New Yorker Secondhandshops fanden.

Above: *The music room overlooks the garden. "All the wall surfaces were redwood – but the poorest grade – and they were all covered in 40 layers of old dust and paper," said Philip Going. "The key was to uncover the wood, then add small-paned windows to let in the light." They took down walls to open up the interiors and lighten and brighten the rooms, while still keeping their low-key, vintage air. "My vision was to make the house fit comfortably into the garden so that it would almost disappear beneath the wisteria and roses," said Dale.*
Right: *china collections in the pantry.*

Ci-dessus: *Le salon de musique donne sur le jardin. «Tous les murs sont en bois rouge, de mauvaise qualité, et tous étaient recouverts de 40 couches de poussière et de papier», raconte Philip. «Il fallait remettre le bois à jour, puis ajouter des fenêtres à petits carreaux pour laisser entrer la lumière.» Les Going ont abattu des murs pour ouvrir les espaces intérieurs et éclairer les pièces, tout en conservant un air ancien. «Je voulais que la maison trouve sa place dans le jardin, qu'elle croule presque sous les glycines et les roses», ajoute Dale.*
A droite: *collections de porcelaine dans l'office.*

Oben: *Das Musikzimmer mit Blick auf den Garten. »Alle Wände waren aus Redwood, in miserablem Zustand allerdings, und bedeckt mit 40 Schichten Staub und Tapete«, sagt Philip Going. »Der Trick bestand darin, das Holz wieder hervorzuzaubern und dann kleine Sprossenfenster einzubauen, die das Licht hereinlassen.« Einige Wände wurden herausgerissen, um die Räume zu öffnen und heller werden zu lassen. Gleichzeitig sollten die Zimmer ihre dezent-nostalgische Atmosphäre behalten. »Ich wollte das Haus so in den Garten einpassen, daß es fast völlig hinter den Glyzinien und Rosenbüschen verschwindet«, erzählt Dale.*
Rechts: *die Porzellansammlung in der Speisekammer.*

Peu après avoir découvert cette rustique maison de rêve dans un canyon de Berkeley, David Bryson, guitariste du célèbre groupe Counting Crows, eut la chance de rencontrer la décoratrice san-franciscaine
Kelly Lasser. Immédiatement sensible à l'élégante façade de bardeaux
de bois rouge, aux cheminées carrelées anciennes, aux matériaux naturels et aux poutres de bois, elle insista pour que Bryson joue sur les
racines originales, celles d'un simple cottage. Cette maison d'été de
185 m² avait été construite dans les années 20 par une élève de l'architecte de San Simeon, Julia Morgan. «David apprécie la simplicité,
aussi avons nous choisi de revenir à la période Arts and Crafts, floris-
sante à Berkeley au tournant du siècle», explique Kelly Lasser. «Les
maisons de ce type sont fondées sur l'idéalisme et exposent leur réalisation soignée et leurs matériaux honnêtes. L'accent a été mis sur les
traditions des constructions vernaculaires, et un moblier neutre et
massif.» Pour David, cette maison est aujourd'hui une retraite.
«Beaucoup de bonnes vibrations … et je ne la quitterai pas avant
longtemps», ajoute le jeune musicien.

David Bryson

Soon after David Bryson, guitarist with the multi-platinum band,
Counting Crows, discovered his rustic dream house in a Berkeley
canyon, he was also fortunate to encounter interior designer Kelly
Lasser. She quickly appraised its handsome redwood plank exterior,
original terracotta tiled fireplace, plain-spoken materials, and timber beams, and insisted that Bryson play up its simple cottage
roots. The 185 sq.m. cottage had been built in the 20s as a summer
house by a student of architect Julia Morgan. "David appreciates
simplicity, so we went back in time to the Arts and Crafts move-
ment that flourished in Berkeley at the turn of the century," says
San Francisco-based Lasser. "Craftsman houses are grounded in
idealism, and showcase fine, honest woods and careful hand-craft-
ing. The emphasis was on unpretentious vernacular building traditions and plain, solid furniture." Bryson says the house today feels
like a retreat. "It has a great vibe – and I don't plan to leave for a
long time," said the young musician.

David Bryson, Gitarrist der Superband Counting Crows, hatte das
große Glück, kurz nach dem Erwerb seines rustikalen Traumhauses
im Berkeley Canyon die Interior-Designerin Kelly Lasser zu finden.
Diese erfaßte mit einem Blick das Potential des Hauses: die hübsche
Redwood-Verschalung außen, den originalen Kamin mit seinen Terra-
kottakacheln, rundum ehrliche Materialien und Holzbalken. Sie
überzeugte Bryson, die Unwüchsigkeit des Cottage unangetastet zu
lassen. Ein Schüler der berühmten Architektin Julia Morgan baute
das 185 m² große Sommerhäuschen in den 20er Jahren. »David mag
es einfach. Deshalb besannen wir uns auf die Arts-and-Crafts-Tradi-
tion von Berkeley zur Jahrhundertwende«, sagt Lasser, die in San
Francisco ihr Büro hat. »Arts-and-Crafts-Häuser entstanden damals
aus schierem Idealismus. Sie sind wunderbare Beispiele für die Ver-
wendung bester Hölzer sowie deren behutsame Verarbeitung. Sie
nahmen einfache, landestypische Bautraditionen auf und sind mit
unprätentiösen, soliden Möbeln eingerichtet.« Für Bryson ist das
Haus mittlerweile eine Fluchtburg. »Es hat eine unglaublich gute
Ausstrahlung. Ich werde hier bestimmt sehr lange bleiben«, sagt der
junge Musiker.

Above: the dining room with Gustav Stickley dining chairs, a dining table crafted after a Stickley design and a green bud-shaped vase.
Facing page: Interior designer Kelly Lasser selected a neutral color palette for David Bryson's living room. Ocher integral-colored plaster was smoothed over the rough-textured walls. The floor is covered by a sage-colored carpet. Furniture is a combination of a William Morris armchair, a Hans J. Wegner chair, an A. Rudin chenille-covered sofa, a coffee table and a "tansu", a Japanese chest of drawers.

Ci-dessus: La salle à manger est meublée de chaises de Gustav Stickley et d'une table réalisée d'après un dessin du même auteur. Sur la table, un vase vert en forme de bulbe.
Page de droite: La décoratrice Kelly Lasser a choisi pour le séjour une palette de couleurs neutres. Un plâtre teinté ocre dans la masse a été passé sur les murs bruts. Le sol est recouvert d'un tapis couleur sauge. Le mobilier associe un fauteuil de William Morris, une chaise de Hans J. Wegner, un canapé recouvert de chenille de A. Rudin, une table basse, et un «tansu», sorte de commode japonaise.

Oben: das Eßzimmer mit Stühlen des Designers Gustav Stickley und einem Eßtisch, der nach einem Stickley-Entwurf geschreinert wurde.
Rechte Seite: Die Innenarchitektin Kelly Lasser verwendete ausschließlich neutrale Farben für Brysons Wohnzimmer. Mit Ocker vermischter Gips glättete die roh verputzten Wände. Auf dem Boden liegt ein Teppich in Salbeigrün. William Morris entwarf den Sessel, Hans J. Wegner einen der Stühle. Das Sofa mit Chenillebezug stammt aus der Werkstatt von A. Rudin. Außerdem stehen hier ein Couchtisch und ein »tansu«, eine japanische Kommode.

Le décorateur angélinien Thomas Beeton est adepte de l'excentricité. «On ne peut imposer des idées bizarres, mais elles donnent toujours beaucoup de charme», constate-t-il. Cette élégante résidence, ancien refuge de la grande actrice Dame Judith Anderson – alias Mrs Danvers, Lady Macbeth ou Médée – se dissimule dans l'un des coins verdoyants du domaine de Montecito. Lorsque Dame Judith à 93 ans rejoignit le théâtre céleste en 1993, ses héritiers australiens cédèrent la maison à un jeune couple new-yorkais. « C'était une ruine», se souvient Thomas Beeton, «mais j'ai immédiatement aimé la qualité ironique de cette maison. On y sent la trace de l'ancien Hollywood. Le minuscule vestibule mène à un grand salon très théâtral, qui est même équipé d'une petite scène.» Thomas a conçu la décoration pour que les meubles puissent être déplacés à volonté, un peu comme un décor de théâtre. Sous sa direction très sûre, la maison a été détournée de sa sensibilité tudorienne vers un style méditerranéen plus approprié au site. Les couleurs sont chaleureuses et naturelles.

A House by Thomas Beeton

Los Angeles interior designer Thomas Beeton believes in eccentricity. "The odd thought can't be forced, but it results in design with charm," he said. This handsome residence, formerly the refuge of the noted actress Dame Judith Anderson, alias Mrs Danvers, Lady Macbeth, Medea, hides in one leafy corner of a Montecito estate. When the 93 year-old Dame Judith went to her heavenly movie-set in 1993, her Australian heirs sold the house to a young New York couple. "It was a shambles," recalled Beeton. "But I loved the tongue-in-cheek quality of the house. There is an imprint of old Hollywood. The miniscule vestibule leads to a very theatrical living room, complete with a stage for dramatic divertimenti." Beeton designed the decor so that furniture can be moved at will, just like stage sets. Under his confident hand, the house was taken from Tudor in sensibility to a more site-appropriate Mediterranean style. Colors are earthy, warm, and luscious.

Der Interior-Designer Thomas Beeton aus Los Angeles mag es exzentrisch. »Einen bizarren Stil kann man nicht erzwingen, als Design hat er aber viel Charme«, sagt er. Dieses bezaubernde Haus, ehemals das Refugium der bekannten Schauspielerin Dame Judith Anderson, alias Mrs. Danvers, Lady Macbeth und Medea, liegt gut versteckt in der grünen Ecke eines Besitzes in Montecito. Als Dame Judith 1993 im Alter von 93 Jahren die himmlische Bühne betrat, verkauften ihre australischen Erben das Haus an ein junges Pärchen aus New York. »Es war ein Bild der Verwüstung«, erinnert sich Beeton. »Aber ich verliebte mich in die ironische Qualität des Hauses. Hier spürt man das alte Hollywood. Durch ein winziges Vestibül gelangt man in das theatralische Wohnzimmer mit Bühne.« Beeton arrangierte den Dekor so, daß man jederzeit die Möbel verrücken kann, genau wie auf einer Bühne. Unter seiner behutsamen Ägide wandelte sich der Tudor-Charakter des Hauses in ein der Umgebung angemesseneres mediterranes Flair. Die Farben sind erdig, warm und lustvoll.

Previous page: A traditional French fruitwood kneading trough stands on a terracotta tiled floor in the main hall.
Above: Beeton introduced swatches of glamor into the 1930s house. "The ottoman is a bit over the top for a country house. But the kids climb on it, and for them it's a movable feast," Beeton noted.
Right: The bed is a reproduction of one Coco Chanel enjoyed in her house in Juan-les-Pins. The Italianate canopy, made of Gretchen Bellinger's "Isadora" pleated silk, is trimmed with antique gilt cord.
Facing page: Cissie Cooper designed the washstand from antique Italian architectural fragments. On the Portuguese marble top, stands a bowl made of French "terre cuite".

Page précédente: dans le hall d'entrée, un pétrin français ancien en bois fruitier campé sur le sol en terre cuite.
Ci-dessus: Thomas a introduit quelques éclats de glamour dans cette maison des années 30. «Le pouf est un peu excessif pour une maison de campagne, mais les enfants adorent l'escalader», fait-il remarquer.
A droite: Le lit est une reproduction de celui de Coco Chanel pour sa maison de Juan-les-Pins. Le ciel en soie plissée «Isadora», de Gretchen Bellinger, est passementé d'une cordelière dorée ancienne.
Page de droite: Cissie Cooper a dessiné cette console de lavabo à partir d'éléments architecturaux italiens anciens. Sur le dessus en marbre du Portugal, une jatte française en céramique.

Vorhergehende Seite: In der Eingangshalle steht ein französischer Weichholztisch, der früher für das Gehen von Teig verwendet wurde.
Oben: Beeton brachte schwungvollen Glanz in das Haus aus den 30er Jahren. »Ich weiß, der dick gepolsterte Tisch ist ein bißchen übertrieben für ein Landhaus, aber die Kinder klettern gerne auf ihm herum. Für sie ist er ein beweglicher Spielplatz«, sagt Beeton.
Rechts: Das Bett ist eine Kopie der Lagerstätte, auf der Coco Chanel in ihrem Haus in Juan-les-Pins ruhte. Der gefältete Seidenstoff

»Isadora« von der Stoffdesignerin Gretchen Bellinger, abgesetzt mit antiken Goldkordeln, bedeckt den italienischen Baldachin.
Rechte Seite: Cissie Cooper entwarf den Waschtisch aus alten italienischen Architekturfragmenten. Auf der Platte aus portugiesischem Marmor steht eine Schüssel aus französischer »Terre cuite«.

Previous pages: *In the new bathroom designed by Cissie Cooper, Eero Saarinen's "Tulip" chair accompanies the Kohler "Vintage" bath. The floor and walls are French limestone.*

Above: *The owner with her cat in her study. Floors here are random-plank oak. "Many of the pieces of furniture were brought out from New York," said Beeton. "I love the mixture of family heirlooms, country antiques, and some newer furniture. The combination paints a vivid picture of continuous life. Its so much more satisfactory in the end than starting out with all new furniture."*

Double page précédente: *Dans la nouvelle salle de bains due à Cissie Cooper, le fauteuil «Tulip» d'Eero Saarinen accompagne la baignoire «Vintage» de Kohler. Le sol et les murs sont en calcaire d'origine française.*

Ci-dessus: *La propriétaire et son chat dans son bureau. Les sols sont ici en lattes de chêne appariées. «Beaucoup de meubles ont été rapportés de New York», précise Beeton, «J'aime le mélange d'héritage familial, d'antiquités rustiques et de quelques meubles plus récents. Cette harmonie donne une image très vivante du cours du temps. C'est beaucoup plus satisfaisant que de tout remeubler à neuf.»*

Vorhergehende Doppelseite: *Eero Saarinens »Tulip«-Sessel und das »Vintage«-Bad von Kohler passen hervorragend in das neue Badezimmer, das Cissie Cooper plante. Wände und Boden sind aus französischem Kalkstein.*

Oben: *Hausherrin und Katze im Arbeitszimmer. Die Böden hier sind aus grob verlegten Eichenbohlen. »Viele der Möbel wurden aus New York mitgebracht«, erzählt Beeton. »Ich liebe die Mischung aus Familienerbstücken, alten Bauernmöbeln und ein paar neueren Stücken, denn sie zeichnet ein lebendiges Bild vom Fluß der Zeit. Am Ende ist das viel befriedigender, als alles neu zu kaufen.«*

In the new children's rooms, steel-framed windows were made to match the existing architecture. "It's important to maintain the integrity of the house during a restoration, but it's not necessary to be slavish about it," said Beeton. "You're not building a period piece, but rather creating a family home."

Dans les nouvelles chambres d'enfants, les fenêtres à châssis métalliques ont été adaptées à l'architecture existante. «Il est important de maintenir l'intégrité de la maison lors d'une restauration, mais sans en être l'esclave», commente Thomas Beeton. «Vous ne faites pas une reconstitution, vous créez une maison pour votre famille.»

Die stahlgefaßten Fenster in den neuen Kinderzimmern passen sich der Architektur des Hauses an. »Es ist wichtig, die Integrität eines Hauses zu erhalten. Es ist aber nicht notwendig, sich sklavisch nach Vorlagen zu richten«, sagt Beeton. »Man muß kein Haus im Stil der Zeit zurechtbasteln. Wichtig ist es, ein Familienheim zu schaffen.«

Laurel Canyon est l'un des secrets les mieux préservés de Los Angeles. A quelques minutes de l'agitation frénétique de Sunset Boulevard, cette petite vallée ombreuse abrite musiciens, acteurs, décorateurs et personnalités du show-business qui préfèrent une vie plus rustique. Par une belle nuit étoilée, il n'est pas rare d'entendre un coyote hurler à la lune. C'est ici que le décorateur et éditeur Paul Fortune, d'origine britannique, a choisi de vivre depuis 17 ans. Son cottage est l'un de ces lieux magiques où ses amis aiment à se retrouver. Quelques pièces, bordées de tous côtés de terrasses-jardins débordent des célèbres collections des trouvailles de Fortune sur les marchés aux puces. «Ce n'est jamais l'étiquette d'un designer qui m'attire vers un fauteuil, un vase de verre ou un bureau», insiste Paul, «je suis plutôt attiré par l'honnêteté de conception, une certaine ligne, le courage du designer d'avoir essayé quelque chose de nouveau. Les meubles dessinés dans les années 30, 40 et 50 semblent aujourd'hui si modernes et si vrais ...»

Paul Fortune

Laurel Canyon is one of the hidden secrets of Los Angeles. Just minutes from frenetic Sunset Boulevard, the shaded valley is home to musicians, actors, interior designers, and entertainment industry types who prefer going the more rustic route. On star-bright evenings, coyotes can be heard howling to the moon. It is here that interior designer and editor Paul Fortune, an English expatriate, has chosen to nest for the last 17 years. His canyon cottage is one of those magical places his friends love to visit. Just a cluster of rooms, filled out with garden terraces on all sides, the house nevertheless captures the eye with virtuoso collections of Fortune's famous flea-market finds. "It's never the designer label that attracts me to a certain chair, a glass vase, or an unusual desk," insisted Fortune. "Rather, I'm drawn to design integrity, a certain line, the designer's courage to try something new. Furniture designed in the 30s, 40s and 50s now looks so modern and real."

Laurel Canyon ist eine der Geheimadressen von Los Angeles. Nur wenige Minuten vom hektischen Sunset Boulevard entfernt, leben hier in einer kühlen Felsschlucht Leute, die es ländlich mögen: Musiker, Schauspieler, Interior-Designer und Leute aus der Unterhaltungsindustrie. An sternklaren Nächten heulen Kojoten den Mond an. Vor 17 Jahren ließ sich hier auch der Redakteur und Interior-Designer Paul Fortune nieder, der ursprünglich aus England stammt. Sein Cottage im Canyon zieht seine Freunde magisch an. Das Haus, das von Gartenterrassen umgeben ist, besteht zwar nur aus wenigen Zimmern, aber Fortunes virtuose und berühmte Sammlung von Flohmarkttrophäen fesselt das Auge. »Designer-Label interessieren mich nicht«, sagt Fortune. »An einem Stuhl, einer Glasvase oder einem ungewöhnlichen Tisch ziehen mich eher die Integrität des Entwurfs und konsequente Linien an. Ich bewundere mutige Designer, die sich auf neues Terrain wagen. Möbel aus den 30er, 40er und 50er Jahren wirken heute immer noch verblüffend modern und anpassungsfähig.«

Previous pages: Designer Paul Fortune waters the gardens surrounding his house. The tall aloe plant in a terracotta pot alludes to the hot, dry, desert climate of Los Angeles. The flamboyant and flourishing ivy on his "breakfast terrace" suggests that Fortune, even so, has green fingers.

Facing page: Paul Fortune uses every nook and cranny of his garden for staging a luncheon, a dinner party, or breakfast "à deux". Here, colorful Southern California art pottery is set for lunch on a tile-topped table. Mexican terracotta pots fill out the garden beds.

Above: Fortune whips up pancake batter in his cheerful kitchen. Art pottery collections cluster above the refrigerator.

Double page précédente: Paul Fortune arrose les jardins qui entourent sa maison. Le grand aloès en pot de terre cuite rappelle le climat chaud et sec de Los Angeles. Le lierre flamboyant et envahissant de la terrasse où l'on prend le petit déjeuner montre que Fortune a la main verte.

Page de gauche: Paul met à profit tous les coins et recoins de son jardin pour mettre en scène ses dîners ou ses petits déjeuners. Ici une poterie artistique de Californie du Sud annonce le déjeuner sur une table carrelée. Des pots mexicains en terre cuite garnissent les parterres.

Ci-dessus: Paul travaille une pâte à crêpes dans sa cuisine pleine de charme. Une collection de poteries d'art surmonte le réfrigérateur.

Vorhergehende Doppelseite: Paul Fortune wässert den Garten, der rund um das Haus angelegt ist. Die große Aloe in dem Terrakottatopf liebt das heiße, trockene Wüstenklima von Los Angeles. Das üppig wuchernde Efeu an der Frühstücksterrasse beweist, daß Fortune ein Händchen für Pflanzen hat.

Linke Seite: Paul Fortune nutzt jeden Winkel seines Gartens für Lunches, Dinner-Parties oder ein Frühstück zu zweit. Hier sieht man einen gekachelten Tisch, der mit farbenfroher südkalifornischer Keramik für ein Lunch gedeckt ist. In den Blumenbeeten stehen mexikanische Tontöpfe.

Oben: Fortune rührt in seiner fröhlichen Küche einen Pfannkuchenteig. Über dem Kühlschrank drängen sich kunstvolle Gefäße aus Ton.

Right: Fortune is particularly adept at arranging rooms so that chairs and sofas have reading lamps and useful tables at hand. The guest bedroom is thoughtfully set out, with an easy chair, and the latest books.
Below: Paul Fortune prepares to put a vase of roses on a table designed by Roy McMakin. Among Fortune's collections are Venini glassware from the 40s, 50s chairs by Paul McCobb, 20s woodcuts by Paul Landacre on the mantel, and 50s Finnish furniture.

A droite: Paul est particulièrement habile dans l'aménagement tout confort de ses pièces: fauteuils et canapés sont équipés de lampes de lecture et de petites tables toujours sous la main. La chambre des invités est sérieusement pensée, avec une chaise longue et les derniers livres parus.
Ci-dessous: Paul se prépare à poser un vase rempli de roses sur une table dessinée par Roy McMakin. Parmi ses collections: des verreries de Venini des années 40, des sièges des années 50 de Paul McCobb, des gravures sur bois des années 20 de Paul Landacre sur le manteau de la cheminée, et des meubles finlandais années 50.

Rechts: Fortune versteht es perfekt, die Möbel in den Zimmern richtig zu plazieren: jeder Sessel und jedes Sofa verfügt über eine Leselampe, und überall stehen praktische kleine Tische. Das Gästezimmer ist wohldurchdacht, mit einem Sessel und den neuesten Büchern zum Schmökern.
Unten: Paul Fortune stellt eine Vase voller Rosen auf einen Tisch, der von Roy McMakin entworfen wurde. Fortunes Sammlung umfaßt unter anderem Venini-Gläser aus den 40er Jahren, Stühle aus den 50ern von Paul McCobb, 20er-Jahre-Holzschnitte von Paul Landacre auf dem Kaminsims und finnische Möbel aus den 50ern.

Above: The living room is welcoming and expansive, with windows and French doors on all four sides. In one corner, Fortune positioned his dining table, its blocky design inspired by the work of Donald Judd. The central stairway, a pirouette in steel, is original to the house.
Right: The bathroom's wall of cabinets, and the plumbing, are original to the house. Fortune believes that the furniture and fittings must be true to the feeling of a modest house. "Gussying up a rustic cottage to make it appear palatial or ultra-modern is simply wrong-headed," insists the designer.

Ci-dessus: Le salon vaste et accueillant est éclairé sur quatre côtés par des fenêtres et des portes-fenêtres. Dans un angle, une table de salle à manger inspirée des sculptures de Donald Judd. L'escalier central, une pirouette d'acier, remonte à l'origine de la maison.
A droite: Les éléments muraux et la plomberie de la salle de bains sont d'origine. Paul pense que le mobilier et les accessoires doivent rester dans l'esprit d'une maison modeste quand c'est le cas. «Déguiser un cottage en palais ou résidence ultra-moderne n'a pas de sens», insiste-t-il.

Oben: Das einladende Wohnzimmer ist großzügig geschnitten. In alle Himmelsrichtungen öffnen sich Glastüren und Fenster. In einer Ecke steht der Eßtisch, dessen gerade Linien von den Arbeiten des Künstlers Donald Judd inspiriert wurden. Die Haupttreppe, eine Pirouette aus Stahl, gehörte immer schon zum Haus.
Rechts: Die Wandschränke und die Wasserleitungen im Bad beließ Fortune so, wie sie ursprünglich angelegt waren. Er weiß, daß Möbel und Ausstattung dem Charakter des Hauses entsprechen müssen. »Es bringt nichts, ein einfaches Cottage pompös oder hypermodern aufzumotzen«, sagt der Designer.

Above: In the study corner of his bedroom, Fortune uses a Finn Juhl desk. Metal-framed windows open to Rousseauesque views of his canyon garden.
Facing page: Paul Fortune was formerly a graphic designer, an art director, and at one time – not his favorite – he worked on television ads. His happy knack for creating a pleasing "mise en scène" is evident in the breakfast room where he pulls together 40s Italian glass flasks, Pakistan-made copies of Finnish 40s chairs, even his perfectly poised black cat.

Ci-dessus: Dans le coin-bureau de sa chambre, Paul a disposé un bureau de Finn Juhl. Les fenêtres à châssis métallique ouvrent sur une vision rousseauiste de son jardin.
Page de droite: Paul a été graphiste, directeur artistique et, à une certaine période – pas celle qu'il préfère – a travaillé pour la publicité télévisée. Son bonheur à créer des mises en scène est évident dans cette pièce de petit déjeuner où il a réuni des flacons de verre italiens des années 40, des copies pakistanaises de fauteuils finnois des années 40, et son chat noir, très content de lui.

Oben: In der Arbeitsecke seines Schlafzimmers steht ein Schreibtisch von Finn Juhl. Die Fenster mit Metallrahmen öffnen sich auf einen Garten, von dem Jean-Jacques Rousseau träumen würde.
Rechte Seite: Früher arbeitete Paul Fortune als Grafiker und Art-Director; zeitweilig kreierte er sogar – wenn auch nicht sehr begeistert – TV-Werbespots. Im Frühstückszimmer setzt Fortune italienische Glasflakons aus den 40er Jahren, Kopien finnischer Stühle aus der gleichen Zeit, made in Pakistan, und seine perfekt posierende Katze in Szene.

Sur Lookout Mountain, loin au-dessus de la rumeur et des lumières de Los Angeles, le réalisateur de films Jeffrey Harlacker vit dans une version bien à lui de cottage hollywoodien, vrai décor de cinéma virtuel. Son domaine, ancien garage d'une propriété dans les bois, est l'œuvre du décorateur et antiquaire dont on parle, Andrew Virtue, personnage de beaucoup d'esprit et d'imagination. «Jeffrey voulait donner à sa maison un tour cinématographique» ajoute celui dont le magasin éponyme, Virtue, s'est spécialisé dans la poterie d'art de Californie du Sud et le mobilier à la Madeleine Castaing. Des strates d'histoires inventées, d'allusions stylistiques et ironiques se révèlent au fur et à mesure que l'on parcourt la maison. Virtue a fait équipe pendant deux ans avec son client pour réunir et remettre en état vieux tableaux, céramiques, lanternes, mobilier à la peinture fatiguée et tissus effrangés qui créent cette mise en scène échevelée à la Carmen Miranda, ou Doris Day. D'exubérantes couleurs citronnées tapissent les murs.

Jeffrey Harlacker

On Lookout Mountain, high above the noise and glitter of Los Angeles, film-maker Jeffrey Harlacker lives in his own version of a Hollywood dream cottage, a virtual movie set. Harlacker's fantasy domain, the former garage of a woodsy estate, is the work of interior designer and antiquaire-about-town Andrew Virtue, a decorator of considerable wit and imagination. "Jeffrey wanted the house to have a cinematic sweep," said Virtue, whose eponymous antiques shop, Virtue, specializes in Southern California art pottery and Madeleine Castaing-lookalike furniture. As you move through the house, layers of invented history, style allusions, and irony are revealed. Virtue teamed with Harlacker for two years to gather and refurbish the old paintings, ceramics, lanterns, chipped-paint furniture, and fringed fabrics that create the giddy Carmen Miranda, Doris Day, 30s Hawaii, "Flying Down to Rio" mise en scène. Exuberant citrus colors are splashed on the walls.

Fern vom Lärm und Glanz von Los Angeles, auf dem Gipfel des Lookout Mountain, lebt der Filmemacher Jeffrey Harlacker in einem traumhaften Cottage wie aus einem Hollywood-Film. Harlackers fantastische Wohnwelt versteckt sich in der ehemaligen Garage eines bewaldeten Anwesens. Schöpfer dieses unglaublichen Werkes ist der Interior-Designer und Antiquitätenhändler Andrew Virtue, ein Mann mit Verstand und vielen Visionen. »Jeffrey wollte die Filmwelt in seinem Haus haben«, sagt Virtue, dessen Antik-Shop Virtue auf südkalifornische Töpferkunst und Möbel im Stil von Madeleine Castaing spezialisiert ist. Eine ausgedachte Geschichte, Anspielungen auf verschiedene Stilrichtungen und Ironie spielen ihre Rollen hier virtuos. Zwei Jahre lang sammelten Virtue und Harlacker alte Gemälde, Keramiken, Laternen, angestoßene Möbelstücke und fransenbesetzte Stoffe, um Carmen Miranda und Doris Day auftreten zu lassen und das schwüle Hawaii der 30er Jahre in Szene zu setzen. Kräftige Zitrusfarben beleben die Wände.

Facing page: In the kitchen, Virtue orchestrated a lively Southern California fruit salad of citrus, greens and tart yellow.
Above: Harlacker crafted his kitchen desk from a salvaged table covered with eucalyptus driftwood. The nostalgic corner includes an untutored artist's portrait of a farmer, vivid Bauer and Fiesta pottery, and ceramics by students.
Right: The Vitamin C-enriched Hermès-orange walls were achieved with six layers of orange glaze.

Page de gauche: Dans la cuisine, Andrew Virtue a orchestré une petite salade californienne à base de citron, verdure et jaune pimpant.
Ci-dessus: Jeffrey Harlacker s'est fabriqué un bureau de cuisine à partir d'une table de récupération plaquée d'écorce d'eucalyptus flotté. Dans une veine encore plus nostalgique, on remarque un portrait anonyme de paysan, des poteries expressives de Bauer et Fiesta, et des céramiques, œuvres d'étudiants.
A droite: Les murs orange Hermès vitaminé ont été obtenus grâce à six couches de glacis orange.

Linke Seite: Für die Küche mischte Virtue einen bunten kalifornischen Obstsalat aus Zitrus, Grüntönen und kräftigem Gelb.
Oben: Harlacker baute den Küchentisch aus einem alten Tisch und verwendete Eukalyptus-Treibholz für die Platte. In der nostalgischen Ecke hängt das Porträt eines Farmers von einem unbekannten Künstler, dazu lebhafte Tonwaren von Bauer and Fiesta sowie Keramiken von Studenten.
Rechts: Die Wände in Hermès-Orange mit einer Prise Vitamin C entstanden aus sechs Schichten orangefarbenen Lacks.

The upstairs bedroom, with its sweeping views of the Pacific Ocean and vistas of a canyon that echoes with coyotes, feels like a far-flung lookout station. Virtue's take on the unpretentious room was to craft a fantasy mountain cabin, a quiet reminder of innocent times. "I saw it as a kind of cross between a 40s sanitarium and an idyllic boy scout camp, so the bed and chair are serviceable and plain," ventured Virtue. Props include an old fan, faux knotty pine walls painted celadon and white, and hand-tinted photos of the "Old Faithful" geyser. The scrubbed steel dresser, whaling bookends, and aged nature paintings conjure up a "boy's adventure" stage set. Jalousie windows, from the 40s, are shaded with roll-up canvas shades.

La chambre de l'étage, aux vues panoramiques sur le Pacifique et un canyon d'où s'élève le hululement des coyotes, fait penser à un belvédère du bout du monde. L'idée d'Andrew Virtue était d'en faire une cabane de montagne, rappel serein d'une époque innocente. «J'y ai vu une sorte de croisement entre un sanatorium des années 40 et un camp scout idyllique, ce qui explique le choix d'un lit et de sièges neutres et pratiques», commente-t-il. Les éléments décoratifs comprennent un vieux ventilateur, des murs peints en faux bois noueux vert céladon et blanc, et des photos colorées à la main du geyser du Vieux Fidèle. Le buffet en acier brossé, les serre-livres en forme de baleiniers et d'anciennes peintures sur le thème de la nature reprennent l'idée des «aventures de jeunes». Les fenêtres des années 40, équipées de jalousies, sont voilées de stores de toile.

Wie das Innere eines Wachturms wirkt das obere Schlafzimmer mit Blick über den Pazifik und eine Felsschlucht, die widerhallt vom Geheul der Kojoten. In diesem Zimmer versuchte Virtue die Illusion einer Berghütte zu schaffen, die an längst vergangene Zeiten erinnert. »Ich sehe den Raum als eine Mischung aus einem Sanatorium der 40er Jahre und einem Pfadfinderlager. Bett und Stuhl dienen deshalb nur der Notwendigkeit«, erzählt Virtue. Ein alter Ventilator steht auf dem Stuhl, sepiagetönte Fotos des Geisirs Old Faithful zieren die seladonfarbenen und weißen Wände aus nachgemachtem knotigen Pinienholz. Die Kommode aus gebürstetem Stahl, die Buchstützen in Walbootform und die Landschaftsmalereien mit Patina beamen einen direkt in die Verfilmung eines Bubenabenteuers à la Huckleberry Finn. Die Jalousienfenster aus den 40er Jahren werden mit Leinenrollos verdunkelt.

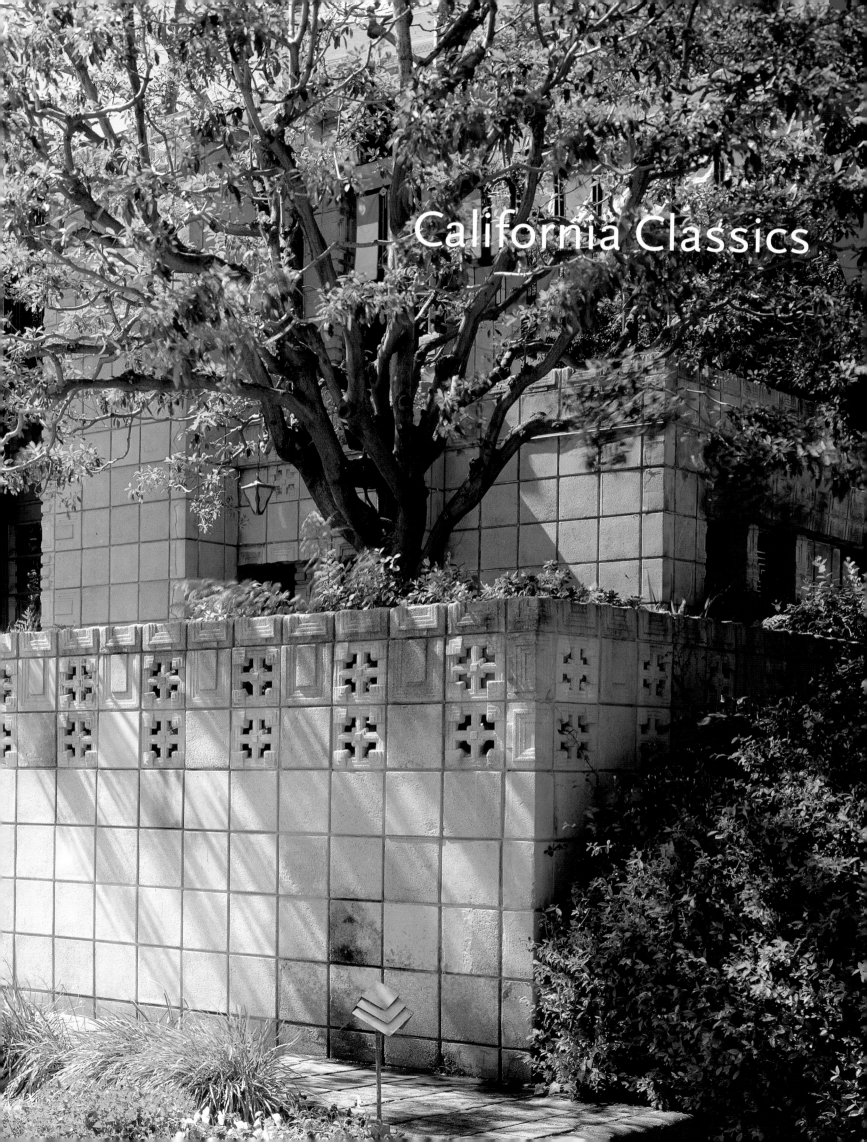

California Classics

Frank Lloyd Wright était déjà réputé à Chicago et à Tokyo lorsqu'il arriva en Californie en 1916. Ce grand novateur, que certains considèrent comme le plus grand architecte américain, trouva rapidement des clients et construisit cinq maisons qui font aujourd'hui partie du patrimoine architectural de Los Angeles. Il pensait qu'une maison devait exprimer et mettre en valeur son objectif humaniste, et donc s'intégrer avec grâce et subtilité dans son environnement. Son architecture était strictement géométrique et ses intérieurs donnent un sentiment d'aisance et de raffinement sans aucun effet forcé. La maison Storer que le producteur de films Joel Silver acheta dans les Hollywood Hills en 1984 avait très besoin que l'on s'occupe d'elle. Pour lui redonner vie, il partit à la recherche d'élèves de Wright, de spécialistes de la restauration et engagea même Eric Lloyd Wright, petit-fils du maître et architecte lui-même. Il rassembla par ailleurs une collection de meubles et de luminaires dessinés par Wright. Le chantier de réparation et de restauration dura plusieurs années.

The Storer House

Frank Lloyd Wright had made his reputation in Chicago and Tokyo when he came to California in 1916. The iconoclastic Wright, whom some regard as the greatest American architect, quickly found clients and built five houses that are considered among the treasures of Los Angeles. Wright believed that a residence should express and enhance its human purpose, and that it must live gracefully and subtly in its setting. His architecture was arranged with strictly ordered geometry, and the interiors have a sense of ease and delight without feeling forced or bombastic. When film producer, Joel Silver, acquired the two-storey Storer House in 1984, it was in disrepair. To revitalize his Hollywood Hills residence, Silver first tracked down Wright scholars and restoration specialists, and then enlisted Wright's architect grandson, Eric Lloyd Wright. Finally, Silver gathered a collection of Wrightdesigned furniture and lighting. The process of repair and rehabilitation took several years.

Frank Lloyd Wright hatte sich bereits in Chicago und Tokio einen Namen gemacht, als er 1916 nach Kalifornien kam. Der Pionier Wright, den manche für den größten amerikanischen Architekten halten, fand schnell Kundschaft und baute fünf Häuser, die heute zu den Schätzen von Los Angeles gehören. Wright glaubte daran, daß ein Haus seine Wohnfunktion ausdrücken und sich gleichzeitig anmutig in seine Umgebung einfügen sollte. Seine Architektur ist streng geometrisch angelegt, das Innere der Gebäude immer sorglos und fröhlich, nie gezwungen oder bombastisch. Als Filmproduzent Joel Silver 1984 das zweistöckige Storer-Haus kaufte, war es ziemlich heruntergekommen. Zunächst suchte er Schüler von Wright und Restaurierungsspezialisten und verpflichtete schließlich Wrights Enkel, Eric Lloyd Wright, um das Haus in den Hollywood Hills wieder zu beleben. Danach trug Silver eine Kollektion von Möbeln und Lampen zusammen, die Wright entworfen hatte. Die Reparaturen und Instandsetzungsarbeiten dauerten mehrere Jahre.

Previous pages: *The exterior of the Wright house is clad in Mayan-influenced concrete blocks which the architect referred to as "textile blocks".*
Above: *the living room and east terrace.*
Right and facing page: *The sunny east terrace was furnished with seagrass and rattan chairs and a sofa, all cushioned with moss green fabric. Silver added the bronze-weighted canvas awning, supported on copper-finialed redwood posts, designed by Frank Lloyd Wright.*

Double page précédente: *L'extérieur de la maison est revêtu de blocs de béton reprenant des motifs maya et surnommés «textile blocks» par l'architecte.*
Ci-dessus: *le séjour et la terrasse est.*
A droite et page de droite: *En plein soleil, la terrasse était meublée de fauteuils et d'un canapé de rotin et d'osier, rembourrés de coussins vert mousse. Silver y a ajouté un auvent de toiles, soutenu par des poteaux de séquoia à faîteau de cuivre, dessinés par Frank Lloyd Wright.*

Vorhergehende Doppelseite: *Die Fassade des von Wright entworfenen Hauses ist mit Betonblöcken verkleidet, deren Muster von der Kunst der Maya inspiriert sind. Der Architekt nannte sie »textile blocks«.*
Oben: *das Wohnzimmer und die östlich gelegene Terrasse.*
Rechts und rechte Seite: *Die sonnige Ostterrasse wurde mit Stühlen aus Seegras und Rattan möbliert sowie einem Sofa mit einem Bezug aus moosgrünem Segeltuch. Die mit Bronzegewichten stabilisierten Segeltuchmarkisen fügte Silver hinzu. Sie werden von Redwood-Pfeilern mit Kupferenden gestützt, die Frank Lloyd Wright entworfen hatte.*

Previous pages: *The upper living room of the 280 sq.m. Storer House, here restored by Joel Silver's team of experts, is awash with sun in the late afternoon. Light emphasizes the iteration, hierarchies and silhouettes of Wright's textile blocks. The oak adjustable chair in the center is by Wright.*
Below and right: *The interiors of the Hollywood Boulevard house are rigorous and pure, thanks to Silver's respectful interpretation of Wright's vision. The dining table was designed by Wright in 1908. The dining chairs are Wright reproductions. A narrow stairway leads from the first-floor dining room up to the 4 m-high living area.*

Double page précédente: *Le séjour supérieur de cette résidence de 280 m² restaurée par l'équipe d'experts réunie par Joel Silver, est baigné de soleil en fin d'après-midi. La lumière met en valeur les cheminements, les hiérarchies et les profils des blocs textiles de Wright. Le fauteuil réglable en chêne est de Wright.*
Ci-dessous et à droite: *L'intérieur est resté absolument rigoureux et pur grâce aux recherches approfondies de Silver et à son interprétation respectueuse de la vision de l'architecte. La table a été dessinée par celui-ci en 1908. Les chaises sont des reproductions de Wright. Un escalier étroit mène de la salle à manger de l'étage au séjour de presque 4 m de haut.*

Vorhergehende Doppelseite: *Das Wohnzimmer im oberen Bereich des fast 280 m² großen Storer-Hauses wurde von Joel Silvers Expertenteam restauriert und wird am Spätnachmittag von der Sonne durchflutet. Das Licht betont die hierarchische Reihung und die Silhouetten der »textile blocks«. Der verstellbare Eichenstuhl in der Mitte ist ein Entwurf von Wright.*
Unten und rechts: *Das Interieur des Hauses am Hollywood Boulevard ist streng und puristisch dank Silvers originalgetreuer Interpretation der Visionen von Wright. Der Eßzimmertisch wurde 1908 von Wright entworfen, die Stühle sind Nachbauten. Eine Treppe führt vom Eßzimmer zum Wohnbereich, der fast 4 m hoch ist.*

Above: Silver's study includes state-of-the art eclectronics and art pottery collections. History may have proven Wright's dream of designing houses to uplift "the common man" impractical, but his architecture has continued to inspire and excite new generations of Wright thinkers. Frank Lloyd Wright died in 1959, at the age of 92.
Right: The wall light fixture in the master bedroom, was custom designed for the Storer House by Wright. The rocking chair is by Kem Webber.

Ci-dessus: Le bureau de Joel Silver comprend un équipement de haute fidélité dernier cri et des collections de poteries artistiques. L'histoire a peut-être prouvé que le rêve de Wright d'élever «l'homme commun» par l'architecture était irréalisable, mais son œuvre continue à inspirer et intéresser de nouvelles générations de praticiens. Frank Lloyd Wright est mort en 1959 à l'âge de 92 ans.
A droite: Le luminaire mural dans la chambre principale, a été spécialement dessiné pour la maison Storer par Wright. Le rocking-chair est de Kem Webber.

Oben: In Silvers Arbeitszimmer befinden sich das allerneueste elektronische Equipment und eine Keramiksammlung. Es mag sein, daß die Geschichte Wrights Traum von Häusern für den »Mann von der Straße« ad absurdum geführt hat, seine Architektur allerdings inspiriert nach wie vor neue Generationen von Wright-Jüngern. Frank Lloyd Wright starb 1959 im Alter von 92 Jahren.
Rechts: Die Wandbeleuchtung im Schlafzimmer ist eine Spezialanfertigung Wrights für das Storer-Haus. Der Schaukelstuhl ist von Kem Webber.

Tellement Hollywood! Niché dans les collines de Hollywood, ce monument historique baptisé maison Samuel, puis maison Ramon Novarro et maintenant maison Diane Keaton est l'une des premières réalisations de Lloyd Wright, fils aîné de Frank Lloyd Wright. Après avoir quitté Chicago pour Los Angeles dans les années 20, il s'était vu commander en 1923 les plans d'une maison pour Ramon Novarro qui venait de triompher dans «Ben Hur». Lorsque Diane Keaton acquit cette résidence en 1989, elle demanda à l'architecte angélinien Josh Schweitzer et au chef de projet Patrick Ousey, de la restaurer dans l'esprit de ses origines. «La maison avait été sauvagement remodelée au cours des années», fait remarquer l'architecte. Un simple projet de rénovation se transforma bientôt en un important chantier de restauration. Le stuc extérieur fut sablé pour retrouver le fini blanc et onctueux de Wright. A l'intérieur, Schweitzer a joué entre rénovation et réinvention sans hésiter à ouvrir des murs ou agrandir des pièces.

Diane Keaton

Only in Hollywood! It's a landmark house that is variously known as the Samuel House, the Ramon Novarro House, and now Diane Keaton's House, after its famous residents. In fact, the house in the Hollywood Hills was one of the first works of architect Lloyd Wright, eldest son of Frank Lloyd Wright. The young Wright left Chicago for Los Angeles in the 20s, and gained in 1923 the commission to design a house for Ramon Novarro, fresh from his triumph in "Ben Hur". When actress Diane Keaton acquired the residence in 1989, she commissioned Los Angeles architect Josh Schweitzer and project architect, Patrick Ousey, to restore the house in the spirit of the original. "The house had been savagely 'remodeled' over the years," noted Schweitzer. What began as simple remodeling soon became a full-tilt restoration. The added-on roughcast stucco was sand-blasted back to its smooth, white plaster cladding. For the interior, Schweitzer balanced renovation and reinvention, cutting away walls and opening up rooms.

So etwas gibt es nur in Hollywood! Dieses Haus ist fast schon ein Wahrzeichen: Erst hieß es Samuel-Haus, dann Ramon-Novarro-Haus, jetzt ist es das Diane-Keaton-Haus. Diese Residenz berühmter Persönlichkeiten war eines der ersten Bauwerke des Architekten Lloyd Wright, des ältesten Sohns des legendären Frank Lloyd Wright. Der junge Wright zog in den 20er Jahren von Chicago nach Los Angeles und erhielt 1923 den Auftrag, eine Bleibe für Ramon Novarro zu entwerfen, der gerade einen triumphalen Auftritt in »Ben Hur« gefeiert hatte. Als Diane Keaton 1989 das Haus erwarb, engagierte sie die Architekten Josh Schweitzer und Patrick Ousey aus Los Angeles, um das Haus im Sinne seines Erbauers zu restaurieren. »Das Haus ist im Lauf der Jahre ziemlich wild ›umgestaltet‹ worden«, berichtet Schweitzer. Was ursprünglich als einfache Umbauarbeit begann, sollte schnell zu einem Mega-Projekt ausufern. Der in späteren Jahren hinzugefügte Rauhverputz wurde mit einem Sandstrahlgebläse entfernt. Zum Vorschein kam der originale glatte Verputz. Bei der Innenausstattung bewegte sich Schweitzer geschickt zwischen Instandsetzung des Vorhandenen und Hinzufügung von Neuem, indem er Wände entfernte und Räume öffnete.

Previous pages, left: Copper trim on the exterior of the Lloyd Wright-designed house is enlivened by an arrowhead motif.
Previous pages, right: The oversized numerals also screen the house from passersby.
Above, right and facing page: Lloyd Wright trained as a landscape architect, and his realization of sunny but private outdoor spaces is particularly successful. During the restoration, begun while Diane Keaton was filming "The Godfather III" in Sicily, copper trim was restored to the exterior.

Double page précédente, à gauche: Le parement de cuivre extérieur est traité selon un motif de pointes de flèche.
Double page précédente, à droite: Les chiffres surdimensionnés de l'adresse contribuent à protéger l'intimité de la maison.
Ci-dessus, à droite et page de droite: Lloyd Wright était architecte paysagiste de formation et ses aménagements extérieurs, à la fois ensoleillés et intimes, sont particulièrement réussis. Le décor de cuivre fut restauré pendant que Diane Keaton tournait en Sicile «Le Parrain III».

Vorhergehende Doppelseite, links: Ein Pfeilspitzenmotiv ziert die Kupferblenden an dem Lloyd-Wright-Haus.
Vorhergehende Doppelseite, rechts: Die überdimensionale Hausnummer schützt obendrein vor neugierigen Blicken.
Oben, rechts und rechte Seite: Lloyd Wright war eigentlich gelernter Landschaftsarchitekt. Das zeigt sich besonders in der Gestaltung der sonnigen und trotzdem intimen Plätze im Freien. Die Renovierungsarbeiten begannen, als Diane Keaton »Der Pate – Teil III« auf Sizilien drehte. Als erstes wurden die Kupferblenden wieder an der Fassade angebracht.

Architect Josh Schweitzer opened up the living room, which had been "modernized" and plaster-boarded over six decades. Schweitzer also united the disparate levels and aspects with large block-like cabinets, smoothly reductive concrete floors, and continuous white plaster walls. "The rooms now are about light and air and volumes – not fussy decorating or period details," said Schweitzer. The former molded stucco fireplace surround has been replaced by a back-lit screen of cast-concrete arrowheads.

L'architecte Josh Schweitzer a ouvert le vaste séjour, qui avait été «modernisé» et plâtré pendant plus de 60 ans. Il a également unifié les niveaux un peu disparates par d'importants meubles-ilôts, des sols en béton qui compriment un peu l'échelle et des murs continus en plâtre blanc. «Les pièces parlent maintenant d'air et de volume, et pas de décoration niaise ou de détails qui datent», commente Schweitzer. L'ancien cadre de cheminée en plâtre moulé a été remplacé par un écran de pointes de flèches en ciment moulé rétroéclairé.

Der Architekt Josh Schweitzer öffnete den Wohnraum, der vor über 60 Jahren mit Trennwänden aus Gips modernisiert worden war. Große, blockförmige Vitrinen, glatte Betonböden und durchgehend weiße Gipswände geben den verschiedenen Ebenen und Blickwinkeln eine ästhetische Einheit. »Diese Räume verlangen Licht, Luft und Volumen – kein kleinkariertes Dekor oder Details aus der Zeit«, bemerkt Schweitzer. Die stuckverzierte Kaminverkleidung wurde durch einen von hinten beleuchteten Gußbetonschirm mit Motiven aus Pfeilspitzen ersetzt.

The lower-level office, study and gallery, were carved from small
maids' rooms and a guest room which Wright himself had remodeled
in the 30s. Bold cabinets of stained ash and a Schweitzer-designed
oversized lamp have a light-hearted quality.

Le bureau du niveau inférieur, le cabinet de travail et la galerie ont
été recréés à partir de petites chambres de service et d'une chambre
d'amis que Wright lui-même avait remodelée dans les années 30. Les
meubles spectaculaires en frêne teinté et la lampe surdimensionnée
dessinée par Schweitzer sont roboratifs.

Das Büro im unteren Stockwerk dient gleichzeitig als Lesezimmer
und Galerie. Früher befanden sich hier kleine Angestellten- und ein
Gästezimmer, das Wright in den 30er Jahren persönlich umgebaut
hatte. Gewagte Schränke aus gebeizter Esche und eine überdimensionale, von Schweitzer entworfene Lampe geben dem Raum
Leichtigkeit.

Josh Schweitzer is unafraid to design oversized furniture and bold cabinetry in tiny rooms. Here in the bedroom and bathroom, an ash-framed bed, broad shelves, and a stained-ash mirror resemble architecture-within-architecture. The small bathroom gains texture and a kinetic quality from an arrowhead-patterned concrete screen. Throughout the house, the architect kept fittings and fixtures that were original to the house, and brought in period-appropriate new hardware and fixtures. Colors range from acid green, celadon, white, and chrome yellow to the muted patina of weather-beaten copper.

Josh Schweitzer ne craint pas de dessiner des meubles hors d'échelle et des rangements audacieux, même pour de petites pièces. Ici, dans la chambre avec salle de bains, le lit en frêne, les larges étagères et le miroir en frêne teinté jouent à l'architecture dans l'architecture. La petite salle de bains a gagné en structuration et en dynamique grâce à un écran en béton à pointes de flèches. Dans toute la maison, l'architecte a conservé les accessoires et équipements d'origine, et apporté lorsque c'était nécessaire des éléments mieux adaptés à cette époque. Les couleurs vont du vert acide, vert céladon, blanc et jaune de chrome aux tonalités assourdies de la patine naturelle du cuivre vieilli.

Josh Schweitzer hat keine Hemmungen, kleine Räume mit überdimensionierten Möbeln und kühnen Schränken auszustatten. Im Schlaf- und Badezimmer schuf er eine Architektur innerhalb der Architektur mit einem Bett mit Eschenrahmen, breiten Regalen und einem Spiegel aus gebeizter Esche. Das kleine Bad gewinnt Substanz und kinetische Qualität durch eine Trennwand aus Beton mit Pfeilspitzenmotiven. Der Architekt beließ die originalen Armaturen und Beschläge, suchte nachgemachte, der damaligen Zeit entsprechende Haushaltswaren und Beschläge. Als Farben wählte er Säuregrün, Seladon, Weiß, Chromgelb und den gedämpften Farbton von altem Kupfer.

Depuis 30 ans, Tony Duquette vit son propre «Conte des deux cités». Ce designer bien connu passe en effet une partie de son temps dans sa résidence de Beverly Hills, où il veille aux destinées de la Elsie de Wolfe Foundation, reçoit son armada d'amis et relations, donne des conférences, peint et conçoit ses bijoux. A San Francisco, il a choisi le cadre théâtral d'une splendide petite maison de capitaine de vaisseau datant de 1860 et presque entièrement dissimulée sous les débordements d'un brugmansia couvert de petites fleurs en trompette parfumées. Sa façade blanche et élaborée évoque les maisons de ville des romans de Tennessee Williams, ou la résidence londonienne d'un gentleman victorien juste revenu de son Grand Tour, chargé de malles de souvenirs et rêvant de recréer un paradis perdu. «Lorsque nous avons décidé d'acheter cette demeure, mon conseiller en affaires me suggéra de m'en débarrasser. Il pensait que c'était une erreur. Or il se trouve que c'est un des meilleurs investissements que j'aie jamais réalisé», raconte Tony, en dégustant une tasse de tisane dans son salon.

Tony Duquette

For 30 years, Tony Duquette has lived his own perfect "Tale of Two Cities". One half of his time is spent at his Beverly Hills mansion, where Tony, an acclaimed designer, attends to the affairs of the Elsie de Wolfe Foundation, entertains a lifetime collection of friends, presents lectures, designs jewelry and paints. In San Francisco, Duquette's "mise en scène" is a splendid 1860 sea captain's refuge, a small house almost completely hidden by a lush Brugmansia tree dripping with fragrant trumpet flowers. The elaborate exterior of Duquette's white house looks like the romantic Southern townhouse of a Tennessee Williams heroine – or the Victorian residence of a London gentleman recently returned from the Grand Tour with trunks of treasures and dreams of recreating a lost paradise. "When we decided to buy the house, my business manager told us to get rid of it. He thought it was a mistake. As it happens, it's one of the best investments I've made," said Tony, drinking sweet herb tea in the drawing room.

Seit 30 Jahren pendelt Tony Duquette zwischen zwei perfekten Welten. Die eine Hälfte seiner Zeit verbringt er in seinem Mansion in Beverly Hills, wo sich der anerkannte Designer um die Elsie de Wolfe Foundation kümmert, eine Reihe lebenslanger Freundschaften pflegt, Vorträge hält, Schmuck entwirft und malt. In San Francisco spielt sich Duquettes Leben in einer kleinen, aber prächtigen Kapitänsvilla aus dem Jahr 1860 ab, die fast völlig hinter einer üppigen Brugmansia mit wohlriechenden Trompetenblüten verschwindet. Die kunstvolle Fassade von Duquettes weißem Haus könnte die romantische Südstaatenbleibe einer Romanheldin von Tennessee Williams sein oder die viktorianische Residenz eines Londoner Gentleman, der gerade mit gefüllten Koffern und voller Sehnsucht nach einem verlorenen Paradies von einer Bildungsreise zurückkehrt. »Als wir beschlossen, das Haus zu kaufen, riet mir mein Manager, es sofort wieder loszuwerden. Er hielt den Kauf für einen Fehler, aber es war die beste Investition meines Lebens«, erzählt Tony bei einer Tasse gesüßtem Kräutertee im Salon.

With the house sale finalized in 1958, Duquette hired Los Angeles
artist Art Fine to paint faux finishes on ceilings, moldings and windows. While Fine painted, the multi-talented Duquette was away in
New York, Paris and Los Angeles designing costumes and sets for
movies with director Vincente Minelli, designing gold necklaces and
creating elegant interiors for the likes of Doris Duke, Norton Simon,
J. Paul Getty and Elizabeth Arden. Among the antique Turkish car-
pets, Chinese screens and Victorian birdcages, Duquette offsets his
precious collections with theatrical displays of faux coral.

Une fois la maison achetée en 1958, Tony Duquette a demandé à
l'artiste de Los Angeles, Art Fine, de peindre en faux bois les plafonds,
les moulures et les fenêtres. Pendant que Fine travaillait, Tony était
monopolisé à New York, Paris et Los Angeles par ses innombrables
activités, dessinant entre autres des costumes et des décors de cinéma
pour Vincente Minelli, des colliers d'or et des décors intérieurs pour
des personnalités comme Doris Duke, Norton Simon, J. Paul Getty et
Elizabeth Arden. Tony a atténué l'effet de ses tapis turcs anciens, de
ses paravents chinois et cages à oiseaux victoriennes par des mises en
scène sophistiquées de faux coraux.

Als 1958 die Kaufverträge unterzeichnet waren, beauftragte Duquette
den Künstler Art Fine aus Los Angeles, Decken, Zierleisten und Fen-
sterrahmen mit Trompe-l'œil-Malereien zu verzieren. Während Fine
malte, war das Multitalent Duquette in New York, Paris und Los Angeles unterwegs, wo er Kostüme und Bühnenbilder für den Regisseur
Vincente Minelli sowie goldene Halsgeschmeide und elegante Interieurs für Doris Duke, Norton Simon, J. Paul Getty und Elizabeth Arden entwarf. Mit Arrangements aus falscher Koralle setzt Duquette
seine wertvollen Sammlungen von antiken türkischen Teppichen, chinesischen Paravents und viktorianischen Vogelbauern in Szene.

"I always decorate as if I were working in the period, rather than merely recreating it," Duquette said. Riches to please the eye include antique Chinese fabrics, a narwhal tusk, Paris green silk cord surrounding an antique English mirror, Japanese lacquer trays, a Portuguese santo, Chinese porcelain bowls, and a bright red Amaryllis. "I use all the rooms," said Duquette. "I have breakfast in the four-poster. Lunch is served in the terrace room with sunshine streaming through a Tiffany glass window."

«J'ai toujours décoré comme si je travaillais dans la période qui m'intéressait plutôt que de me contenter de la recréer», précise Tony. Parmi ses merveilles, d'anciens tissus chinois, une corne de narval, un miroir anglais ancien orné d'une cordelette de soie verte de Paris, des plateaux de laque japonais, un saint portugais, des coupes de porcelaine chinoise, et d'éclatantes amaryllis. «J'utilise toutes les pièces. Je prends mon petit déjeuner dans le lit à baldaquin. Le lunch est servi dans la salle à manger d'été éclairée par le soleil qui vient caresser un vitrail de Tiffany», raconte Duquette.

»Ich dekoriere immer so, als lebte ich in der jeweiligen Epoche. Das ist einfacher, als Dinge einfach nachzustellen«, erklärt Duquette. Die sinnenfreudige Dekoration beinhaltet antike chinesische Stoffe, den Stoßzahn eines arktischen Narwals, grüne Seidenkordeln aus Paris, die einen alten englischen Spiegel rahmen, japanische Lacktabletts, eine portugiesische Heiligenfigur, chinesische Porzellanschüsseln und flammendrote Amaryllis. »Das Frühstück nehme ich im Himmelbett ein. Das Mittagessen wird im Wintergarten serviert, wo das Sonnenlicht durch ein Fenster aus Tiffany-Glas fällt«, sagt Duquette.

«Je voulais acheter une vieille maison en Europe, mais ma vie est à Los Angeles et j'ai donc fait construire à Bel Air», confesse la créatrice de meubles et «antiquaire» Rose Tarlow. Perfectionniste, elle insista pour que sa résidence qui s'élève sur 1,5 hectare de terrain ombragé dans les collines, ait l'air ancien, mais ni faux-ancien ni pseudo-ancien. «J'ai fait venir tous les matériaux d'Angleterre, y compris des planchers et des dalles du 17e siècle, des poutres du 11e siècle», poursuit-elle. «La base devait être juste.» L'extérieur, qui disparaît sous des glycines mauves et le lierre, est en pierre couleur sable et en brique. «J'aime ma maison, parce qu'elle m'entraîne dans un autre monde, la Californie historique ou la France profonde. Tout est très paisible ici et presque mystique aussi bien la nuit que le jour», aime-t-elle à dire. En fait, elle ne se trouve qu'à un quart d'heure du célèbre Sunset Boulevard. Le jardin caché est très simple, car 15 daims vivent sur le domaine. «Ils broutent mes haies, mais heureusement ils n'aiment pas les pins et les glycines», a remarqué Rose.

Rose Tarlow

"I wanted an old house in Europe, but my life is in Los Angeles, so I built it in Bel Air," admitted "antiquaire" and furniture designer Rose Tarlow. A perfectionist, she insisted that the house, which stands on 1.5 sq.m. of sheltered hillside land, should be old-looking, not faux-ancient, nor pseudo-antique. "I brought all the materials over from England, including 17th-century oak floor planks, 11th-century beams, and 17th-century slate for the floors. The background must be right," she said. The exterior, now draped in mauve wisteria and ivy, is sand-colored stone and brick. "I love my house because it takes me to another world – early California or deepest France. It's very peaceful here and quite mystical day and night," Tarlow mused. In fact, she is 15 minutes from star-struck Sunset Boulevard. The secluded garden is very simple because 15 deer live on the property. "They chomp on my bay hedges – but fortunately not the stone pines and wisteria," Tarlow noted.

»Ich wollte immer ein altes Haus in Europa, aber jetzt lebe ich in Los Angeles. Also habe ich in Bel Air ein Haus gebaut«, sagt Rose Tarlow, Antiquitätenhändlerin und Möbeldesignerin. Das Haus steht auf 1,5 Hektar geschütztem Hügelland. Es sollte alt, aber nicht nachgemacht oder gar pseudo-antik aussehen. »Das gesamte Baumaterial kam aus England, inklusive der Eichendielen und Schieferplatten aus dem 17. Jahrhundert sowie der Balken aus dem 11. Jahrhundert. Der Hintergrund muß stimmen«, erklärt sie. Das Haus aus sandfarbenem Stein und Ziegeln ist mit malvenfarbenen Glyzinien und Efeu bewachsen. »Ich liebe mein Haus, denn es führt mich in eine andere Welt – ins frühe Kalifornien oder mitten in das Herz von Frankreich. Hier ist es friedlich und fast mystisch, bei Tag und bei Nacht«, sagt Tarlow. Tatsächlich ist sie nur 15 Minuten vom glamourösen Sunset Boulevard entfernt. Der abgeschirmte Garten ist sehr einfach, da 15 Rehe auf dem Grundstück leben. »Sie fressen meine Lorbeerhecken in Grund und Boden, die Pinien und Glyzinien lassen sie Gott sei Dank in Frieden«, bemerkt Tarlow.

Previous page: Los Angeles "antiquaire" Rose Tarlow swathed her house in ivy and wisteria. The metal garden furniture is by her company, Melrose House.
Above and facing page: The study is furnished with linen-slipcovered Regency chairs. The floor is slate. Vellum-bound books and design magazines line her bookcases. Tarlow uncovered the antique spiral stairway on an excursion to a Paris flea market. "Finding it was the easy part," said the designer, a veteran of shipping, restoring, and handling quirky architectural dimensions.

Double page précédente: L'antiquaire de Los Angeles a recouvert sa maison de lierre et de glycine. Le mobilier de jardin métallique vient de sa galerie, Melrose House.
Ci-dessus et page de droite: Le bureau est meublé de sièges Regency houssés de lin. Le sol est en ardoise. Les livres reliés en parchemin et les magazines de décoration remplissent la bibliothèque. Rose Tarlow a découvert l'escalier en spirale ancien au marché aux puces de Paris. «Le trouver fut bien le plus facile», commente la décoratrice, habituée des transports internationaux, restaurations et adaptations.

Vorhergehende Doppelseite: die Antiquitätenhändlerin Rose Tarlow; die Gartenmöbel stammen von ihrer Firma Melrose House.
Oben und rechte Seite: Das Arbeitszimmer ist mit Regency-Stühlen möbliert, die in Leinenüberzügen stecken. Die Bodenplatten sind aus Schiefer. In den Bücherregalen stehen Designzeitschriften und in Pergament gebundene Bücher. Die alte Wendeltreppe entdeckte Tarlow auf einem Pariser Flohmarkt. »Sie zu finden, war der leichtere Teil«, sagt die Expertin im Versenden, Restaurieren und Anpassen.

On a sunny Southern California afternoon, a hand-crafted Welsh farmhouse chair is poised in front of an antique Basque desk. Tarlow's passions: deep window reveals, superb old wood, time-worn plank floors. Every detail is thought out. The walls are integral-color plaster, loosely applied and mixed with local clay to give it the right texture and authentic color.

Après-midi californien ensoleillé: une chaise de ferme galloise est disposée devant un bureau basque ancien. La passion de Rose: les volets intérieurs, les vieux bois patinés, les planchers usés par le temps. Chaque détail est réfléchi. Les murs sont en plâtre coloré dans la masse, appliqué à la main et mélangé à de l'argile du terrain pour lui donner une texture intéressante et une couleur authentique.

An einem sonnigen südkalifornischen Nachmittag steht der handgemachte Bauernstuhl aus Wales vor einem antiken baskischen Tisch. Tarlows Leidenschaft sind Fensterläden, wunderbares altes Holz und von der Zeit abgenutzte Bohlen. Hier stimmt jedes Detail. Die Wände sind aus durchgefärbtem Gips, der lose verputzt und mit Tonerde vom Grundstück versetzt wurde, um ihm die richtige Textur und eine authentische Farbe zu verleihen.

Tarlow's linen-draped bed is a rare early 18th-century settee which folds out into a comfortable bed. All her textiles are handwoven. The bench, one of Tarlow's favorite objects, is a Welsh farmhouse piece.

Le lit aux draps de lin est en fait un rare canapé du début du 18ᵉ siècle qui se déplie en lit confortable. Tous les textiles sont tissés à la main. Le banc, l'un des objets favoris de la propriétaire, provient d'une ferme galloise.

Tarlows mit Leinen bezogenes Bett ist eine Rarität aus dem frühen 18. Jahrhundert, eine Polsterbank, die im Nu in ein gemütliches Bett verwandelt werden kann. Die Stoffe sind von Hand gewebt. Die Bank, eine von Tarlows Lieblingsstücken, stand früher in einem walisischen Bauernhaus.

Comme Jean-Michel Frank qui disait de ses créations «On ne travaille pas en centimètres, mais en millimètres», le décorateur de San Francisco John Dickinson était un perfectionniste. Il ne laissait rien au hasard. Et pourtant ses réalisations n'avaient jamais l'air figé, intimidant ou prétentieux. Les chaises étaient là pour s'asseoir et être déplacées, les oreillers pour s'appuyer. Les lampes étaient conçues pour lire ou dessiner, les tables pour présenter à bonne hauteur ses livres, ses boissons ou ses journaux. Dickinson aimait le paradoxe de ce que son amie Andrée Putman appelle «le riche et le pauvre»: détails de rembourrage coûteux sur une toile banale, élégante dormeuse recouverte de Naugahyde blanche, rideaux de mousseline traités dans le style le plus «Balenciaga» possible. John Dickinson vivait dans sa plus belle création, une caserne de pompiers de 1893. Avec ses laitons, ses portières drapées de toile, sa Jaguar aux portières cannées, ses tables de plâtre blanc, sa cheminée chromée, et ses murs peints couleur topaze, c'était un lieu magique, mystérieux, élégant et théâtral à la fois.

John Dickinson

Just like Jean-Michel Frank, who said of his designs, "One doesn't work in centimeters but in millimeters", San Francisco designer John Dickinson was a perfectionist. Nothing about his rooms was left to chance. Still, they never looked stiff, intimidating, or pretentious. Chairs were to be used and moved, cushions were to be leaned on. Lights were for reading or drawing, tables were the right height for books, drinks, newspapers. Dickinson loved the paradox of what his friend, the French designer Andrée Putman, calls, "rich and poor": expensive upholstery details on plain fabric, an elegant slipper chair upholstered in white Naugahyde, muslin curtains done in the most "Balenciaga" way. John Dickinson lived in his finest design, a towering 1893 firehouse. With its brass name plates, fabric-draped portière, cane-sided Jaguar, white plaster tables, chrome-plated fireplace, and hand-painted topaz walls, it was a remarkable place to visit. There was magic there, and mystery, elegance and theatricality.

Der Designer John Dickinson aus San Francisco war Perfektionist – genau wie sein Vorbild Jean-Michel Frank, der sagte: »Ich arbeite nicht mit Zentimetern, sondern mit Millimetern.« Dickinson überließ bei der Gestaltung seiner Räume nichts dem Zufall. Trotzdem wirken sie weder steif noch einschüchternd oder prätentiös. Stühle sind zum Sitzen da und Kissen, um es sich gemütlich zu machen. Unter Lampen wird gelesen oder gezeichnet, die Tische haben genau die richtige Höhe, um darauf Bücher, Getränke oder Zeitungen abzustellen. Dickinson liebte das Paradoxon »Reich und Arm«, wie es seine Freundin, die französische Designerin Andrée Putman, nennt. Er setzte es um mit exquisitem Dekor auf einfachem Leinen, einem eleganten Stuhl, der mit weißer Baumwolle bezogen ist, oder Musselinvorhängen, die dramatisch à la Balenciaga drapiert werden. John Dickinson lebte selber im nobelsten aller seiner Entwürfe, einem gewaltigen Feuerwehrhaus aus dem Jahr 1893. Ein wahrhaft bemerkenswerter Ort, mit einem Namensschild aus Messing, einer kunstvoll drapierten Leinenportiere, mit weißen Tischen aus Gips, einem verchromten Kamin und handbemalten topasfarbenen Wänden. Ein Jaguar mit Seiten aus Rohrgeflecht steht vor der Tür. Es war eine magische Stätte, geheimnisumwittert, elegant und theatralisch.

Le cadre ne pourrait être plus merveilleux. Ou plus paisible. A l'extrémité d'une longue allée de Pacific Palisades, un pré sauvage et un
bosquet d'eucalyptus cadrent des vues sur le Pacifique que l'on aperçoit à distance au travers de la brume de chaleur. C'est ici que
Charles et Ray Eames décidèrent de construire une maison de 140 m²
en 1949. En compagnie, au départ, de leur ami l'architecte Eero Saarinen, ils sélectionnèrent des matériaux industriels, dessinèrent une façade extérieure simple, pure et presque transparente et édifièrent ainsi
une maison et un atelier qui restent parmi les créations architectu-
rales les plus admirées de Californie du Sud. Conçue à l'origine dans
le cadre du célèbre programme des Case Study lancé par le magazine
«Arts & Architecture», pour promouvoir la production industrielle et
la préfabrication, la maison se compose de deux «boîtes» de structure
métallique à châssis de fenêtre standard et répété. Si quelques étudiants en architecture restent béats devant le jeu de l'ombre et de la
lumière sur les surfaces planes serties d'acier, d'autres préfèrent les intérieurs ouverts aux matériaux simples et apparents.

Ray and Charles Eames

The setting could not be more beautiful or peaceful. At the end of a
long drive in Pacific Palisades, a wild meadow and eucalyptus
grove frame views of the Pacific Ocean in the heat-hazy distance. It
was here that Ray and Charles Eames chose to build their 140 sq.m.
house in 1949. Working first with their friend Eero Saarinen, the
Eameses selected standard, machined building materials, limned a
pure and almost transparent exterior, and built a house and studio
that are still among the most admired in Southern California. Originally conceived as part of "Arts & Architecture" magazine's famous Case Study House program, which advocated mass production and prefabrication, it consists of two metal-framed boxes with
repetitions of standard sash. While some architecture students
stand in awe as they watch the play of light and shadow across the
steel-framed surfaces, other guests admire the open interior.

Die Szenerie könnte nicht schöner, nicht friedvoller sein. Am Ende
einer langen Auffahrt in Pacific Palisades wird der Blick auf den Pazifischen Ozean, der in der Ferne in der Hitze flimmert, gerahmt von
einer wilden Wiese und einem Eukalyptushain. An dieser Stelle bauten 1949 Ray und Charles Eames ihr 140 m² großes Domizil. Aus
standardisierten, vorgefertigten Materialien errichteten sie, zunächst
gemeinsam mit ihrem Freund Eero Saarinen, ein Haus und ein
Atelier mit klaren Linien und fast transparenter Fassade. Die Stahl-
skelettbauten mit einer Folge von standardisierten Schiebefenstern
zählen immer noch zu den meistbewunderten Gebäuden in Südkalifornien. Ursprünglich entstanden sie im Rahmen der Case Study
Houses, die die Zeitschrift »Arts & Architecture« initiiert hatte, um
Massenproduktion und Fertigteilherstellung zu fördern. Während
manche Architekturstudenten begeistert das Spiel von Licht und
Schatten auf der stahlgerahmten Fassade beobachten, bewundern
andere das offene Innere des Hauses mit seinen Sichtmaterialien.

Previous pages: *Like a Mondrian painting, the Eames House stands within yet visually apart from its setting. Ray and Charles Eames' house was nominated by the Los Angeles Conservancy to the Los Angeles Cultural Heritage Commission, in 1986, as an important monument to "off-the-shelf" use of industrial materials for its architecture. Solid panels on the exterior are painted in primary colors to correspond to the character of the functions taking place there.*
Above and right: *The interior of the house has been maintained and furnished much as it was during the Eames's long tenure. Ray lived in the house continually from 1949 until her death in 1988. Surprisingly, few pieces of Eames furniture were used day-to-day: the couple favored a looser, cozier, collections-textiles-and-Thonet approach. Moroccan, Mexican and Indian fabrics and crafts are souvenirs of many trips abroad. The steel and plywood bookcase has been emulated by the many architectural students and practicing architects who visit the house, which is open, by appointment, to visitors. A sleeping gallery overlooks the 5 m-high living room.*
Facing page: *Japanese lanterns punctuate the double-height living room. The house reaches out toward the Pacific Ocean and a wooded hillside.*

Double page précédente: *Telle un tableau de Mondrian, la maison des Eames s'élève, à la fois isolée et intégrée à son cadre. Elle fut classée monument historique en 1986 par la Los Angeles Conservancy to the Los Angeles Cultural Heritage Commission, pour son utilisation de matériaux industriels courants. Les panneaux pleins de l'extérieur sont peints de couleurs primaires pour exprimer les fonctions qu'ils dissimulent.*
Ci-dessus et à droite: *L'intérieur de la maison a été préservé et meublé à peu près comme du temps des Eames. Ray vécut ici de 1949 à sa mort en 1988. Curieusement, peu de leurs meubles ont été utilisés. Le couple préférait une approche plus textile, plus Thonet,*

plus décontractée et cosy. Les tissus et objets décoratifs marocains, mexicains et indiens sont des souvenirs de voyage. La bibliothèque en acier et contreplaqué a inspiré de nombreux étudiants en architecture et architectes visitant de la maison qui est ouverte sur rendez-vous. Une chambre-galerie domine le séjour haut de plus de 5 m.
Page de droite: *Des lanternes japonaises ponctuent le volume du séjour double-hauteur. La maison est orientée vers le Pacifique et une colline boisée.*

Vorhergehende Doppelseite: *Wie ein Gemälde von Mondrian fügt sich das Haus einerseits harmonisch in die Umgebung ein, andererseits hebt es sich visuell ab. Die Kommission der Los Angeles Conservancy to the Los Angeles Cultural Heritage ernannte das Eames-Haus 1986 zu einem wichtigen architektonischen Beispiel für die Nutzung von industriell gefertigten, für jedermann erhältlichen Baustoffen. Die soliden Paneele an der Fassade wurden in Primärfarben bemalt, um die jeweilige Raumfunktion zu betonen.*
Oben und rechts: *Die Einrichtung und Ausstattung des Hauses blieben erhalten, wie sie zur Zeit der Eames war, die viele Jahre hier lebten: Ray wohnte hier von 1949 bis zu ihrem Tod im Jahr 1988. Überraschenderweise benutzten die Eames nur wenige Möbel für den täglichen Gebrauch: Das Ehepaar schätzte einen legeren, gemütlichen Lebensstil mit Sammlerstücken, Textilien und Thonet-Möbeln. Die marokkanischen, mexikanischen und indischen Stoffe sowie die Folk-Art-Objekte sind Souvenirs vieler ausgedehnter Fernreisen. Das Bücherregal aus Stahl und Preßholz wurde schon von vielen Architekturstudenten und Architekten nachgebaut. Eine Schlafgalerie thront über dem mehr als 5 m hohen Wohnzimmer. Das Haus kann nach Anmeldung besichtigt werden.*
Rechte Seite: *Japanische Lampen akzentuieren das Wohnzimmer mit doppelter Raumhöhe. Das Haus liegt zwischen Pazifik und bewaldeten Hügeln.*

Facing page: The modular rythms of 2.3 m bays articulate the volumes of the house, which measures seven bays long.
Above: The Eames family has worked hard to maintain the house, and has been particularly successful in giving the contents a lived-in appearance, as if Ray and Charles had merely stepped across the courtyard to their studio.
Right: The small, neat bedroom is like an aerie in the dappled shadow of eucalyptus trees.

Page de gauche: Le rythme modulaire des travées de 2,30 m articule les volumes de la maison, qui mesure sept travées de long.
Ci-dessus: La famille Eames s'est efforcée de préserver la maison, et a réussi à lui conserver un caractère vivant, comme si Charles et Ray venaient juste de traverser la cour pour se rendre dans leur atelier.
A droite: La petite chambre, sans fioriture, est comme suspendue dans l'ombre pommelée des eucalyptus.

Linke Seite: Der Rhythmus der aufeinanderfolgenden, 2,30 m breiten Erker betont das Volumen des Hauses, das sich aus sieben Modulen zusammensetzt.
Oben: Die Familie Eames ist sehr bemüht, das Haus zu erhalten. Es ist ihr gelungen, die Räume bewohnt wirken zu lassen, gerade so, als ob jeden Moment Ray und Charles über den Hof zu ihrem Atelier gehen würden.
Rechts: das Schlafzimmer im Schatten der Eukalyptusbäume.

«En fait je ne cherchais pas une maison de style traditionnel», avertit Orlando Diaz-Azcuy, architecte paysagiste et décorateur dont l'atelier aux murs blancs se dresse dans une rue historique du centre de San Francisco. Il avait vendu son luxueux appartement de Russian Hill et joué un instant avec l'idée d'une maison moderniste et simple. Puis on lui présenta une construction de style colonial espagnol datant de 1938, avec vue sur l'océan. Il fut immédiatement séduit par les gracieuses arches de pierre, la loggia au lumineux carrelage, les balcons chargés d'ornements et les murs de plâtre finis à la main. «J'ai eu l'impression de me retrouver à Cuba. C'est exactement comme la maison dans laquelle j'ai grandi à La Havane», poursuit-il. Comment aurait-il pu résister? Le séjour possède des plafonds de 5,50 m de haut à poutres équarries à la main. Les planchers de chêne sont à lattes sciées «comme à la main». «Pour moi l'essentiel était de maintenir un décor simple et même légèrement austère. C'est l'architecture que l'on doit vivre, pas un principe de décoration ...»

Orlando Diaz-Azcuy

"I really wasn't looking for a traditional-style house," commented Orlando Diaz-Azcuy, a landscape architect and interior designer whose white-walled studio stands on an historic lane in downtown San Francisco. Diaz-Azcuy had sold his rather grand apartment on Russian Hill and briefly entertained the idea of a Modernist house, something simple. Then Diaz-Azcuy was shown a 1938 Spanish Colonial-style house with views of the ocean. The designer was immediately drawn to its graceful stone arches, the sunny tiled loggia, ornate balconies, and hand-plastered walls. "I felt as if I were back in Cuba. It's just like the house where I grew up in Havana," said the designer. How could he resist? The living room has 5.5 m ceilings, with hand-carved beams. Oak floors were added to look as if they were hand-sawn. "For me, the key was to keep the interiors simple and somewhat sparse. It's the architecture you should experience and enjoy, not a design statement," said Diaz-Azcuy.

»Eigentlich wollte ich gar kein traditionelles Haus«, sagt Orlando Diaz-Azcuy, ein Landschaftsarchitekt und Interior-Designer, dessen weißes Atelier in einer historischen Gasse in Downtown San Francisco steht. Diaz-Azcuy hatte sein großzügiges Apartment im Viertel von Russian Hill verkauft und spielte kurz mit der Idee, ein einfach gestaltetes modernistisches Haus zu kaufen. Dann sah er sich ein Haus aus dem Jahr 1938 an, mit Blick über den Ozean und im spanischen Kolonialstil gehalten. Der Designer fühlte sich sofort zu den anmutigen Steinbögen, der sonnendurchfluteten gekachelten Loggia, den verzierten Balkonen und den handverputzten Wänden hingezogen. »Ich fühlte mich wieder wie in Kuba. Es sah so aus wie das Haus in Havanna, in dem ich aufgewachsen bin«, erzählt Diaz-Azcuy. Wie konnte er da widerstehen? Das Wohnzimmer hat 5,50 m hohe Decken mit handgeschnitzten Balken. Die Eichenböden wirken wie handgesägt. »Der Clou für mich war, das Innere des Gebäudes einfach, fast spartanisch zu halten. Es geht darum, die Architektur zu erleben und zu genießen, und nicht um Designprinzipien«, sagt Diaz-Azcuy.

First pages: The long desk in the bedroom is topped with 17th-century Italian volumes and galvanized-tin drawing models.

Previous pages: In the dining room, an Eero Saarinen table is surrounded by George III gilded chairs with plain linen upholstery. Diaz-Azcuy designed the chandelier.

Facing page: For the white-walled living room, the designer planned a versatile grouping, including a circular white-lacquered coffee table, and linen-upholstered slipper chairs.

Above and right: In the taupe-walled study, Kraft paper-lined cabinet doors disguise electronic equipment and volumes on design and art. The terracotta tiled floor is original to the house.

Première double page: sur le long bureau dans la chambre, des livres italiens anciens du 17e siècle et des objets en zinc galvanisé qui servaient de modèle aux peintres.

Double page précédente: Dans la salle à manger, la table d'Eero Saarinen est entourée de chaises en bois doré George III recouvertes de toile unie. Le lustre a été dessiné par le propriétaire.

Page de gauche: Dans le séjour aux murs blancs, Orlando Diaz-Azcuy a mis en scène divers regroupements de meubles dont une table basse circulaire laquée blanc, et des chauffeuses habillées de toile.

Ci-dessus et à droite: Dans le bureau au mur taupe, des portes fermées au papier Kraft dissimulent l'équipement de haute fidélité et des livres sur l'art et le design. Le sol en carrelages de terre cuite est d'origine.

Eingangsseiten: der lange Tisch im Schlafzimmer mit italienischen Büchern aus dem 17. Jahrhundert und galvanisierten Zeichenmodellen aus Blech.

Vorhergehende Doppelseite: Im Eßzimmer stehen ein Tisch von Eero Saarinen und vergoldete georgianische Armlehnstühle mit einfachen Leinenbezügen. Den Kronleuchter entwarf Diaz-Azcuy.

Linke Seite: Vor den weißen Wänden des Wohnzimmers arrangierte der Designer eine verrückbare Sitzgruppe aus Sesseln mit Leinenbezügen um einen weißlackierten Couchtisch.

Oben und unten: Im Arbeitszimmer verbergen Wandschränke, deren Türen mit preiswertem, widerstandsfähigem Papier verkleidet sind, das elektronische Equipment sowie Kunst-und Designbücher. Der Terrakottaboden ist original.

Right: Silk taffeta cushions are piled on the linen slip-covered sofa in the living room. The floor lamp is a Diaz-Azcuy design.
Below: The guest bedroom is filled with light in the early morning. Natural linen draperies hang from simple wrought-iron rods. Diaz-Azcuy used plain fabrics throughout the house to highlight the architectural details and perfect symmetry of the rooms.

A droite: Sur le canapé de lin du séjour s'empilent des coussins en taffetas de soie. Le lampadaire est signé Orlando Diaz-Azcuy.
Ci-dessous: Au petit matin, la chambre d'amis est envahie de lumière. Les tentures de lin naturel sont suspendues à des tringles de fer battu. Orlando préfère les tissus unis, pour mettre en valeur les détails architecturaux et la symétrie parfaite des pièces.

Rechts: Auf dem Sofa mit Leinenbezug im Wohnzimmer türmen sich seidene Taftkissen. Die Stehlampe stammt von Diaz-Azcuy.
Unten: In das Gästezimmer scheint die Morgensonne. An einfachen schmiedeeisernen Stangen hängen Vorhänge aus Naturleinen. Diaz-Azcuy verwendet ausschließlich einfache Stoffe, damit nichts von den architektonischen Details und der perfekten Symmetrie der Räume ablenkt.

Orlando Diaz-Azcuy's ocean-view bedroom opens onto a quiet terrace. He had the pristine white-lacquered desk custom-made as both
a work surface and for displaying his fine book collection. The designer wanted the simplest bed – really just a pencil sketch of a four-
poster – and adorned it with an oversized cover of crunchy acid-yellow
silk taffeta. The weathered teak chairs on the terrace are popular
Diaz-Azcuy designs.

La chambre du maître de maison donne sur l'océan et ouvre sur une
terrasse tranquille. Le grand bureau inhabituel laqué blanc a été réalisé sur mesure et sert à la fois de plan de travail et de présentoir pour
sa collection de livres anciens. Il souhaitait le plus simple des lits, juste
une ébauche, mais à baldaquin. Il l'a habillé d'un couvre-lit surdi-
mensionné en taffetas de soie jaune acide. Les chaises de teck vieilli
sur la terrasse sont des modèles connus, dessinés par Orlando.

Orlando Diaz-Azcuys Schlafzimmer mit Meeresblick öffnet sich auf
eine ruhige Terrasse. Der ungewöhnliche weißlackierte Tische ist maß-
gefertigt und dient gleichzeitig als Arbeits- und als Ablagefläche für
die exquisite Büchersammlung. Der Designer wünschte sich eine ganz
einfache Schlafstätte. Es ist eigentlich nur der Hauch eines Himmel-
bettes, bedeckt mit einem übergroßen grellgelben Überwurf aus
Seidentaft. Die verwitterten Teakholzstühle auf der Terrasse sind
bekannte Entwürfe von Diaz-Azcuy.

Les peintures de Wade Hoefer évoquent un passé romantique de paysages de collines battues par les vents, de soleils écrasants, et de rivières dolentes. Son atelier d'Healdsburg envahi de lumière suggère des temps plus anciens, plus sereins. Ses proportions de loft et ses meubles extravagants venus des Puces de Paris, cachent qu'il a été construit en mezzanine sous le plafond en béton armé d'un ancien supermarché Purity des années 40. C'est à la fermeture de l'établissement, que Wade a découvert cet espace poussiéreux. Il y passa un premier printemps à peindre, dans un splendide isolement. «L'atelier est près du cinéma Raven, du Ravenous Café, des librairies, du centre de la ville, mais reste à la fois très privé et très calme. La construction en béton est extrêmement solide et bien isolée», fait-il remarquer. «Avec mes 335 m², je peux imaginer toutes sortes de possibilités». Côté glamour, le cottage qu'occupe le couple à deux pas a plus à offrir : «C'est un peu de Paris et de l'Isle-sur-la-Sorgue en Californie du Nord ...»

Myra and Wade Hoefer

Wade Hoefer's evocative paintings allude to a romantic past, with invented landscapes of sun-faded, wind-combed hillsides, and placid rivers. So, too, his light-struck painting studio suggests a yearning for an ideal, quieter time. Hoefer's Healdsburg studio, with its lofty proportions and unconventional Paris flea-market furnishings, was built on a mezzanine beneath the reinforced concrete ceiling of a former 40s Purity supermarket. When the store closed, Wade discovered the dusty raw space and during one fine spring he painted there in splendid isolation. "The loft is near the Raven cinema, Ravenous café, book shops, the bustle of town, but it's very private and silent," noted Wade. "The concrete construction's extremely sound and well-insulated. With 335 sq.m. of open space available, I can imagine all kinds of possibilities." The couple's Ivy Cottage, just a hop and a skip from the studio, is a residence of stepped-up glamor. "It's our little bit of Paris and L'Isle-sur-la-Sorgue in Northern California," said Myra.

Wade Hoefers Gemälde von imaginären Landschaften mit sonnengebleichten, windzerzausten Hügeln und friedlichen Flüssen beschwören eine romantische Vergangenheit. So ist es nicht verwunderlich, daß sein lichtdurchflutetes Atelier in Healdsburg diese Sehnsucht nach einer »idealen«, unbeschwerten Zeit widerspiegelt. Das Atelier mit seinen loftartigen Proportionen und der exaltierten Einrichtung von Pariser Flohmärkten lag im Mezzanin unter der verstärkten Betondecke eines ehemaligen Purity-Supermarktes aus den 40er Jahren. Als der Laden geschlossen wurde, entdeckte Wade den nackten, staubigen Raum und malte dort in vollkommener Einsamkeit ein ganzes Frühjahr lang. »Er liegt nahe bei dem Raven-Kino und Ravenous-Café, den Buchläden und dem Getümmel der Stadt. Trotzdem ist es sehr ruhig hier, denn die solide Betonverschalung isoliert gut«, sagt Wade. Das prachtvolle Ivy Cottage des Paares liegt nur einen Katzensprung vom Atelier entfernt. »Es ist unser Stückchen Paris und L'Isle-sur-la-Sorgue im Norden Kaliforniens«, schwärmt Myra.

Previous pages, left: *Artist Wade Hoefer and his wife, an interior designer; Myra and her daughter, Gina, dine in the garden.*
Previous pages, right: *In Wade's studio, a suite of French neoclassical chairs upholstered in ivory silk contrasts with an improvised work table decorated with vintage auto license plates.*
Above: *Wade spends most of the day painting, working and mulling over multiple canvases to stay stimulated.*
Right: *A series of "grisaille" panels encountered in Paris lines the center of the loft. Pine planks march down the studio, from end to end.*

Double page précédente, à gauche: *Le peintre Wade Hoefer et son épouse; Myra, décoratrice, et sa fille Gina dînent dans le jardin.*
Double page précédente, à droite: *Dans l'atelier de Wade, une rangée de chaises néoclassiques françaises tendues de soie ivoire en contraste parfait avec une table de travail improvisée, décorée de plaques d'immatriculation de voitures anciennes.*
Ci-dessus: *L'artiste passe le plus clair de ses journées à peindre, travaillant et réfléchissant à de multiples toiles à la fois.*
A droite: *Une série de panneaux en grisaille trouvés à Paris marque le centre du loft. D'épaisses lattes de pin recouvrent le sol de l'atelier.*

Vorhergehende Doppelseite, links: *Künstler Wade Hoefer und seine Frau, eine Interior-Designerin; Myra und Tochter Gina im Garten.*
Vorhergehende Doppelseite, rechts: *In Wades Atelier steht eine Reihe neoklassizistischer französischer Stühle, die mit elfenbeinfarbener Seide bezogen sind. Auf dem improvisierten Arbeitstisch liegen alte Autonummernschilder.*
Oben: *Wade verbringt die meiste Zeit des Tages mit Malen.*
Rechts: *Die großformatigen Gemälde in Grisaille-Technik stöberte Wade in Paris auf.*

California Interiors   Myra and Wade Hoefer

Right: The bold curve of the concrete ceiling is punctuated with a row of skylights. Wade props larger paintings along the central axis so that he may view them as he goes about his work.
Below: The Hoefers lived for a while in the painting studio, and some of the accouterments of their life linger on. An oversized Mexican rusted-iron mirror reflects the length of the studio and becomes, in a sense, a window on the process.
Following pages: Wade Hoefer works on sketches at this long plank table, made from recycled barn wood. The jar-shaped wire lamp was designed by Ron Mann.

A droite: La belle courbe tendue du plafond de béton est ponctuée par une rangée de verrières. Wade dispose ses plus grandes toiles le long de l'axe central pour les examiner à loisir.
Ci-dessous: Les Hoefer ont vécu un certain temps dans l'atelier, et y ont laissé quelques traces de cette vie antérieure. Un énorme miroir mexicain à cadre de fer rouillé reflète l'atelier dans toute sa longueur et se transforme, du même coup, en fenêtre.
Double page suivante: Wade travaille à ses projets sur cette grande table faite de planches récupérées dans une vieille grange. La lampe de fil de fer en forme de jarre a été dessinée par Ron Mann.

Rechts: In der kühn geschwungenen Betondecke öffnet sich eine Reihe von Dachfenstern. Wade stellt die größeren Gemälde entlang der Mittellinie auf, so daß er sie während der Entstehung genau betrachten kann.
Unten: Eine Zeitlang wohnten die Hoefers im Atelier, und einige Dinge ihres häuslichen Lebens stehen immer noch herum. Ein übergroßer mexikanischer Spiegel mit einem Rahmen aus rostigem Eisen spiegelt das Atelier in seiner gesamten Länge und wird damit gewissermaßen zu einem Fenster.
Folgende Doppelseite: Wade Hoefer skizziert an diesem langen Tisch, dessen Planken aus einer alten Scheune stammen. Die Drahtlampe in Form eines Kruges ist ein Design von Ron Mann.

Right: In their Ivy Cottage, which was built in 1918 for the local piano teacher, the Hoefers prefer a pale, more neutral palette. In the center of the kitchen, a marble-topped breakfast counter.
Below: Myra, a renowned interior designer, is partial to mirrors. Here, a wall-sized mirror is framed with bleached fir. The salon-style velvet-upholstered slipper chairs are a prim counterpoint to the dog's favorite armchair. The painting, right, is by Wade Hoefer.

A droite: Dans leur Ivy Cottage, construit en 1918 pour un professeur de piano, les Hoefer ont opté pour une palette plus neutre. Au centre de la cuisine, un petit comptoir à dessus de marbre pour prendre le petit déjeuner.
Ci-dessous: Myra, décoratrice très connue, a un goût marqué pour les glaces. Ici, un miroir de la taille du mur est encadré de pin décoloré. Les chauffeuses élégantes en velours viennent en contrepoint du fauteuil favori du chien de la maison. Le tableau de droite est de Wade Hoefer.

Rechts: In ihrem Ivy Cottage, das 1918 für einen Klavierlehrer aus dem Ort gebaut wurde, bevorzugen die Hoefers gedämpfte, neutrale Farben. In der Mitte der Küche steht der Frühstückstisch mit Marmorplatte.
Unten: Myra, eine bekannte Interior-Designerin, liebt Spiegel. Dieser ist wandhoch und mit gebleichtem Tannenholz gerahmt. Der mit Samt bezogene Salonstuhl bildet einen Gegenpol zum Lieblingssessel des Hundes. Das Gemälde rechts ist von Wade Hoefer.

Above: Summers in Healdsburg are scorchers. As respite, Myra favors country glamor, silk-draped windows, and cooling, muted colors. The Portuguese table and Louis Seize-style chair, upholstered in Henry Calvin silk, are from Michael Taylor Designs. The Chinese table, right, is from Sloan Miyasato. Angelo Garo forged the iron candlestick. "The house is a springboard for our travels to Paris and Provence," said Myra. "It's so quiet and private. We love coming home."
Right: The family's Jack Russells lay claim to the linen-dressed bed of the Hoefers' teenage son, Zane.

Ci-dessus: Les étés sont torrides à Healdsburg. Pour s'en protéger, Myra a adopté les rideaux de soie aux fenêtres et les couleurs assourdies et rafraîchissantes. La table portugaise et le fauteuil de style Louis Seize, recouvert de soie d'Henry Calvin, sont de Michael Taylor Designs. La table chinoise, à droite, est de Sloan Miyasato. Angelo Garo a forgé le bougeoir en fer. «La maison est un point de départ pour nos voyages vers Paris et la Provence; tout est si calme et si intime ici. Nous aimons revenir chez nous», ajoute Myra.
A droite: Les deux jack-russell terriers de la famille ont pris possession du lit de lin du jeune fils des Hoefer, Zane.

Oben: Da die Sommer in Healdsburg glühend heiß sind, bevorzugt Myra einen gehobenen Landhausstil mit Seidenvorhängen und kühlen, gedämpften Farben. Der portugiesische Tisch und der Louis-Seize-Stuhl, der mit Henry-Calvin-Seide bezogen ist, sind von Michael Taylor Designs. Den Tisch im chinesischen Stil rechts entwarf Sloan Miyasato. Angelo Garo schmiedete den eisernen Kerzenleuchter. »Das Haus ist Sprungbrett für unsere Reisen nach Paris und in die Provence«, erklärt Myra. »Es ist so herrlich ruhig. Wir lieben es, nach Hause zu kommen.«
Rechts: die Jack-Russell-Terrier auf dem Bett von Teenage-Sohn Zane.

Le décorateur Michael Smith est souvent qualifié, à tort, d'enfant terrible. Les journalistes spécialistes du design sont un peu jaloux de voir qu'il ne se contente pas d'imposer à ses nombreux clients un style bien rôdé. Au contraire, ce créateur encore jeune, désinvolte et facilement lassé, approche chacun de ses projets avec un regard frais et souvent provocant. Pour une demeure de style colonial espagnol à Montecito, ou la maison de plage de Richard Gere à Malibu, il a ainsi choisi de robustes meubles anciens portugais et indiens, de sinueux fauteuils sculptés trouvés chez un grand antiquaire parisien, ou de chastes drapés de lin irlandais. Une semaine, il s'occupe de l'appartement décontracté de Cindy Crawford à Manhattan, la suivante de la ferme d'un président de société dans le Connecticut. Une fois chez lui, Michael y applique la même souplesse et la même invention. Il est passé sans problème de son ancienne penthouse de Santa Monica avec vue sur l'océan et de ses voluptueux canapés recouverts de soie, à une simple maison des années 60 «moderniste en adobe d'Arizona» dans un canyon de Brentwood. Austère et robuste à la fois, c'était une intéressante table rase pour de nouvelles expériences.

Michael Smith

Los Angeles interior designer, Michael Smith, is often mislabeled an "enfant terrible". What shocks many design editors is that he never foists one tried-and-true trademark style upon his many clients. Rather, the breezy, easily-bored 30-something decorator approaches each new project with a fresh, creative and often irreverent eye. For a Spanish Colonial mansion in Montecito or Richard Gere's beachhouse in Malibu, it's robust Portuguese-Indian antiques, quirky hand-carved chairs from a noble Paris "antiquaire", or chaste Irish handkerchief linen draperies. One week it's Cindy Crawford's cool apartment in Manhattan, the next an executive's Connecticut farmhouse. Home at last, Smith applies the same flexibility and invention. Leaping from his former Santa Monica seaview penthouse and glamorous silken sofas, he pounced upon a simple "Arizona adobe and Modernist" 60s house in a Brentwood canyon. Spare but robust, it was a clean slate for experimentation.

Der Interior-Designer Michael Smith aus Los Angeles wird oft fälschlicherweise als »Enfant Terrible« bezeichnet. Die meisten Design-Journalisten irritiert, daß er sich auf keinen Stil festlegt. Der lebhafte, schnell gelangweilte Dekorateur um die 30 nähert sich jedem neuen Projekt mit frischen, kreativen, manchmal respektlosen Ideen. Für ein Herrenhaus im spanischen Kolonialstil in Montecito oder Richard Geres Strandhaus in Malibu kombinierte er robuste portugiesisch-indische Antiquitäten mit schrulligen handgeschnitzten Stühlen eines bekannten Pariser Antiquitätenhändlers und Vorhängen aus schlichtem irischen Taschentuchleinen. Heute kümmert er sich um Cindy Crawfords modernes Apartment in Manhattan, morgen um das Farmhaus eines Managers in Connecticut. Endlich daheim, ist Smith genauso flexibel und erfindungsreich. Er verließ sein Penthouse mit Meeresblick und seidenbezogenen Sofas in Santa Monica und zog in ein einfaches Haus aus den 60er Jahren im Brentwood Canyon, das Moderne und Adobe-Architektur miteinander verbindet. Spartanisch, aber solide gebaut, ist es eine fantastische Kulisse für stilistische Experimente.

Previous page: *"I'm opposed to narrowness of taste and lazy design,"* said interior designer Michael Smith, who also has a studio in Santa Monica. In his office, Smith matched a Gio Ponti table with an antithetical leather chair from his own Jasper collection.
Facing page, above and right: The massive beams of the living room ceiling were exposed when Smith stripped the house down to its bones. The aesthetic here: International Modernist Style tempered with organic materials such as terracotta tiles and white-painted brick walls.

Page précédente: «Je suis opposé à toute étroitesse de goût et paresse de conception», déclare le décorateur Michael Smith qui possède également un studio à Santa Monica. Dans son bureau, il a disposé une table de Gio Ponti près d'un fauteuil totalement discordant, sélectionné dans sa propre collection «Jasper».
Page de gauche, ci-dessus et à droite: Les poutres massives du plafond du séjour sont apparues lorsque Michael a dégagé la structure de la maison «jusqu'à l'arête ...». Son choix esthétique: un style moderniste international tempéré par des matériaux naturels, tels des carrelages de terre cuite et des murs de brique peints en blanc.

Vorhergehende Doppelseite: »Ich verabscheue engstirnigen Geschmack und träges Design«, bekennt Interior-Designer Michael Smith, der auch ein Atelier in Santa Monica besitzt. In seinem Büro bildet der Lederstuhl aus seiner »Jasper«-Kollektion einen Gegensatz zu dem Tisch von Gio Ponti.
Linke Seite, oben und rechts: Die massiven Balken im Wohnzimmer kamen zum Vorschein, als Smith das Haus innen komplett aushöhlte. Der modernistische International Style wird durch natürliche Materialien wie Terrakottafliesen und weißgestrichene Ziegelwände gedämpft.

Facing page and right: *Michael Smith insists on natural materials and low-key colors that are at one with the surroundings. He remodeled his three bathrooms with Ann Sacks glass tiles, a Kohler whirlpool, simple glass windows, and a limestone steam shower. It's peaceful here, although often coyotes howl in the canyon beyond the terrace.*
Above: *The dining room looks onto the entry courtyard, with its olive trees, river stones, and a small reflecting pool. The table is 19th-century Spanish; his chairs are American Empire style.*

Page de gauche et à droite: *Michael insiste sur les matériaux naturels et les couleurs subtiles qui se marient avec leur environnement. Il a remodelé ses trois salles de bains avec des carrelages d'Ann Sacks, un bain à remous Kohler, de simples fenêtres, et une douche à vapeur en pierre calcaire. Le grand calme, même si l'on entend parfois un coyote dans le canyon, de l'autre côté de la terrasse ...*
Ci-dessus: *la salle à manger donne sur la cour d'entrée, décorée d'oliviers, de galets et d'un petit bassin qui réfléchit le ciel. La table est 19ᵉ siècle espagnol, les fauteuils américains de style empire.*

Linke Seite und rechts: *Michael Smith besteht auf natürlichen Materialien und gedämpften Farben, die mit der Umgebung harmonieren. Er renovierte die drei Badezimmer mit Glasfliesen von Ann Sacks, einem Whirlpool von Kohler, einfachen Fenstern und einer Dampfdusche aus Kalkstein. Hier herrscht Friede, auch wenn manchmal die Kojoten in dem Canyon unterhalb der Terrasse heulen.*
Oben: *Das Eßzimmer geht auf einen Eingangshof mit Olivenbäumen, Flußsteinen und einem kleinen glitzernden Wasserbassin. Der Tisch ist spanisches 19. Jahrhundert, die amerikanischen Stühle im Empire-Stil gearbeitet.*

Ses décors d'un grand raffinement et d'un superbe équilibre valent, depuis vingt ans, une réputation enviable au designer new-yorkais John F. Saladino. Il manifeste un goût tellement prononcé pour l'Antiquité et la période classique, qu'il serait difficile de l'associer au modernisme. Sa nouvelle résidence de Montecito, dans les collines boisées qui dominent Santa Barbara, se distingue néanmoins par ses lignes nettes, ses détails minimalistes et ses espaces ouverts. «J'ai eu envie d'acheter cette maison pour son environnement quasi sauvage et ses vues qui portent à près de 160 km», confesse le décorateur. «Elle possède des fenêtres toute hauteur et des terrasses sur toutes ses faces». L'intérieur est traité sans détour. Une grande pièce de 18 m de long, équipée d'une cuisine à une extrémité, a été découpée sans hésitation en salle à manger, séjour et salon. Dans ces espaces décontractés, quelques objets rappellent le passé: canapés à profusion de coussins de lin, fauteuils recouverts de voile, urne de plomb de Robert Adam, architecte écossais du 18e siècle, gravures classiques, tapis Ušak, et fauteuil de cuir clouté argenté Louis Treize.

John Saladino

New York interior designer John F. Saladino has made a distinguished name for himself over the last 20 years, creating rooms imbued with great refinement and balance, and a pervasive sense of the antique and classic past. Few would associate him with Modernism. But Saladino's new house in Montecito, in the wooded hills above Santa Barbara, is all clean lines, minimalist details, and open spaces. "I was compelled to buy the house for its wild setting and hundred-mile views," admitted Saladino. "It has floor-to-ceiling windows and terraces on all sides." Best of all, the interior is straightforward. One 18 m-long room, with the kitchen at one end, has been informally divided into a dining room, a living room, and a sitting area. Into these cool cubes were introduced remembrances of things past: cushioned linen sofas, gauze-covered armchairs, a lead urn from the 18th century by the Scottish architect Robert Adam, classical etchings, Ušak rugs, and a silver-leafed tooled leather Louis Treize chair outlined in nailheads.

Der New Yorker Interior-Designer John F. Saladino kreiert seit 20 Jahren mit überzeugendem Gespür für Antiquitäten und klassischen Stil perfekt ausgewogene und raffinierte Räume. Nur wenige würden ihn deshalb mit Modernismus in Zusammenhang bringen. Saladinos neues Haus allerdings, das in Montecito in den bewaldeten Hügeln oberhalb von Santa Barbara liegt, besteht aus klaren Linien, minimalistischen Details und offenen Räumen. »Ich mußte das Haus kaufen, allein wegen seiner Lage mitten in der Wildnis und wegen der fantastischen Aussicht«, gibt Saladino zu. »Die Fenster reichen vom Boden bis zur Decke, und auf allen Seiten gibt es Terrassen.« Innen präsentiert sich das Haus völlig schnörkellos. Ein 18 m langer Raum, mit der Küche an einem Ende, wurde locker und leicht in Eßzimmer, Wohnzimmer und Sitzecke unterteilt. Diese kühlen Kuben wurden mit Gegenständen gefüllt, die an längst vergangene Zeiten erinnern: schwer gepolsterte Leinensofas, gazebezogene Lehnstühle, eine Bleiurne aus dem 18. Jahrhundert des schottischen Architekten Robert Adam, klassizistische Radierungen, Ušak-Teppiche und ein mit Blattsilber verzierter, lederner Louis-Treize-Stuhl mit Nagelbespannung.

Previous pages: Saladino turned a former carport into a shady loggia for afternoon napping.
Facing page: the double-height entry hall of the house, designed by architect Richard Martin. The floor is of practical terracotta pavers.
Above: The guest-house has its own private patio overlooking the hillside garden. Walls are stuccoed in taupe to harmonize with the eucalyptus trunks and the indigenous clay.
Right: outdoors: languid wraparound terraces, olive trees, rosemary, verbena and lavender. Life takes place outdoors in the summer, and Saladino has imbued each terrace with its own character.

Page précédente: John a transformé un ancien auvent pour voitures en loggia ombragée pour la sieste.
Page de gauche: Le hall d'entrée dessiné par l'architecte Richard Martin, monte jusqu'au toit. Le sol est en grosses dalles de terre cuite.
Ci-dessus: La maison d'amis possède son propre patio qui donne sur le jardin à flanc de colline. Les murs sont en plâtre taupe pour s'harmoniser à la couleur des troncs des eucalyptus et à l'argile du terrain.
A droite: De langoureuses terrasses, plantées d'oliviers, de romarin, de verveine et de lavande entourent la maison. En été, la vie se déroule au dehors.

Vorhergehende Seite: Einen ehemaligen Autostellplatz verwandelte Saladino in eine schattige Loggia, ideal für die Siesta.
Linke Seite: Die Eingangshalle hat doppelte Raumhöhe und wurde von dem Architekten Richard Martin entworfen. Der Boden ist mit praktischen Terrakottafliesen belegt.
Oben: Das Gästehaus hat seinen eigenen Patio. Die Wände sind mit graubraunem Mörtel verputzt, um mit den Eukalyptusstämmen und der Tonerde zu harmonisieren.
Rechts: lässige Terrassen, Olivenbäume, Rosmarin, Eisenkraut und Lavendel: Im Sommer findet das Leben draußen statt.

Right: Practical and portable campaign chairs with canvas seats afford easy-going comfort in the guest sitting room. The leather-upholstered sofa, a Saladino design, opens into a comfortable double bed.
Below: John F. Saladino makes peace with Modernist lines, adding multi-cushioned chairs and sofas, and quirky antique chairs complete with silver-leafed leather. The periwinkle blue linen-upholstered "Shelter" sofa is a classic Saladino design. Beyond the sofa is the dining room, and the kitchen is concealed behind a pewter-colored scrim curtain.

A droite: Des sièges de campagne à assise de toile, pratiques et facilement transportables, donnent une note de confort décontracté au salon de la maison d'amis. Le canapé de cuir, un modèle de Saladino, se transforme en confortable lit à deux places.
Ci-dessous: John a fait la paix avec le modernisme, non sans glisser quelques fauteuils et canapés couverts de coussins, ou des sièges anciens en cuir argenté. Le canapé «Shelter» recouvert de lin bleu pervenche est une création classique de John Saladino. Derrière, le coin salle à manger. La cuisine est dissimulée par un rideau en toile légère gris étain.

Rechts: Praktische, leichte Stühle mit Leinensitzen bieten Komfort in den Gästezimmern. Das Ledersofa, ein Design von Saladino, läßt sich zu einem bequemen Doppelbett ausziehen.
Unten: Saladino hat mit der modernistischen Ästhetik Frieden geschlossen. Er stellt Sessel und Sofas mit vielen üppigen Kissen sowie eigenwillige, antike Stühle auf, deren Ledersitze mit Blattsilber verziert sind. Das »Shelter«-Sofa mit blaßblauem Leinenbezug ist ein klassischer Entwurf des Hausherrn. Dahinter schließt sich das Speisezimmer an, die Küche verschwindet hinter einem zinngrauen, leichten Leinenvorhang.

Above and right: *The 3.65 m-tall wraparound windows in the living room afford views of ravines and the distant Pacific Ocean. The designer's constructions of lacquered Chinese and Japanese boxes echo the cube-on-cube architecture. Saladino is not a decorator who relies on pattern for effect: his favored mood-enhancing materials include tone-on-tone textiles, age-patinated metals and time-lined woods.*
Following pages: *Saladino did not desert his signature antiquities and classics when he came west of Montecito. In his bedroom and bathroom, old urns, a column, and finials reference the designer's classical bent.*

Ci-dessus et à droite: *Les vastes baies de 3,65 m de haut qui entourent le séjour offrent des vues superbes sur les ravins et le Pacifique dans le lointain. La composition de boîtes de laque chinoises et japonaises fait écho à l'architecture cubiste. John Saladino ne s'intéresse guère aux motifs pour créer des effets. Ses matériaux préférés sont les tissus ton sur ton, les métaux patinés et les bois vieillis par le temps.*
Double page suivante: *John n'a pas abandonné son goût connu pour les antiquités en s'installant à Montecito. Dans sa chambre et sa salle de bains, des urnes anciennes, une colonne, et des éléments architecturaux le rappellent.*

Oben und rechts: *Die 3,65 m hohen Fenster im Wohnzimmer geben den Blick auf Schluchten und den fernen Pazifik frei. Das Arrangement aus lackierten, chinesischen und japanischen Schachteln ist die Antwort des Designers auf die kubistische Architektur. Saladino bevorzugt Stoffe mit stimmungsvoll aufeinander abgestimmten Farbtönen, Metalle mit Patina und in Würde gealterte Hölzer.*
Folgende Doppelseite: *Saladino hat sein Faible für die Antike und Klassik nicht abgelegt. In seinem Schlafzimmer und im Bad bezeugen das antike Urnen, eine Säule und Fialen.*

Design Catalogue
Le catalogue de design

Los Angeles

First-time visitors must deal with their fear of freeways. Shopping in Los Angeles and nearby Santa Monica and Beverly Hills means miles of driving. Most of these hand-picked stores and galleries are in easily accessible neighborhoods. Still, it helps to have a parking angel on your shoulder – and a good map in your hand. North Robertson Avenue, Melrose Avenue and La Cienega Boulevard are good places to begin. Then hop to Melrose Place (the real one), along Beverly Boulevard, over to Sunset Plaza, up and down La Brea Avenue, then to tidy Larchmont Avenue, through hip Silver Lake, and out into sunny Santa Monica. Sidewalk merchandizing is a Los Angeles tradition. It's essential to catch the eye of drive-by customers within seconds, because few potential clients walk to their destinations. The weather's generally sunny all-year, so there's no risk of weather damage. Thus, creative store owners display ziggurats of pneumatic sofas, hand-carved beds, cartoony armchairs, painted urns and Mexico-made pine tables in front. Chock-a-block streets like Melrose Avenue, La Brea Boulevard, and Beverly Boulevard often look like a swap-meet. It's ad hoc, cheerful, casual, and very Los Angeles.

Le visiteur nouveau venu doit oublier son angoisse des freeways. Faire du shopping à Los Angeles, Santa Monica et Beverly Hills vous oblige en effet à dévorer les kilomètres. La plupart des magasins et galeries se trouvent dans des quartiers facilement accessibles, mais il est toujours utile d'avoir un plan à portée de la main, et le dieu tutélaire du parking à ses côtés. North Robertson Avenue, Melrose Avenue et La Cienega Boulevard sont un bon point de départ. Puis poussez jusqu'à Melrose Place, le long de Beverly Boulevard, jusqu'à Sunset Plaza, la Brea Avenue (des deux côtés)? jusqu'à la proprette Larchmont Avenue, en passant par Siver Lake très mode en ce moment, et Santa Monica. Le trottoir est un lieu de vente privilégié à Los Angeles. Il faut absolument attirer le regard des clients envoiturés, puisque peu d'entre eux vont à pied. Le temps est généralement au beau tout au long de l'année, et ne pose donc pas de problème. Tous plus créatifs les uns que les autres, les commerçants disposent donc des ziggourats de canapés, de lits sculptés de bois, de vases peinturlurés, de tables en pin mexicaines. Les artères commerçantes comme Melrose Avenue, La Brea Boulevard et Beverly Boulevard font souvent penser à une décharge chic. C'est pratique, gai, concret, et définitivement Los Angeles.

Neuankömmlinge dürfen sich nicht vor Freeways fürchten. Einkaufen in Los Angeles oder dem nahen Santa Monica und Beverly Hills bedeutet kilometerweite Autofahrten. Die meisten der unten aufgeführten Läden und Galerien liegen in gut erreichbaren Gegenden. Trotzdem ist es sinnvoll, eine Straßenkarte in der Hand und einen Parkplatzengel zur Seite zu haben. Am besten beginnt man an der North Robertson Avenue, Melrose Avenue und am La Cienega Boulevard. Von dort ist es ein Katzensprung zum Melrose Place (dem echten!). Über den Beverly Boulevard geht's zur Sunset Plaza, dann die La Brea Avenue hinauf und hinunter, ein Abstecher in die Larchmont Avenue und ein Bummel über den hippen Silver Lake bis zum sonnigen Santa Monica. Es ist eine alte Tradition in Los Angeles, seine Ware auf dem Bürgersteig zum Verkauf anzubieten. Da fast niemand zu Fuß geht, müssen die Ladenbesitzer innerhalb von wenigen Sekunden die Aufmerksamkeit der vorbeifahrenden potentiellen Kunden auf sich ziehen. Fast das ganze Jahr über scheint die Sonne, so daß sich auf dem Bürgersteig gefahrlos Sofas, handgeschnitzte Betten, Sessel und mexikanische Kieferntische türmen können. Hauptstraßen wie Melrose Avenue, La Brea Boulevard und Beverly Boulevard wirken oft wie ein Treff von Tauschhändlern. Das ist praktisch, fröhlich und typisch Los Angeles.

Algabar
920 North La Cienega Boulevard
Exotic accessories, French teas, fine glassware, and East-West furniture. Fragrant breezes from the east waft here – and it's a very cosmopolitan mix.
Les brises parfumées de l'Orient viennent jusqu'ici, et la sélection est vraiment très cosmopolite: accessoires exotiques, services à thé français, verrerie de qualité et meubles.
Exotische Accessoires, französische Teeservices, feine Gläser sowie Möbel aus Ost und West – eine wahrhaft kosmopolitische Mischung.

American Rag Cie
Maison et Cafe
148 South La Brea Avenue
Los Angeles loves France. Easy-going and colorful French country-hand-crafted glasses, wish-I-were-in-Provence plates, cosy custom upholstery. Style books, ceramics, and accessories for every room – plus a tiny cafe.
Los Angeles aime la France. Verrerie française artisanale colorée, plats qui rappellent la Provence, tissus au mètre, livres sur les styles, céramiques et accessoires pour toute la maison, plus un petit café.
Ganz Los Angeles liebt Frankreich. Farbenfrohe, handgefertigte Gläser aus Frankreich, Teller, die Erinnerungen an den letzten Urlaub in der Provence wecken, und gemütliche Polsterstoffe nach

Maß. Lifestyle-Bücher, Keramiken, Accessoires für das ganze Haus und ein kleines Café.

Brenda Antin
7319 Beverly Boulevard
Brenda's well-edited antique French and English garden decor catches the eye. In this hushed place, the senses are thrilled by monogrammed white linen slip-covers and lampshades, French quilts, vintage French textiles, combinations of unusual colors.
La collection d'accessoires de jardin français et anglais de Brenda vaut le coup d'œil. Dans ce lieu feutré, les sens sont néanmoins réveillés par des dessus de lit en lin blanc monogrammés, des abat-jour, des quilts français, des tissus français anciens qui marient avec audace les couleurs.
Brendas gut sortierte, antike französische und englische Accessoires für den Garten sind wahre Eyecatcher. An diesem verwunschenen Ort betören weiße Leinenüberzüge mit Monogramm, Lampenschirme, französische Quilts, antike französische Stoffe und ungewöhnliche Farbzusammenstellungen die Sinne.

Blackman/Cruz
800 North La Cienega Boulevard
Where national style trends start. Remember the mania for stripped stainless steel clinic furniture? Started here! Trends set, energetic

David and Adam, the cool partners, inevitably move on. Fast turnover, so it's essential to keep coming back. Rooms full of style icons, and must-have 20th-century objects and furniture. Architectural fragments. A favorite with interior designers, architects, and Hollywood set designers.
Point de départ de beaucoup de tendances qui s'imposeront coast-to-coast. Vous vous souvenez de la manie des mobiliers d'hôpitaux en acier? C'est parti d'ici. David et Adam, associés et pleins d'énergie sont toujours sur la brèche. La rotation du stock est rapide, aussi faut-il revenir souvent. Les salles sont bourrées d'objets célèbres et de tous les meubles style 20ᵉ siècle dont on ne saurait se passer. Eléments d'architecture. Lieu hanté par les designers, les architectes et les décorateurs de cinéma d'Hollywood.
Hier entstehen amerikanische Trends. Erinnern Sie sich an die Manie der Klinikmöbel aus rostfreiem Stahl? Sie begann hier! Kaum ist ein Trend etabliert, sind die beiden Inhaber David und Adam schon einen Schritt weiter. Trends sind schnellebig. Schauen Sie also oft vorbei. Bis unter die Decke stapeln sich berühmte Designobjekte und Möbel des 20. Jahrhunderts, die man einfach haben muß. Dies ist natürlich ein Lieblingsladen der Interior-Designer, Architekten und Set-Designer von Hollywood.

Book Soup
8818 Sunset Boulevard
West Hollywood
Would-be novelists, along with big-name script writers, set designers, stars and memoirists love all-day and midnight browsing. Superb selections of interior design, architecture, art, and photography books. Open-air magazine mews has every international design magazines. Bistro.
Romanciers en devenir, scénaristes connus, décorateurs de cinéma, stars et biographes viennent jeter un œil ici du matin à minuit. Superbe sélection d'accessoires et de livres sur la décoration, l'architecture, l'art et la photographie. Stand de presse en plein air où se retrouvent les magazines de design du monde entier. Bistro.
Möchtegern-Schriftsteller, aber auch bekannte Drehbuchautoren, Set-Designer, Stars und ihre Biographen wühlen hier mit Begeisterung Tag und Nacht. Eine exquisite Auswahl an Büchern über Interior-Design, Architektur, Kunst und Fotografie. Der Open-Air-Pressestand bietet jede internationale Designzeitschrift. Bistro.

Decades
8214 Melrose Avenue
Los Angeles has a special taste for the old. Perhaps it's from watching and loving the style of all those early films. Vintage clothing and accessories, mostly, but also vintage Georg Jensen holloware and

silver. Watch for stars scavenging for Gucci, Pucci, Gernreich and Norell. Seriously good.
Los Angeles aime tout ce qui a déjà bien vécu. Peut-être est-ce dû à la culture des films anciens. Vous trouverez essentiellement ici des vêtements et accessoires de mode d'occasion, mais aussi de la vaisselle et de l'argenterie de Georg Jensen. Quelques stars viennent se fournir en Gucci, Pucci, Gernreich et Norell. Maison sérieuse.
Los Angeles hat ein ausgeprägtes Faible für alles Alte, wahrscheinlich weil es die schönen alten Filme liebt. Decades bietet hauptsächlich Secondhand-Kleider und Accessoires, aber auch Geschirr und Silber von Georg Jensen. Hier grabbeln die Stars nach Gucci, Pucci, Gernreich und Norell. Richtig gut.

Demolicious
7912 Melrose Avenue
Vivian Levy and Carter Anderson gather handsome old garden furnishings, lavish iron urns, fountains, architectural salvage from all over the world. Garden style-indoors and outdoors is a great passion. Here, pêle-mêle, are benches, picnic baskets, romantically rusted gates, cafe tables, shells, Bauer pots, Belgian hand tools, watering cans, outdoor lighting, and old fences in ever-changing array and disarray. It's a great jumble of superb old style icons. There's no sign out front.
Vivian Levy et Carter Anderson cherchent et trouvent dans le monde entier des vieux meubles de jardin, de superbes vases de fer, des fontaines, des éléments d'architecture récupérés. Le style jardin, pour l'intérieur comme pour l'extérieur, est leur grande passion. Ici, vous trouvez pêle-mêle bancs, paniers de pique-nique, portails à la rouille, tables de café, coquillages, pots, outils belges, arrosoirs, éclairage de jardin et vieilles barrières dans un désordre – ou un ordre – qui évolue de jour en jour. Aucun panneau sur la façade.
Vivian Levy und Carter Anderson bieten hübsche alte Gartenmöbel, prächtige eiserne Urnen, Brunnen und Architekturelemente aus der ganzen Welt an. Accessoires für innen und außen sind ihre große Leidenschaft. Bänke, Picknickkörbe, romantisch verrostete Gartentore, Kaffeetische, Muscheln, Keramik, Gartenwerkzeuge aus Belgien, Gießkannen, Außenbeleuchtungen und alte Zäune türmen sich in ständig wechselnden Arrangements. Ohne Ladenschild.

Diamond Foam & Fabric
611 South La Brea Avenue
Helpful Jason Asch's textiles empire is legendary in the design trade. Off-the-rack, instant fabric gratifications, no back orders. Upstairs at Diamond is a not-so-secret source for well-priced this-minute fabrics. Basic and luxurious textiles – velvets, linen, chintz, silk, damask, twills, challis, terry, all in the right weaves and colors. Don't forget to hop across the street to the La Brea Bakery for sour cherry and chocolate chip bread, jet-fuel coffee ... and dog biscuits!
L'empire textile du serviable Jason Asch jouit d'une réputation légendaire auprès des décorateurs. Choisissez, profitez des promotions, le stock disponible est énorme. L'étage est la source inépuisable – et pas si secrète qu'on veut bien le dire – de tissus à prix d'appel. Velours, lins, chintz, soies, damas, twills, éponge, dans les bons tissages et les couleurs que vous cherchez. N'oubliez pas de passer à La Brea Bakery, de l'autre côté de la rue, pour un «chip bread» aux griottes et au chocolat, pour un café énorme ou des biscuits de chien!
Das Textilimperium des zuvorkommenden Jason Asch ist Legende in Designerkreisen: er hat alles auf Lager, es gibt keine Wartezeiten, dafür aber Herstellerrabatte. In der ersten Etage kann man – kein Geheimtip mehr! – preiswert brandaktuelle Stoffe ergattern. Einfache und aufwendigere Textilien: Samt, Leinen, Chintz, Seide, Damast, Köper und Frottee, alle natürlich in der richtigen Webart und Farbe. Bei der Gelegenheit sollten Sie unbedingt bei der La Brea Bakery auf der anderen Strasseneite einkaufen: Sauerkirsch- und Schokobrot, eine Tankladung Kaffee ... und Hundekuchen!

Domestic Furniture
6150 Wilshire Boulevard
Roy McMakin's understated furniture is a top 20th-century collectible – for some of the most style-conscious beings around. Simple, unpretentious, pleasing.
Le mobilier raffiné de Roy McMakin est déjà l'objet de toutes les attentions des collectionneurs de classiques du 20e siècle. Simple, sans prétention, agréable.
Die Understatement-Möbel von Roy McMakin sind für Stilbewußte die Top-Sammlerstücke des 20. Jahrhunderts. Schlicht, unprätentiös, angenehm.

Getty Center
1200 Getty Center Drive
Richard Meier's impressive complex stands on the summit of a hill – master of all it surveys. Reservations are required to view the treasury of Greek and Roman statuary, illuminated texts, "that" Van Gogh, and days' worth of paintings, formal interiors, architectural juxtapositions.
L'impressionnant complexe muséal conçu par Richard Meier s'élève au sommet d'une colline d'où il domine le panorama. Réservations nécessaires pour admirer la statuaire grecque et romaine, les manuscrits enluminés, un célèbre Van Gogh, des tableaux, des pièces reconstituées, des meubles et des objets d'art somptueux.
Der beeindruckende Komplex von Richard Meier steht auf einem Hügel mit fantastischem Ausblick. Vor den griechischen und römischen Statuen, »dem« van Gogh, den illuminierten Handschriften, Gemälden, Interieurs und Architekturelementen kann man ganze Tage verbringen. Die Besichtigung ist nur nach Anmeldung möglich.

Indigo Seas
123 North Robertson Boulevard
Lynn von Kersting's style: part Cecil Beaton, part Zelda and Scott Fitzgerald and the Murphys, a dash of laid-back Anglo-Indian, a splash of Caribbean Colonial outpost, with swatches of the French Riviera, all infused with romanticized England. Witty. Sofas, silver, soaps.
Le style Lynn von Kersting: moitié Cecil Beaton, moitié Zelda and Scott Fitzgerald, un soupçon de nonchalance anglo-indienne, une touche de Caraïbes, avec quelques réminiscences de la Côte d'Azur, le tout baigné dans une nostalgie romantique pour l'Angleterre. Beaucoup d'esprit. Sofas, argenterie, savons.
Lynn von Kersting kombiniert Cecil Beaton mit Zelda und Scott Fitzgerald, gibt eine Prise entspanntes Anglo-Indien, einen Spritzer Karibik zur Kolonialzeit, einen Hauch von französischer Riviera dazu – und mariniert all das mit romantischem England. Wirklich witzig. Bietet auch Sofas, Silber und Seifen.

James Jennings Furniture
8471 Melrose Avenue
The custom-crafted James Jennings Furniture collections, plus lines by Kerry Joyce and Madeline Stuart. Excellent craftsmanship – plus gentleman James, and the lovely Constance.
Les collections de meuble sur mesure de James Jennings, plus celles de Kerry Joyce et de Madeline Stuart. Réalisation très soignée, sans compter l'accueil de gentleman de James et celui de la charmante Constance.
Maßgefertigte James-Jennings-Möbel, außerdem Möbel von Kerry Joyce und Madeline Stuart. Exzellente Handarbeit plus Gentleman James und die liebenswürdige Constance.

Liz's Antique Hardware
453 South La Brea Avenue
Superior and solid collections of antique, vintage and new hardware. Antique bathroom fittings, lighting, original pieces from the 1860s onward.
Stock de qualité de quincaillerie ancienne ou nouvelle. Accessoires anciens pour salles de bains, luminaires, pièces originales à partir des années 1860.
Eine gute Auswahl an hochwertigen, soliden, antiken und neuen Haushaltswaren. Alte Badezimmerarmaturen, antike Leuchten und Originalstücke ab 1860.

Pat McGann
748 North La Cienega Boulevard
Modernist designs, quirky accessories, art, antiques. Pat has a great eye and terrific taste – and all the top decorators shop here.
Meubles modernistes, accessoires curieux, antiquités, œuvres d'art. Pat a l'œil et le goût fantastiques: tous les grands décorateurs lui rendent régulièrement visite.
Design der Moderne, eigenwillige Accessoires, Kunst und Antiquitäten. Pat hat einen großartigen Blick und einen tollen Geschmack, weshalb die besten Interior-Designer hier einkaufen.

Modern Props
5500 West Jefferson Boulevard
Love 50s or 70s design icons but can't afford them until that script is sold? Hop over to Modern Props, with 35 000 objects from sets of "RoboCop", "Blade Runner" and "Lethal Weapon" and other blockbusters. It's all for rent, so try it, return it, then test something from another time zone. Only in Los Angeles.
Vous adorez les meubles des années 50 ou 70, mais ne pouvez vous les offrir tant que vous n'avez pas vendu votre scénario? Ils sont tous ici – 35 000 références – et proviennent des décors de «Robocop», «Blade Runner», «Arme fatale» et autres succès. Tout est à louer. Essayez-les et rapportez-les pour en tester d'autres. Exclusivement Los Angeles.
Sie lieben Design aus den 50er oder 70er Jahren, können es sich aber nicht leisten, bis Sie Ihr Drehbuch verkauft haben? Schauen Sie bei Modern Props vorbei, wo man unter 35 000 Objekten wählen kann, die bei »RoboCop«, »Blade Runner«, »Lethal Weapon« und anderen Kassenschlagern mitgespielt haben. Man kann sie mieten – also nichts wie hin und ausprobieren. Zurückgeben kann man sie immer und sich dann in eine neue Zeitzone beamen. Gibt es nur in Los Angeles.

Richard Mulligan-Sunset Cottage
8157 Sunset Boulevard
To the trade only: by appointment ++1–213–650–86 60. With your decorator in tow, view furnishings imbued with the Mulligan's chic and sophisticated country style. Richard and Mollie have star and staying power – and an avid following among old-timers, Hollywood designers, and zesty celebs. Finely finessed reproductions and collectible one-of-a-kind lamps.
Réservé aux professionnels et sur rendez-vous: ++1–213–650–86 60. Escorté de votre décorateur, venez repérer les accessoires de décoration qui illustrent le style «country chic» et sophistiqué de Richard Mulligan. Richard et Mollie règnent ici et possèdent d'ailleurs leur cour de vieux fidèles, de décorateurs d'Hollywood et de célébrités du moment. Belles reproductions et lampes en modèles uniques.
Nur für Händler nach Absprache: ++1–213–650–86 60. Nehmen Sie mit Ihrem Interior-Designer im Schlepptau die feinen und eleganten Einrichtungen im Landhaus-Stil in Augenschein. Richard und Mollie besitzen Starqualitäten sowie Durchhaltevermögen und werden von Anhängern der guten alten Zeit, von Hollywood-Designern und der Prominenz gleichermaßen verehrt. Exquisite Stilmöbel und Unikat-Lampen mit Sammlerwert.

Neiman-Marcus
9700 Wilshire Boulevard
Beverly Hills
The revamped Gift Galleries and decor boutiques in the lower level are of the highest quality. This bright and bold bazaar is one-stop global shopping for decorative home gifts, porcelain, witty and chic gold-edged plates by Annieglass, myriad throws, spectacular and colourful drinking glasses, trays, paintings, rugs, and chairs.
Rénovées, la galerie des cadeaux et les boutiques de décoration du sous-sol atteignent au plus haut niveau de qualité. Ce bazar de grand luxe propose le choix total en matière de cadeaux pour la maison, porcelaines, amusants plats d'Annieglass bordés d'or, myriades de couvertures et jetés, verres à boire spectaculaires et multicolores, plateaux, peintures, tapis et sièges.
Die renovierten Boutiquen für Geschenk- und Dekorartikel im Untergeschoß bieten allerbeste Qualität. In dem hellen Basar findet man Porzellan, witzige und elegante Teller von Annieglass mit Goldrand, Myriaden an Tagesdecken, farbenfrohe Trinkgläser, Tabletts, Gemälde, Teppiche und Stühle: Shopping total.

Odalisque
7278 Beverly Boulevard
Linger among the funky antiques, vintage silks, chandeliers, and cushions. Super-chic and quirky. Antique fabrics. One-of-a-kind cushions and draperies made from embroidered old ecclesiastical fabrics and other obscure sources.
Vous hésiterez entre les antiquités curieuses, les soies anciennes, les lustres et les coussins. Super chic et parfois bizarre. Tissus anciens. Coussins et tentures exclusifs fabriqués à partir de vieilles nappes d'autel brodées et d'autres sources mystérieuses.
Stromern zwischen eigenartigen Antiquitäten, alten Seidenstoffen, Kronleuchtern und Kissen. Elegant und bizarr: alte Stoffe, einzigartige Kissen, Vorhänge aus bestickten Stoffen, die aus Kirchen und anderen obskuren Quellen stammen.

Orange
245 South Robertson Boulevard
Great interior artifacts of California's vanished industrial age. Steel desks, lamps, lockers, file cabinets,

gritty metal office manager chairs, 60s stuff all cleaned up.
Superbes objets décoratifs pour la maison issus du passé industriel de la Californie en cours de disparition. Bureaux d'acier, lampes, placards de vestiaire, efficaces et solides fauteuils de direction en métal, trucs des années 60, le tout remis à neuf.
Großartige Interior-Artefakte aus dem längst untergegangenen kalifornischen Industriezeitalter. Tische, Lampen, Spinde und Aktenschränke aus Stahl sowie Bürostühle aus angerauhtem Metall und aufgearbeiteter Krimskrams aus den 60er Jahren.

Outside
442 North La Brea Avenue
Vintage outdoor furniture. William Haines-designed patio sets and other movie star-handsome furniture with a pedigree. Colors, too, are of the period.
Mobilier de jardin ancien. Ensembles pour patio dessinés par William Haines et mobilier de stars, avec pedigree s'il vous plaît. Les couleurs, elles aussi, sont d'époque.
Alte Gartenmöbel. Von William Haines entworfene Ensembles für den Innenhof, außerdem Möbel mit Starqualitäten und Pedigree. Die Farben entsprechen natürlich auch der Epoche.

Pacific Design Center
8687 Melrose Avenue
To-the-trade essential design resource. Showrooms such as Mimi London, Donghia, Bradbury Collection, Oakmont, Randolph & Hein, Snaidero, McGuire, Brunschwig & Fils, Baker, Michael Taylor Designs, Dakota Jackson and Kneedler-Fauchere present the finest fabrics, furniture, lighting, rugs, hardware, reproductions, decorative accessories, fixtures. These showrooms are the crème de la crème of design – all very professional, totally top-of-the-line.
Un lieu professionnel entre tous. Des dizaines de show-rooms comme ceux de Mimi London, Donghia, Bradbury Collection, Oakmont, Randolph & Hein, Snaidero, McGuire, Brunschwig & Fils, Baker, Michael Taylor Designs, Dakota Johnson et Kneedler-Fauchere présentent ici leurs plus beaux tissus, meubles, luminaires, tapis, reproductions, accessoires de décoration et pour l'équipement de la maison. Ces show-rooms sont certainement ce qu'il y a de mieux à Los Angeles: très professionnels, très haut de gamme.
Eine wichtige Designquelle für den Handel: Showrooms von Mimi London, Donghia, Bradbury Collection, Oakmont, Randolph & Hein, Snaidero, McGuire, Brunschwig & Fils, Baker, Michael Taylor Designs, Dakota Jackson und Kneedler-Fauchere präsentieren hier die feinsten Stoffe, Möbel, Leuchten, Teppiche, Haushaltswaren, Stilmöbel, dekorative Accessoires und Armaturen – die Crème de la Crème des Design, professionell und absolut top.

Residences Bis
4464 West Adams Boulevard
Joyce McRae, a former design editor, and her partner Lindsay Shuford have a sweet setting for antiques with grace and charm. Selections might include East-Coast estate finds, old porcelain, and garden accessories.
Joyce McRae, ancienne journaliste de décoration, et son associé Lindsay Shuford ont l'œil pour les antiquités pleines de grâce et de charme. Leur choix est riche en meubles et objets venus de grandes demeures de la côte Est, de porcelaines anciennes et accessoires de jardin.
Die ehemalige Designjournalistin Joyce McRae und ihr Partner Lindsay Shuford haben ein Faible für Antiquitäten mit Anmut und Charme. Ihre Auswahl umfaßt Stücke aus Herrenhäusern an der Ostküste, antikes Porzellan und Gartenaccessoires.

Rizzoli Bookstore
9501 Wilshire Boulevard
Outstanding selection of design, photography and architecture books. Browse among the stacks. Open late. Also excellent, large stores in Santa Monica, Costa Mesa, San Francisco.
Remarquable sélection de livres sur le design, la photographie et l'architecture. N'hésitez pas à fouiller dans les piles. Ouvert jusque tard dans la nuit. Aussi des grands magasins à Santa Monica, Costa Mesa, San Francisco.
Herausragende Auswahl an Design-, Foto- und Architekturbüchern. Die Bücherstapel laden bis spätabends zum Wühlen ein. Auch exzellente, große Filialen in Santa Monica, Costa Mesa und San Francisco.

Rubbish
1627 and 1630 Silverlake Boulevard
Ha! It's not! Elegant and curvy mid-century furniture, lighting, and accessories. Collected in these two small stores, which face each other across the street, are hard-to-find decorative objects that decorators love to snap up. They're often the kinds of Ray and Charles Eames pieces, pop decor, and architect-designed furnishings that once stood neglected at estate sales and flea markets by those rushing toward shabby chic design or country looks.
Ce n'en est certainement pas (rubbish = ordures)! Mobilier curviligne élégant des années 50, luminaires et acessoires. Dans ces deux petits magasins face à face, vous trouverez rassemblés des objets de décoration rares, que les décorateurs s'arrachent. Sélection souvent dans l'esprit Eames, pop, et mobilier d'architectes délaissés par ceux qui préfèrent le shabby chic et le look campagne.
Bestimmt kein »Rubbish«! Elegant geschwungene Möbel, Leuchten und Accessoires der 50er Jahre. In den beiden kleinen, einander gegenüberliegenden Läden ergattern Interior-Designer Objekte, die sonst schwer zu finden sind, darunter Design von Ray und Charles Eames, Pop-Dekor und von Architekten entworfene Möbel, die die Fans von Shabby Chic und Landhaus-Stil nicht beachten.

Shelter
7920–7926 Beverly Boulevard
In a city where embellishment is all, it is refreshing to cast a glance over the chic, simple, modern furniture and accessories at Shelter. Beds, framed photography, tables and chairs with spare and versatile lines. OK, a vintage shop within Shelter sells "à la mode" mid-century dinnerware, old Italian espresso machines, 50s and 60s handblown glass, vintage European culinary gizmos, and other neat stuff gleaned by Larry Schaffer.
Dans une ville où le paraître est essentiel, il est rafraîchissant de trouver encore les meubles et les accessoires de décoration chics, simples et modernes de chez Shelter. Lits, photographies encadrées, tables et sièges aux lignes calculées. On y trouve aussi une petite boutique intégrée consacrée aux antiquités «à la mode» comme la vaisselle des années 50, les vieilles machines à espresso italiennes, le verre soufflé des années 50 et 60, les accessoires de cuisine européens et autres objets sympathiques glanés par Larry Schaffer.
In einer Stadt, in der nur Schönheit zählt, ist es geradezu erfrischend, sich die eleganten, einfachen, modernen Möbel und Accessoires von Shelter anzusehen: Betten, gerahmte Fotografien, Tische und Stühle mit klaren, abwechslungsreichen Formen. In dem Geschäft bietet ein kleiner Shop Geschirr aus den 50er Jahren an, das gerade »in« ist, alte italienische Espressomaschinen, mundgeblasenes Glas aus den 50er und 60er Jahren, alte Küchenutensilien aus Europa und andere nette Dinge, die Larry Schaffer aufgespürt hat.

Rose Tarlow Melrose House
8454 Melrose Place
Design Queen – or Empress – Rose Tarlow has an unerring sense of color and scale, along with a dash of humor. Her furniture collections spell out her deep understanding of design history, luxury, elegance, line and grace. A certain Continental and English sensibility, languor, and timeless glamour.
Reine, voire impératrice du design, Rose Tarlow possède un sens inouï de la couleur et des proportions, non dénué d'une pointe d'humour. Ses collections de meubles expriment une connaissance profonde de l'histoire du design, du luxe, de l'élégance, de la ligne et de la grâce. Une certaine sensibilité continentale et britannique, d'où une certaine langueur et un glamour hors du temps.
Rose Tarlow, die Königin des Design – eigentlich sogar die Kaiserin – hat ein unfehlbares Urteil, wenn es um Farben und Proportionen geht, und außerdem Sinn für Humor. Ihre Möbelkollektionen sind Luxus, Eleganz, Stil und Anmut pur und spiegeln auch ihre profunde Kenntnis der Geschichte des Design. Eine gewisse europäische und britische Sensibilität sowie zeitloser Glamour gehören einfach dazu.

Therien & Co.
716 North La Cienega Boulevard
Eclectic, elegant antiques, discovered by antiquaire Robert Garcia on global forays. Also superbly edited Therien Studio reproductions that are collector's items themselves. Also in San Francisco.
Antiquités éclectiques et élégantes découvertes par Robert Garcia au cours de ses expéditions d'exploration dans le monde entier. Egalement superbes reproductions de Therien Studio, qui sont en soi des pièces de collection. Même maison à San Francisco.
Robert Garcia hat eklektizistische und elegante Antiquitäten aus der ganzen Welt zusammengetragen, dazu wunderbar präsentierte Stilmöbel des Therien Studio, die ihrerseits Sammlerstücke sind. Auch in San Francisco vertreten.

Virtue
149 South La Brea Avenue
Superior collections of ceramics. Very L.A, but cosmopolitan, too. Andrew Virtue's chic antiques and decoration shop is part Madeleine Castaing, a dash of Elsie de Wolfe. Witty, and joyful. Garden furniture to bring indoors, paintings by untutored artists, sweet cushions
Impressionnante collection de céramiques, définitivement Los Angeles, mais cosmopolite aussi. L'élégante boutique d'antiquités et de décoration d'Andrew Virtue fait penser à Madeleine Castaing, avec cependant une touche d'Elsie de Wolfe. Beaucoup d'esprit et de gaîté. Mobilier de jardin, que l'on peut installer à l'intérieur, peintures d'artistes autodidactes, coussins.
Exquisite Keramiken. Typisch Los Angeles und trotzdem kosmopolitisch. Andrew Virtues witziger und fröhlicher Antik- und Dekor-Shop erinnert an Madeleine Castaing mit einem Spritzer Elsie de Wolfe, geistreich und fröhlich. Die Gartenmöbel sehen auch im Haus gut aus, außerdem gibt es hier Gemälde von autodidaktischen Künstlern und Kissen.

W Antiques and Eccentricities
8925 Melrose Avenue
Fine Chinoiserie, plus excellent collections of rare style books. Melissa Wallace Dietz's sunny gallery sells everything from 18th-century gilded ottomans, cinnabar chairs and birdcage-shaped chandeliers to stone fountains, iron urns, art deco furniture. It's one-of-a-kind and ever-changing.
Art chinois de qualité, et bel ensemble de livres rares sur le design. La galerie ensoleillée de Melissa Wallace Dietz vend de tout, des poufs dorés du 18e siècle, sièges de Cinnabar et cages en forme de lustres, à des fontaines de pierre, des urnes de métal et des meubles Art Déco. Unique et toujours «on the move».
Feines Kunsthandwerk aus China und eine exzellente Auswahl an seltenen Designbüchern. Melissa Wallace Dietz verkauft in ihrer sonnigen Galerie alles, von vergoldeten Hockern aus dem 18. Jahrhundert, zinnoberroten Stühlen und Kronleuchtern in Form von Vogelkäfigen bis zu steinernen Brunnen, Urnen aus Eisen und Art-déco-Möbeln – alles ständig wechselnde Unikate.

Worldware at Fred Segal Melrose
8118 Melrose Avenue
Fresh, original and colorful decor and gifts. Design books, frames, pens, vintage mementoes, cushions, dinnerware glasses in the bright and cheerful Los Angeles mode. After buying a book or two, it's fun to grab an iced latte and sit outside on the sunny terrace. Watch stars park their own Range Rovers! View a famous comedian lunching with his kids! Then go upstairs to try on Martin Margiela, Paul Smith, Dries van Noten. Pure Los Angeles.
Objets de décoration et cadeaux, frais, colorés et originaux. Livres sur la décoration, cadres, stylos, carnets anciens, vaisselle, verres, tout donne dans l'éclatant et la bonne humeur. Après avoir acheté un livre ou deux, dégustez un café au lait glacé sur la terrasse ensoleillée. Vous pourrez y contempler des stars du cinéma garant leur Range ou un célèbre comédien déjeuner avec ses enfants. Puis passez à l'étage supérieur pour essayer quelque chose de Martin Margiela, Paul Smith ou Dries van Noten. Du pur Los Angeles.
Frische, originelle und farbenfrohe Dekor- und Geschenkartikel, außerdem Designbücher, Rahmen, Stifte, alte Hefte, Kissen, elegante Gläser im fröhlichen Los Angeles-Stil. Wenn man ein oder zwei Bücher gekauft hat, sitzt man gerne mit einem Eiskaffee auf der sonnigen Terrasse und beobachtet die Stars, wie sie ihren Range Rover parken, oder einen Komiker beim Lunch mit seinen Kindern. Und dann geht es wieder nach oben zu Martin Margiela, Paul Smith und Dries van Noten. Das ist Los Angeles pur.

San Francisco

Just as San Francisco has a multitude of micro-climates, so it also has micro-villages dotted around its lovely square-mileage. Presidio Heights, Pacific Heights, North Beach, Mission District, Hayes Valley, Union Square, South of Market and so on all have their own characters and eccentricities. The most interesting design and style stores are on Fillmore Street, Hayes, Brady Street – actually a lane off Market Street –, downtown Post and Sutter Streets, Sacramento Street in Pacific Heights, the western end of Polk Street, Jackson Square and around Union Square. Explore Fillmore Street from Jackson Street to Bush Street. Outer Sacramento Street, Noe Valley and mid-Market Street all have their own neighborhood flavor. Tech-gulchy South Park, funky South of Market, and the edgy Mission District house design stores. There's even Interieur Perdu under the South pier of the Bay Bridge.

De même que San Francisco bénéficie d'une multitude de micro-climats, elle se répartit en de multiples micro-villages qui se succèdent tout au long de ce merveilleux site. Presidio Heights, Pacific Heights, North Beach, Mission District, Hayes Valley, Union Square, South of Market etc., chacun possède son caractère et sa touche d'excentricité personnelle. Les magasins de décoration et de design les plus intéressants se trouvent sur Fillmore Street, Hayes, Brady Street – en fait une allée donnant sur Market Street –, Post and Sutter Streets dans le centre, Sacramento Street à Pacific Heights, l'extrémité ouest de Polk Street, Jackson Square et autour de Union Square. Explorez également Fillmore Street de Jackson Street à Bush Street. Les alentours de Sacramento Street, Noe Valley et de la partie centrale de Market Street sont des quartiers en soi. South Park, sous le signe des technologies nouvelles, South of Market plutôt funk, et le quartier marginal de Mission District abritent aussi des boutiques de décoration. On trouve même un magasin intitulé Interieur Perdu au pied de la pile sud du Bay Bridge.

So wie San Francisco eine Vielzahl von Mikroklimata vereint, gibt es hier auch Minidörfer, die sich um das wunderschöne Zentrum gruppieren. Presidio Heights, Pacific Heights, North Beach, Mission District, Hayes Valley, Union Square und South of Market haben alle einen eigenen Charakter. Die interessantesten Design- und Einrichtungsgeschäfte liegen an der Fillmore Street, Hayes, Brady Street – die eigentlich eine Nebenstraße der Market Street ist –, Post Street und Sutter Street im Zentrum, Sacramento Street in Pacific Heights, dem westlichen Ende der Polk Street, Jackson Square und rund um den Union Square. Erforschen Sie auch die Fillmore Street von der Jackson bis zur Bush Street. Die äußere Sacramento Street, Noe Valley und der mittlere Teil der Market Street haben jede ihr ganz unverkennbares Flair. South Park wird von den neuen Technologien geprägt, South of Market ist ausgeflippt, und auch der am Rand gelegene Mission District verfügt über Designläden. Sogar unter dem südlichen Pier der Bay Bridge gibt es ein Geschäft: Interieur Perdu.

Alabaster
597 Hayes Street, corner of Laguna Street
Owners Nelson and Paul dream in white. White pillows, ivory pottery, mother-of-pearl spoons, white chairs, clear pressed vintage glass, plus pale and interesting prints and photographs. Chic!
Nelson et Paul, les propriétaires, rêvent en blanc. Coussins blancs, objets en ivoire, cuillères en nacre, sièges blancs, verre pressé ancien, gravures et photographies intéressantes et pâlies. Très chic.
Die Besitzer Nelson und Paul träumen in Weiß. Weiße Kissen, Elfenbeingefäße, Perlmuttlöffel, weiße Stühle, durchsichtiges Preßglas und interessante, verblichene Drucke und Fotos. Très chic!

Antique & Art Exchange
3419 Sacramento Street
All the top California decorators drop into this chock-a-block emporium for displays of eclectic California plein-air paintings, Chinoiserie chests, small Japanese "tansus", English silverware, painted furniture of fine provenance, rare porcelain, vermeil frames. Connoisseurs love the Gustav III boxes, shell-encrusted frames, fine tramp art, Venetian glass, furnishings from notable mansions.
Tous les grands décorateurs californiens viennent de temps en temps jeter un coup d'œil dans cet emporium éclectique et bourré: peinture de paysages californiens, coffres chinois, petits «tansus» japonsais, argenterie anglaise, meubles peints de bonne provenance, porcelaines rares, cadres en vermeil. Les connaisseurs aiment les boîtes Gustave III, les cadres décorés de coquillages, l'art de la rue de qualité, les verreries vénitiennes, les meubles de noble provenance.
Kaliforniens Top-Interior-Designer suchen hier nach kalifornischen Landschaftsmalereien, chinesischen Kisten, japanischen »tansus«, englischem Silber, bemalten Möbeln, seltenem Porzellan und feuervergoldeten Rahmen. Kenner lieben die Dosen im Gustavian Style, die muschelverzierten Rahmen, Straßenkunstwerke, edlen Möbel und das venezianische Glas.

Arkitektura
650 Ninth Street
This showroom offers Artemide lighting, Droog designs, and clean-lined furniture, storage, accessories and lighting by the likes of Flexform, Herman Miller, Saarinen Collection, Josef Hoffmann, Vitra Edition, Kartell, Miele, Fiam Italia, Leucos, Flos, Luceplan and Casamilano. Art exhibits, too.
Ce show-room propose des objets de Droog Design, des meubles aux lignes nettes, des rangements, des accessoires et luminaires de marques comme Artemide, Flexform, Herman Miller, Saarinen Collection, Josef Hoffmann, Vitra Edition, Kartell, Miele, Fiam Italian, Leucos, Flos, Luceplan et Casamilano. Egalement expositions d'art.
Dieser Showroom zeigt Entwürfe von Droog, Möbel mit klaren Linien, Schränke, Accessoires und Leuchten von Artemide, Flexform, Herman Miller, Saarinen Collection, Josef Hoffmann, Vitra Edition, Kartell, Miele, Fiam Italia, Leucos, Flos, Luceplan und Casamilano.

Banana Republic
Flagship store on corner Grant Avenue and Sutter Street
Banana Republic goes home! Most of the larger Banana Republic stores around the country now display tempting decor – to buy along with jeans and t-shirts. Well-priced, basic home accessories, nothing fussy. Superbly edited home collection of linens, glassware, barware, throws, silverware, napkins, cushions, vases, decor ... all with the noted casual-chic Banana Republic sensibility. Many other California locations.
Banana Republic chez elle! La plupart des vastes magasins Banana Republic des Etats-Unis affichent maintenant un décor séduisant pour inciter à acheter jeans et T-shirts. Accessoires de base pour la maison à prix sensés, pas de chichis. Belle collection de draps, de verrerie, d'accessoires pour le bar, de couvertures, de couverts, de serviettes, coussins, boîtes, objets décoratifs, le tout avec le style chic quotidien et la sensibilité Banana Republic. Nombreuses autres adresses en Californie.
Banana Republic kommt zu Ihnen nach Hause! Die meisten größeren Banana Republic Stores in den Vereinigten Staaten stellen jetzt zwischen Jeans und T-Shirts auch verführerisches Dekor aus. Günstige Preise, schlichte Wohnaccessoires, kein Schnickschnack. Eine wunderbare Auswahl an Leinen, Glas, Utensilien für die Hausbar, Tagesdecken, Besteck, Servietten, Kissen, Vasen ... alles mit dem bekannten unauffällig-sensiblen Chic von Banana Republic. Viele Zweigstellen in Kalifornien.

Bauerware
3886 17th Street
The sunshine-bright (shocking pink! mango! chartreuse!) exterior will draw you in. Interior designer Lou Ann Bauer's new hardware shop sells more than 1 600 pulls and knobs and other decorative delights. Traditional polished brass, vintage Bakelite, resin, wood, and rock knobs. Customers often walk in with drawers in hand.
Comment cette façade éclatante (rose shocking, mangue et chartreuse) n'attirerait-elle pas votre regard? La nouvelle boutique de quincaillerie de la décoratrice Lou Ann Bauer propose plus de 1 600 boutons, poignées et autres charmants accessoires décoratifs. Laiton poli traditionnel, Bakélite ancienne, résines, boutons et poignées en bois et pierre. Des clients viennent même ici leur tiroir à la main.
Die knallbunte Fassade in Pink, Mango und Chartreuse zieht einfach an. Der neue Haushaltswarenladen der Interior-Designerin Lou Ann Bauer verkauft über 1 600 Türgriffe, Klinken und andere Schätze aus traditionellem, poliertem Messing, altem Bakelit, Harz, Holz und Stein. Manche Kunden bringen ihre Schubladen gleich mit.

Bell'Occhio
8 Brady Street
Claudia Schwartz and Toby Hanson – charm and grace personified – run this whimsical little boutique offering French postcards, old-time Florentine soaps, hand-painted ribbons, French silk velvet flowers. Their frequent sorties to Paris produce witty antiques, hats, posters, and Leclerc face powders.
Claudia Schwartz et Toby Hanson – le charme et la grâce personnifiés – animent cette fantasque petite boutique qui propose des cartes postales françaises, des savonnettes florentines à l'ancienne, des rubans peints à la main, des fleurs en velours de soie français. De leurs fréquentes expéditions à Paris, ils rapportent des antiquités amusantes, des chapeaux, des affiches et la poudre Leclerc.
Claudia Schwartz und Toby Hanson, beide personifizierter Charme und Anmut, führen diese skurrile, kleine Boutique mit französischen Postkarten, alten Florentiner Seifen, handbemalten Schleifen und französischen Seidensamtblumen. Von ihren häufigen Reisen nach Paris bringen sie witzige Antiquitäten, Hüte, Poster und Gesichtspuder von Leclerc mit.

Bloomers
2975 Washington Street
Floral designer Patrick Powell stocks simply the freshest cut flowers, branches, bulbs, and orchids in terracotta pots. Hundreds of vases, rolls of French ribbons and decorative baskets. Nothing fussy here – just nature's natural beauty.
Le fleuriste-créateur Patrick Powell vend des fleurs coupées d'une fraîcheur exceptionnelle, mais aussi des feuillages, des bulbes et des orchidées en pots de terre cuite. Des centaines

de vases, de rouleaux de rubans français et de paniers décoratifs. Rien de mignard ici, juste la simple beauté de la Nature.
Der Florist und Designer Patrick Powell hat die schönsten Schnittblumen, Zweige, Knollen und Orchideen in Terrakottatöpfen. Hunderte von Vasen, rollenweise französische Schleifen und dekorative Körbe. Kein Schnickschnack, nur die Schönheit der Natur.

Bulgari
237 Post Street
The chic-est diamonds and fine accessories, yes, but the temptations grow. Browse in the elegant upstairs silver and accessories department. Now there are scarves, scents as well as all things sparkling and elegant.
Sophistication, diamants et accessoires de luxe. A l'étage, argenterie et objets de table. On y vend aussi maintenant des foulards, des parfums et tout ce qui brille.
Atemberaubende Diamanten und feine Accessoires. Die elegante erste Etage mit Silber und Accessoires ist einen Besuch wert. Jetzt gibt es auch Schals, Düfte und alles, was glitzert und elegant ist.

Cartier
231 Post Street
Every home should have a little Cartier. In this glamor setting are clocks and other worldly musthaves, elegant accessories, silver, crystal, vases, porcelain.
Chacun devrait avoir un peu de Cartier chez soi. Dans ce cadre «glamour» des pendules et autres Must, accessoires élégants, argenterie, cristaux, vases, porcelaine.
Jedes Haus sollte ein bißchen Cartier haben. In diesem glamourösen Umfeld gibt es Uhren und andere Dinge, die man unbedingt haben muß, elegante Silberaccessoires, Kristallglas, Vasen und Porzellan.

De Vera
580 Sutter Street
Federico de Vera's wordly "museum" of style. A soulful, one-of-a-kind store. "Objets trouvés", antique sculptures. Refined Venetian glass, small-scale finds, and original chair designs by de Vera himself. Ceramics, pottery, superb Scandinavian glass, antique and rare handhewn tables, santos, paintings, furniture, jewelry.
C'est le petit musée du style créé par Federico de Vera. Boutique inspirée d'objets uniques. «Objets trouvés», sculptures antiques. Verrerie vénitienne raffinée, brimborions et sièges dessinés par de Vera lui-même. Céramiques, poteries, superbe verrerie scandinave, tables anciennes et rares fabriquées artisanalement, saints mexicains, tableaux, mobilier et bijoux.
Das »Museum of Style« von Frederico de Vera ist einmalig. Es zeigt verschiedenste Fundstücke,

antike Skulpturen, raffiniertes venezianisches Glas, begehrenswerte Kleinigkeiten und von de Vera selbst entworfene Stühle, außerdem Keramik, Töpferwaren, superbes skandinavisches Glas, antike und seltene handgefertigte Tische, Heiligenfiguren, Gemälde, Möbel und Schmuck.

Fillamento
2185 Fillmore Street
For more than 14 years this bustling store has been a must-see for design aficionados. Iris Fuller, the cheerful owner, stocks three floors with a variety of style-conscious furniture, tableware, soaps, fixtures, towels, mirrors, glass, toiletries, and gifts. Iris is first with new designers and supports local talent including Nik Weinstein, Willsea O'Brien, Ann Gish, Annieglass and Cyclamen Studio.
Depuis plus de 14 ans, ce magasin très animé est un must pour les aficionados de la déco. Iris Fuller, son accueillante propriétaire, a bourré ses trois niveaux de tout un achalandage de meubles qui ne s'en laissent pas compter, d'objets pour la table, de savons, d'accessoires de décoration, de serviettes, miroirs, verres, accessoires pour la salle de bains et cadeaux. Iris est toujours la première à découvrir de nouveaux designers et soutient les créateurs locaux comme Nik Weinstein, Willsea O'Brien, Ann Gish, Annieglass et Cyclamen Studio.
Seit mehr als 14 Jahren ist der betriebsame Laden Anlaufstelle für Design-Fans. Die gut gelaunte Iris Fuller verkauft auf drei Etagen eine große Bandbreite an stilvollen Möbeln, Tafelzubehör, Seifen, Armaturen, Handtüchern, Spiegeln, Glas, Toiletten- und Geschenkartikeln. Iris endeckt neue Designer immer als erste und unterstützt Lokaltalente wie Nik Weinstein, Willsea O'Brien, Ann Gish, Annieglass und Cyclamen Studio.

Fioridella
1920 Polk Street
A joyful and fun floral celebration. Flower-lovers love this zesty place. Kelly Schrock's fine selection of decorative accessories and versatile vases make flower-buying a pleasure.
Hommage joyeux et amusant à l'art du bouquet, apprécié des amoureux des fleurs. La sélection raffinée d'accessoires décoratifs et de vases de toutes formes de Kelly Schrock fait que l'on achète ici vraiment par plaisir.
Spaß und Freude an Blumen. Blumenliebhaber verehren diesen reizvollen Laden. Kelly Schrocks exzellente Auswahl an dekorativen Accessoires und Vasen in verschiedensten Formen läßt den Kauf zum Vergnügen werden.

George
2411 California Street
Canine style for loved pets – and cats are not neglected. Pet fashions

including pieces by Todd Oldham and Tom Bonauro, charms, toys, cedar chushions, bowls and accessories. Best dog treats: handmade whole-grain biscuits.
Le grand style pour votre chien favori – ou votre chat, pourquoi pas? Accessoires pour animaux de Todd Oldham et Tom Bonauro, dont jouets, coussins, écuelles et accessoires. Les chiens adorent leurs biscuits au blé complet.
Der Salon für heißgeliebte Haustiere – Katzen eingeschlossen. Mode fürs Tier unter anderem von Todd Oldham und Tom Bonauro: Spielzeug, Kissen, Freßnäpfe und Accessoires. Der Hund schätzt die selbstgebackenen Vollkornbiskuits.

Gump's
135 Post Street
When in San Francisco, everyone comes to Gump's, a century-old must-visit! This chic Gump's, next to Rizzoli, has superb fine crafts, art, ceramics, classic Orient-inspired accessories, plus quality names in silver, crystal, elegant bed linens. Bunny Williams' Treillage garden antiques shop, and the decorative glass departments are favorites.
A San Francisco, tout le monde va chez Gump's et ce depuis un siècle. Ce Gump's chic, juste à côté de Rizzoli, présente de magnifiques céramiques, des créations artisanales et artistiques, des accessoires d'inspiration orientale, quelques grands noms de l'argenterie et du cristal et parures de drap très classe. La boutique d'antiquités de jardin Treillage de Bunny William et le département de verrerie sont à voir absolument.
Jeder geht bei einem Besuch in San Francisco bei Gump's vorbei, und das schon seit 100 Jahren. Das elegante Gump's neben Rizzoli verkauft feines Kunstgewerbe, Kunst, Keramik, klassische, orientalisch inspirierte Accessoires, Qualitätssilber und Kristallglas sowie elegante Bettwäsche. Treillage, der Laden für antike Gartenmöbel von Bunny Williams, und die Abteilung für dekorative Glaswaren sind ebenfalls sehenswert.

Ed Hardy San Francisco
188 Henry Adams Street
Elegant, eclectic, surprising, and desirable antiques in a Palladian villa-inspired gallery. The stylish and schorlarly staff here is especially gracious and helpful, and clients love to wander for hours, often ending up with lunch – by invitation – in the garden among the stone urns, Victorian benches, lions, cranes and fountains.
Antiquités élégantes, éclectiques, suprenantes, en un mot très désirables, installées dans une galerie inspirée d'une villa palladienne. Le personnel tout aussi stylé et décoratif est particulièrement avenant et serviable, et les clients adorent y passer des heures, terminant souvent par un lunch dans le jardin au milieu d'urnes

de pierre, de bancs victoriens, de lions, de grues et de fontaines.
In dieser von einer palladianischen Villa inspirierten Galerie finden sich elegante, eklektizistische, überraschende und begehrenswerte Antiquitäten. Das stilbewußte Personal ist besonders hilfsbereit. Kunden spazieren stundenlang herum und werden oft zum Lunch im Garten eingeladen, umgeben von steinernen Urnen, viktorianischen Bänken, Löwen und Kranichen.

Hermès
212 Stockton Street
Classic, collectible Hermès silk scarves here are the ultimate in timeless style, but zip past them for now to discover ceramics, modernist vases, tableware, cashmere blankets, cashmere throws, picnicware, silver and chic decor.
Bien entendu, vous y trouverez les carrés de soie au style intemporel, mais vous y découvrirez aussi des céramiques, des vases modernistes, des accessoires pour la table, des couvertures et des couvre-lits en cachemire, des ustensiles de pique-nique et de l'argenterie.
Die klassischen Hermès-Seidentücher stehen für ultimative, zeitlose Eleganz. Aber hier gibt es außerdem Keramiken, Vasen der Moderne, Tafelzubehör, Kaschmirdecken und -überwürfe, Picknickausstattungen, Silber und elegante Accessoires zu entdecken.

Richard Hilkert Books
333 Hayes Street
Great place to start a design library. Give Richard a tinkle to order unusual style books and new and practical design books.
Richard ne pouvait trouver un lieu plus indiqué pour ouvrir une librairie de design. N'hésitez pas à commander des livres rares sur le style ou des ouvrages nouveaux et pratiques sur le design.
Ein großartiger Standort für eine Designbuchhandlung. Animieren Sie Richard dazu, ungewöhnliche Lifestyle-Bücher oder neue und praktische Designbücher zu bestellen.

House of Mann
2727 Mariposa, no. 104
Bold California decor by Ron Mann and Louise La Palme Mann. Cleverly located in a former mayonnaise factory, this striking interior design studio is far from white bread! Ron Mann's muscular Douglas fir sofas, sculptural chairs and steel tables are highly collectible. Louise Mann's handpainted fabrics are boldly patterned.
Décor audacieux et typiquement californien de Ron Mann et Louise La Palme Mann. Astucieusement logé dans une ancienne fabrique de mayonnaise, ce superbe studio de décoration n'a rien de banal. Les puissants canapés en pin de Douglas signés de Ron Mann, les fauteuils

sculpturaux et les tables d'acier savent séduire. Tissus peints à la main de motifs audacieux par Louise Mann.
Kühnes, typisch kalifornisches Design von Ron Mann und Louise La Palme Mann. Dieses eindrucksvolle Interior-Design-Studio in einer ehemaligen Mayonnaisefabrik hat Pfiff! Ron Manns mächtige Sofas aus Douglasfichte, seine geschnitzten Stühle und Stahltische haben hohen Sammlerwert. Dazu gibt es handbemalte Stoffe von Louise Mann.

Interieur Perdu
340 Bryant Street
Warning: It's a little hard to find. Hint: Look in the loading dock. Trend-setting country French antiques – of the rusted, fusty, funky, charming, hard-to-find kind. Owners Fritzi, Coco and Fred have turned their French lessons into an excellent adventure!
Vous êtes prévenu: l'adresse est un peu difficile à trouver. Un conseil: repérez la baie de déchargement. Antiquités françaises à la mode, du type rouillé, bizarre, suranné, charmant et difficile à trouver. Fritzi, Coco et Fred, les propriétaires, ont bien mis à profit leurs cours de français!
Achtung: Der Laden ist schwer zu finden! Suchen Sie bei den Docks. Trendige, rustikale, französische Antiquitäten der seltenen, verrosteten, morbiden, verrückten und charmanten Art. Die Besitzer Fritzi, Coco und Fred haben ihren Französischkurs abenteuerlich umgesetzt!

Juicy News
2453 Fillmore Street
Neighborhood haunt. Tall racks display every possible international fashion, design, architecture and style magazine. Gretchen also offers fresh fruit refreshments named for favorite publications.
Une boutique de quartier. Sur de hautes étagères s'étalent tous les magazines internationaux sur la mode, le design, l'architecture et le style. Gretchen propose également des jus de fruit frais baptisés du nom de grands magazines.
Treffpunkt für die Nachbarschaft. Auf hohen Ständern gibt es hier jede erdenkliche internationale Mode-, Design-, Architektur- und Lifestyle-Zeitschrift. Gretchen serviert dazu frisch gepreßte Fruchtsäfte, die nach berühmten Zeitschriften benannt sind.

Sue Fisher King
3067 Sacramento Street
Also: Sue Fisher King Home at Wilkes Bashford
375 Sutter Street
Luscious and elegant style for bathrooms, dining rooms, bedrooms. Class-act Sue King's Italian, French and English bed linens, cashmere throws and tableware are the richest, most unusual and prettiest. Thick winter blankets, hand-dyed

Himalayan cashmere fringed throws, handcrafted glass accessories, design books, French soaps, furniture and Diptyque candles.
Style élégant et presque sensuel pour des accessoires de salle de bains, de salle à manger, de chambres à coucher. Sue King a sélectionné des parures de draps d'origine italienne, française et anglaise, des couvre-lits de cachemire, et son choix de vaisselle est à la fois luxueux, inhabituel et plein de charme. Epaisses couvertures pour l'hiver, couvre-lits himalayens en cachemire à franges et teints à la main, accessoires en verre faits main, livres sur le design, savonnettes françaises, meubles et bougies Diptyque.
Wollüstiges und Elegantes für Bade-, Eß- und Schlafzimmer. Sue King hat die üppigsten, ungewöhnlichsten und schönsten Tischaccessoires, Kaschmirdecken sowie Bettwäsche aus Italien, Frankreich und England. Dicke Winterdecken, handgefärbte, fransenbesetzte Kaschmirdecken aus dem Himalaja, handgefertigte Gläser, Designbücher, französische Seifen, Möbel und Kerzen von Diptyque.

Limn
290 Townsend Street
Visionary Dan Friedlander has slowly built an empire! Design fans visit on Saturday afternoons – after buying their frisee and Babcock peaches at the Farmers' Market at Ferry Plaza. Surprisingly, this is only one of a handful of Northern California stores selling top-of-the-line and often avant-garde contemporary furniture, accessories, and lighting by over 300 international manufacturers. Well-priced off-the-floor collections plus (plan to be patient) to-order pieces by Philippe Starck, B&B Italia, Andrée Putman. Visit the "piazza" and edgy gallery behind the store. Also in Sacramento.
Visionnaire, Dan Friedlander s'est peu à peu construit un empire. Les fous de design lui rendent visite le samedi après-midi, après avoir fait leurs emplettes au Farmer's Market de Ferry Plaza. C'est l'un des rares magasins de Californie du Nord a vendre des meubles, des accessoires et des luminaires contemporains haut de gamme et souvent d'avant-garde de plus de 300 marques internationales. Important stock disponible à prix abordables mais vous pouvez aussi commander (soyez patient) des créations de Philippe Starck, B&B Italia, Andrée Putman. Visitez la «piazza» et la galerie derrière le magasin. Même maison à Sacramento.
Der visionäre Dan Friedlander hat sich langsam ein Reich aufgebaut. Design-Fans schauen am Samstag nachmittag vorbei, nachdem sie auf dem Bauernmarkt an der Ferry Plaza Friséesalat und Babcock-Pfirsiche gekauft haben. Dies ist eines von den überraschend wenigen Geschäften in Nordkalifornien, das hochwertige Avantgarde-Möbel, Accessoires und Leuchten von über 300 internationalen Herstellern verkauft. Es gibt eine große Auswahl direkt zum Mitnehmen zu günstigen Preisen. Man kann auch Entwürfe von Philippe Starck, B&B Italia und Andrée Putman bestellen (braucht aber Geduld). Besuchen Sie auch die »Piazza« und die betriebsame Galerie hinter dem Geschäft. Auch in Sacramento vertreten.

MAC
1543 Grant Avenue
Chris Ospital's charming salon sells style inspiration, womenswear, home accessories. Talent and trend-spotter Chris knows who's new. Walk through Chinatown to the menswear MAC at oh-so-French Claude Lane, between Bush and Sutter Streets, to visit Ben Ospital, and see San Francisco-based USDA's selection of handsome modernist furniture.
La charmante boutique de Chris Ospital vend mode féminine et accessoires pour la maison, avec style et inspiration. Talentueuse et dotée d'un flair certain pour les tendances, Chris sait ce qui est vraiment nouveau. Traversez Chinatown pour jeter un coup d'œil à MAC – mode masculine – à Claude Lane, si française, entre Bush et Sutter Streets, et jetez un œil sur la sélection d'élégant mobilier moderniste de USDA de San Francisco.
In Chris Ospitals charmanter Boutique findet man Damenmode und Wohnaccessoires, die viele Anregungen bieten. Talent- und Trendforscher Chris weiß immer, was neu auf dem Markt ist. Spazieren Sie durch Chinatown zum MAC für Herrenmode in der sehr französischen Claude Lane zwischen Bush und Sutter Street. Dort finden Sie Ben Ospital und eine Auswahl an schönen Möbeln der Moderne von der ebenfalls in San Francisco ansässigen Firma USDA.

Jefferson Mack Metals
2094 Oakdale Avenue
Jefferson Mack is a remarkable being of the digital age: He's a blacksmith and hand-forges gates, fences, furniture, decorative metalwork. He crafts the old-fashioned way – with his hands, with his own hand-made tools, and his fired-up forge. Visit Jefferson and see the white-hot metal, the heavy-lifting, the one-of-a-kind, heirloom-quality gazebos, tools, tables. Mack is one of four blacksmiths in San Francisco city boundaries: Angelo Garo, Frank Trousil and James Austin of Alchemy Metalworks work at this physically demanding craft, too.
A l'ère numérique, Jefferson Mack est une exception: il est ferronnier, et fabrique des portails, des barrières, des meubles, des éléments de décor en métal. Il travaille à l'ancienne, avec ses mains, ses propres outils, et sa forge à soufflet. Il faut voir le métal chauffé à blanc, les gloriettes, outils et tables d'un poids énorme qu'il fabrique et sont autant de pièces uniques. Mack est l'un des quatre ferronniers à exercer ce métier très physique à San Francisco avec Angelo Garo, Frank Trousil et James Austin d'Alchemy Metalworks.
Der Schmied Jefferson Mack ist eine bemerkenswerte Ausnahme im digitalen Zeitalter. Er schmiedet Tore, Zäune, Möbel und dekorative Metallarbeiten noch auf althergebrachte Weise mit seinen Händen, handgefertigten Werkzeugen und der heißen Esse. Schauen Sie bei Mack vorbei und beobachten Sie, wie weißglühendes Metall in Schwerstarbeit zu einmaligen Pavillons, Werkzeugen und Tischen verarbeitet wird. Außer Mack üben in San Francisco auch Angelo Garo, Frank Trousil und James Austin von Alchemy Metalworks dieses körperlich anstrengende Handwerk aus.

The Magazine
528 Folsom Street
Also: 1823 Eastshore Highway Berkeley
Rainer and Brian are among the few entrepreneurs in Northern California offering the best contemporary furniture. In this loft-like store are lined up designs by Aalto, Starck, Cappellini, Nelson, Jacobsen and Eames and all the other design icons that are the darlings of design magazines.
Rainer et Brian sont parmi les rares spécialistes à offrir le meilleur du mobilier contemporain en Californie du Nord. Dans ce magasin-loft s'alignent les modèles d'Aalto, de Starck, de Cappellini, Nelson, Jacobsen et Eames et tous ces objets-symboles du design qu'adorent les magazines.
Rainer und Brian gehören zu den wenigen Spezialisten in Nordkalifornien, die bestes aktuelles Möbeldesign anbieten. In ihrem loftartigen Store finden sich Entwürfe von Aalto, Starck, Cappellini, Nelson, Jacobsen, Eames und all der anderen Koryphäen, die von den Designzeitschriften bejubelt werden.

Maison d'Etre
92 South Park
Fred's collections of prints, eccentric vintage garden furniture (for indoors), handblown glass bowls by local artists, vintage candlesticks, new metal vases, sculptural candles. All selected and presented with spirit. Walk across this hidden-away park to discover Isda & Co.'s outlet, then sip an espresso at South Park Cafe or Caffe Centro.
A voir, pour tout ce que Fred a rassemblé de gravures, meubles de jardin anciens et excentriques (à utiliser à l'intérieur), coupes en verre soufflé par des artistes locaux, vieux bougeoirs, vases en métal, bougies sculpturales. Tout est choisi et présenté avec esprit. Traversez le discret South Park pour découvrir Isda & Co., avant de déguster un espresso au South Park Cafe ou au Caffe Centro.
Fred verkauft Drucke, exzentrische alte Gartenmöbel für Innenräume, mundgeblasenes Glas von lokalen Künstlern, alte Kerzenleuchter, neue Metallvasen und monumentale Kerzen – alles geistreich ausgewählt und präsentiert. Ein kurzer Spaziergang durch den South Park führt zu Isda & Co., danach trinkt man Espresso im South Park Cafe oder Caffe Centro.

Mike Furniture
Corner Fillmore and Sacramento Streets
Mike Moore, partner Mike Thakar and their energetic crew enliven this sunny store which offers updated furniture classics-with-a-twist. Fresh food for thought from Mike Studio, Beverly and other national manufacturers. Custom and bespoke design here is very accessible. Fresh accessories, excellent lamps.
Mike Moore, son associé Mike Thakar et leur personnel énergique animent ce magasin ensoleillé qui propose des mobiliers classiques, revus et corrigés. Nouveautés de Mike Studio, Beverly et autres grands fabricants américains. Réalisations sur commande et sur mesure à des prix très accessibles. Accessoires amusants et belles lampes.
Mike Moore, sein Partner Mike Thakar und die geschäftige Crew verkaufen in diesem sonnigen Laden aufgearbeitete Möbelklassiker mit dem gewissen Etwas. Neuheiten von Mike Studio, Beverly und anderen amerikanischen Herstellern. Maßanfertigungen und Bestellungen zu sehr günstigen Preisen. Frischer Wind auch bei den Accessoires, fabelhafte Leuchten.

Modernism
685 Market Street
Cosmopolitan, outstanding, long-time favorite art gallery. Represents top international artists.
Remarquable galerie d'art internationale. Etablie depuis longtemps, elle représente des artistes célèbres.
Diese seit langem beliebte Galerie vertritt berühmte Künstler aus der ganzen Welt.

Naomi's Antiques To Go
1817 Polk Street
Collectible American art pottery! Festive Bauer and Fiesta plus small-production studio pottery. International collectors dote on dinnerware and vases from defunct American railroad, hotels, luxury liners, the navy, dude ranches, and bus depots.
Poterie d'art américaine. Lignes Bauer, Fiesta, plus des céramiques d'atelier en séries limitées. Les collectionneurs du monde entier se précipitent ici pour la vaisselle de wagons-restaurants, de paquebots, d'hôtels, de vaisseaux de la Navy, de ranches pour des touristes et de gares routières, tous aujourd'hui disparus.
Amerikanische Töpferkunst mit Sammlerwert! Festliches von Bauer und Fiesta sowie Töpferwaren aus kleinen Werkstätten. Internationale Sammler schwören auf Geschirr aus Eisenbahnrestaurants, Hotels, Busbahnhöfen, Navyschiffen und Luxuskreuzfahrtschiffen sowie von Touristen-Ranches.

Nest
2300 Fillmore Street
On a romantic Victorian corner, formerly a neighborhood pharmacy, Marcella Madsen and Judith Gilman have feathered their seductive Nest. Treasures include Paris flea-market finds, books, antique beds, rustic French antiques, vintage Italian prints, lavender sachets, sofas, Bravura lampshades and cushions. Virtuoso windows.
A un angle de rue victorien, Marcella Madsen et Judith Gilman se sont aménagé ce «nid» douillet dans une ancienne pharmacie de quartier. Leurs trésors qui proviennent des marchés aux puces de Paris se composent de livres, de lits anciens, de meubles rustiques français, de gravures italiennes anciennes, de sachets de lavande, de canapés, d'abat-jour Bravura et coussins. Merveilleuses vitrines.
In einer ehemaligen Apotheke in einem romantischen viktorianischen Eckhaus richteten Marcella Madsen und Judith Gilman ihr verführerisches »Nest« ein. Ihre Schätze beinhalten Fundstücke von Pariser Flohmärkten, Bücher, alte Betten, rustikale französische Antiquitäten, alte italienische Drucke, Lavendelsäckchen, Sofas, Lampenschirme und Kissen. Virtuose Schaufenster.

The Painters Place
355 Hayes Street
Artists' and designers' favorite framing resource. Extraordinary custom-made frames – all handcrafted and hand-finished. Water gilding, gesso-ing, handpainting, and many arcane arts. Beautifully designed mats, bevels, French lines and Florentine frames and a multitude of styles.
L'encadreur favori des artistes et des décorateurs. Extraordinaires encadrements sur mesure. Dorure à l'eau, plâtre, peinture à la main, et multiples techniques mystérieuses. Superbes marie-louises, boîtes à biseaux, marques françaises et cadres florentins et une multitude de styles.
Hier kaufen Künstler und Designer am liebsten ein: qualitativ hervorragende Rahmen: handwerklich einwandfrei und auf Maß gearbeitet, handbemalt, wasservergoldet, mit Gips überzogen und in geheimnisvollen Techniken bearbeitet. Dazu exquisite Passepartouts, schräg geschliffene Aufziehpappen, Produkte französischer Hersteller und Florentiner Rahmen in verschiedensten Stilrichtungen.

Polanco
393 Hayes Street
Colorful! Excellent Mexican fine arts, photography and crafts. Museum curator Elsa Cameron says you can't find finer quality, even in Mexico City.
Très coloré! Œuvres d'art, photographies et artisanat mexicains de qualité. La conservatrice de musée Elsa Cameron pense que l'on ne trouve pas mieux à Mexico.
Farbenfroh! Exzellente mexikanische Kunst, Fotografie und Kunsthandwerk. Die Museumskuratorin Elsa Cameron behauptet, es gäbe nirgendwo Besseres, auch nicht in Mexico City.

Rayon Vert
3187 16th Street
Discover brilliant floral designer Kelly Kornegay's garden of earthly delights, which just got bigger-and better. Vintage furniture, hand-painted chests, charming Oriental porcelain, fresh flowers – this is, at heart, a flower shop – flea-market artifacts, vintage glasses, architectural fragments and a full-tilt, humble-chic setting.
Découvrez le jardin édenique du brillant fleuriste-créateur Kelly Kornegay, en amélioration constante. Mobilier ancien, armoires peintes à la main, porcelaines orientales, fleurs fraîches puisque nous sommes chez un fleuriste, objets trouvés au marché aux puces, verrerie d'avant-guerre, éléments d'architecture, le tout dans un cadre faussement modeste.
Gönnen Sie sich eine Entdekkungsreise in den Garten Eden der brillanten Designerin und Floristin Kelly Kornegay, der stetig wächst und immer besser wird: antike Möbel, handbemalte Kommoden, charmantes Porzellan aus Fernost, Schnittblumen – denn es ist eigentlich ein Blumenladen –, Fundstücke vom Flohmarkt, altes Glas und Architekturelemente in elegant-bescheidenen Rahmen.

Rizzoli Books
117 Post Street
Action Central for design books. Well-located near GAP flagship, plus Cartier, TSE, Bulgari, Giorgio Armani, Emporio Armani, Gump's, Polo. Outstanding collection of local design, architecture and photography books.
Passage obligé pour les amateurs de livres sur la décoration. Bien situé près du vaisseau amiral de GAP, de Cartier, TSE, Bulgari, Giorgio Armani, Emporio Armani, Gump's et Polo. Remarquable ensemble d'ouvrages sur la décoration locale, l'architecture et la photographie en Californie.
Die erste Adresse für Designbücher liegt günstig in der Nachbarschaft des GAP Hauptgeschäfts, von Cartier, TSE, Bulgari, Giorgio Armani, Emporio Armani, Gump's und Polo. Herausragende Auswahl an Büchern über lokales Design, Architektur und Fotografie.

San Francisco Design Center: Galleria, Garden Court and Showplace
Henry Adams Street, near 15th Street
This South of Market design center is open to the public, but it is wise to visit with a decorator or architect. So many lines and collections of selections of furnishings, and fittings can make the temptations extraordinary and possibly confusing. Along with Showplace West and other nearby showrooms, the Galleria and Showplace offer top-of-the-line furniture, fabrics and furnishings. Randolph & Hein, Kneedler-Fauchere, Sloan Miyasato, Shears & Window, Ann Sacks Tile and Stone, Baker Knapp & Tubbs, Clarence House, Jack Lenor Larsen, Palacek, Brunschwig & Fils, Schumacher, WaterWorks, the Garden Court, Milieux, McRae Hinckley, Donghia, Summit Furniture, Enid Ford Atelier, Barbara Beckmann Studio, Soraya Rugs, and Houlès are among personal favorites. Purchases may also be made through a buying service. Explore the neighborhood and find Therien & Co. (Scandinavian, Continental and English antiques), Therien Studio Workshops (fine reproductions designed by Robert Garcia), along with Drum & Co., McGuire, Robert Hering antiques, and the handsome Palladian outpost of Ed Hardy San Francisco (superb eclectic antiques, accessories, garden antiques).
Ce Design Center de South of Market est ouvert au public, mais il est préférable de s'y rendre en compagnie d'un décorateur ou d'un architecte. Sa richesse, sa surabondance rendent le choix difficile et la tentation trop facile. Comme Showplace West et d'autres show-rooms proches, la Galleria et Showplace proposent un choix de mobilier, de tissus et d'accessoires haut de gamme. Randolph & Hein, Kneedler-Fauchere, Sloan Miyasato, Shears & Window, Ann Sacks Tile and Stone, Baker Knapp & Tubbs, Clarence House, Jack Lenor Larsen, Palacek, Brunschwig & Fils, Schumacher, WaterWorks, the Garden Court, Milieux, McRae Hinckley, Donghia, Summit Furniture, Enid Ford Atelier, Barbara Beckmann Studio, Soraya Rugs, et Houlès sont à voir en particulier. Les achats peuvent également être pilotés par un service de conseil. Dans le voisinage, Therien & Co. (antiquités anglaises, scandinaves et continentales), Therien Studio Workshops (belles reproductions d'après des dessins de Robert Garcia) ainsi que Drum & Co., McGuire, Robert Hering Antiques, et l'élégante ambassade palladienne de Ed Hardy San Francisco (superbes antiquités éclectiques, accessoires, antiquités de jardin).
Das Design Center im South of Market District ist der Öffentlichkeit zugänglich, man sollte es aber mit einem Interior-Designer oder Architekten besuchen. Die Vielfalt an Möbel- und Einrichtungskollektionen verwirrt und führt leicht in Versuchung. Gemeinsam mit Showplace West und anderen nahgelegenen Showrooms zeigen die Galleria und der Showplace Top-Möbel, Stoffe und Accessoires. Besonders zu empfehlen sind Randolph & Hein, Kneedler-Fauchere, Sloan Miyasato, Shears & Window, Ann Sacks Tile and Stone, Baker Knapp & Tubbs, Clarence House, Jack Lenor Larsen, Palacek, Brunschwig & Fils, Schumacher, WaterWorks, the Garden Court, Milieux, McRae Hinckley, Donghia, Summit Furniture, Enid Ford Atelier, Barbara Beckmann Studio, Soraya Rugs und Houlès. Ein Kaufservice erleichtert das Shoppen. In der Nachbarschaft finden Sie Therien & Co. (Antiquitäten aus Mitteleuropa, England und Skandinavien), Therien Studio Workshops (feine Stilmöbel von Robert Garcia), Drum & Co., McGuire, Robert Hering Antiques und das schöne palladianische Geschäft von Ed Hardy, San Francisco (hervorragende, eklektizistische Antiquitäten, Accessoires und alte Gartenmöbel).

San Francisco Museum of Modern Art Store
151 Third Street
Busy, especially for evening openings. Street-level store offers extensive selections of design and art books, modernist accessories, framed posters, hand-crafted designs by local artists. Browse ... then surge upstairs into the Mario Botta-designed galleries. The Fisher Family Galleries, top floor, are the best.
Boutique très active, en particulier lors des soirées de vernissage. Au rez-de-chaussée, elle offre une vaste sélection de livres sur le design et l'art, des accessoires modernes, des posters encadrés, des créations d'artistes locaux. En montant, vous accédez aux galeries de ce grand musée conçu par Mario Botta. Ne pas manquer les Fisher Family Galleries au dernier étage.
Immer gut besucht, besonders an den Abendöffnungen. Der Laden im Erdgeschoß bietet eine große Auswahl an Design- und Kunstbüchern, moderne Accessoires, gerahmte Poster und Entwürfe lokaler Designer. Stöbern Sie in Ruhe, danach geht es nach oben in die Galerien, die Mario Botta entworfen hat. Versäumen Sie nicht die Fisher Family Galleries in der letzten Etage.

William Stout Architectural Books
804 Montgomery Street
The best! Floor-to-ceiling books. Architect Bill Stout's fine store specializes in old and new, basic and obscure 20th-century architecture monographs, along with new and out-of-print interior design and garden books. Catalogues.
Le meilleur! Des livres du sol au plafond. La belle librairie de l'architecte Bill Stout est spécialisée dans les monographies anciennes et nouvelles d'architectes connus ou obscurs du 20ᵉ siècle, ainsi que dans les livres nouveaux ou épuisés sur la décoration et le jardin. Catalogues.
Der beste! Bücher vom Boden bis zur Decke. Der Architekt Bill Stout hat sich auf alte und neue Monographien zur Architektur des 20. Jahrhunderts spezialisiert, von Standardwerken bis hin zu obskuren Titeln. Außerdem gibt es neue und vergriffene Interior-Design- und Gartenbücher. Kataloge.

Swallowtail
2217 Polk Street
Also: 1429 Haight Street
Haight Ashbury
Quirky and chic antiques – with eccentricity and flea-market charm. Glamorous all-white "studio" setting for one-of-a-kind furniture, old glassware, odd paintings. Passionate collectors love their steel cabinets and movie-star mirrors and visit weekly for best finds, especially Sunday.
Antiquités chic et peu courantes. Le charme et l'excentricité d'un marché aux puces. Dans le studio tout blanc des meubles uniques glamour, verrerie ancienne et tableaux curieux. Les collectionneurs passionnés qui adorent les meubles en acier et les miroirs de stars reviennent chaque semaine pour surveiller les nouveaux arrivages, en particulier le dimanche.
Bizarre, exzentrische und elegante Antiquitäten mit Flohmarkt-Charme. Der elegante Laden ganz in Weiß bietet Möbelunikate, alte Gläser und eigenwillige Gemälde. Einmal pro Woche, am liebsten am Sonntag, sehen hier leidenschaftliche Sammler die Stahlschränkchen und Spiegel von Filmstars durch.

Williams Sonoma
150 Post Street, and around the country
Scrumptious! Everything for diners, cooks and kitchens. Flagship for the Williams Sonoma cookware empire founded in Sonoma by Chuck Williams. Stores throughout the United States, including Corte Madera, Palo Alto, Pasadena. Quality, lifetime basics for both serious and dilettante cooks. Excellent catalogues.
E-pa-tant! Tout pour la cuisine et les cuisiniers. Vaisseau amiral de l'empire d'articles pour la cuisine fondé à Sonoma par Chuck Williams. Magasins dans tous les Etats-Unis, dont Corte Madera, Palo Alto, Pasadena. Qualité et durabilité pour le cuisinier dilettante ou l'amateur sérieux. Excellents catalogues.
Toll! Alles für Köche und Küche. Hauptfiliale des Küchenimperiums, das Chuck Williams in Sonoma gegründet hat. Läden überall in den Vereinigten Staaten, unter anderem in Corte Madera, Palo Alto und Pasadena. Qualitätsprodukte für echte und Hobbyköche, die ein Leben lang halten. Exzellente Kataloge.

Worldware
336 Hayes Street
This is a great street for a stroll – and for easy-going shopping. Stylish Shari Sant's eco-store sells cozy sheets and blankets, and delights such as chenille throws, patchwork cushions, aromatherapy (!) candles.
Superbe rue pour flâner et faire un shopping décontracté. L'éco-boutique de grand style de Shari Sant vend des draps et des couvertures confortables, et des «delights» comme des jetés en chenille, des coussins en patchwork, ou des bougies d'aromathérapie (!).
Eine herrliche Straße zum Bummeln und entspannten Shoppen. Shari Sants eleganter Öko-Laden verkauft kuschelige Laken und Decken, Frivolitäten wie Chenilletagesdecken, Patchwork-Kissen und Aromatherapie-Kerzen (!).

Zinc Details
1905 Fillmore Street
Well-priced contemporary furniture, Pro Arte Finnish ceramics, glass, colorful lighting. Handblown glass vases and lamp shades by California artists. Domain of Wendy Nishimura and Vasilios Kiniris – no, they don't sell anything made of zinc.
Mobilier contemporain à des prix accessibles, céramiques finlandaises Pro Arte, verres, luminaires colorés. Vases en verre soufflé et abat-jour d'artistes californiens. C'est le domaine de Wendy Nishimura et de Vasilios Kiniris. Non, ils ne vendent rien en zinc.
Aktuelles Möbeldesign zu günstigen Preisen, finnische Keramik von Pro Arte, Glas, farbenfrohe Leuchten. Mundgeblasene Glasvasen und Lampenschirme von kalifornischen Künstlern. In Wendy Nishimuras und Vasilios Kiniris' Reich gibt es rein gar nichts aus Zink.

Zonal
2139 Polk Street
Also: 568 Hayes Street
Partners Scott Kalmbach and Russell Pritchard tiptoe in fresh fields and pastures new. Leather chairs, custom upholstery, cosy bed linens – plus lots of painted furniture.
Scott Kalmbach et Russell Pritchard s'aventurent sur tous les terrains nouveaux. Fauteuils de cuir, rembourrage de sièges à la demande, parures de draps et dessus de lits sympathiques et beaucoup de meubles peints.
Die Partner Scott Kalmbach und Russell Pritchard bewegen sich gerne auf unbekanntem Terrain: Ledersessel, Polsterungen nach Maß, weiche Bettwäsche und bemalte alte Möbel.

Berkeley, Elmwood

Builders Boursource
1817 Fourth Street
Also: Ghirardelli Square
San Francisco
Designers and architects admire this store. Definitive selection of "shelter" books. Well-considered design, architecture, gardening and building volumes.
Designers et architectes admirent ce magasin. Choix qui fait autorité de livres sur le style «abri». Sélection choisie d'ouvrages sur le design, l'architecture, le jardinage et la construction.
Designer und Architekten lieben diesen Laden. Ultimative Auswahl an Büchern über den »Shelter«-Stil und gut sortiert in den Bereichen Design, Architektur, Garten und Hausbau.

Camps and Cottages
2109 Virginia Street
Visit the café at Chez Panisse or the great Cheese Board, then zip in for a visit to this shop and garden. Sweet little shop sells homey furniture and low-key accessories. Owner Molly Hyde English has perfect pitch for Adirondack styles.
Faites un stop au café Chez Panisse ou chez le fromager Cheese Board, avant de jeter un œil sur cette boutique et son jardin. Mobilier sympathique et accessoires passe-partout. Molly Hyde English adore les meubles de style rustique Adirondack.
Nach einem Besuch im Café Chez Panisse oder bei dem fantastischen Käsegeschäft Cheese Board geht es zu diesem hübschen kleinen Laden mit Garten, der heimelige Möbel und unaufdringliche Accessoires verkauft. Molly Hyde English hat definitiv eine Neigung für den rustikalen Adirondack-Stil.

The Gardener
1836 Fourth Street
Style-setting Alta Tingle's brilliant, bustling garden-style store. Superbly displayed glass vases, design books, stone-topped tables, Indonesian chairs, practical clothing and tools for garden lovers who have a garden or are just dreaming. Zen-cool Asian antiques, Italian terracotta pots. Consistently original, classic style. See also the new country store in Healdsburg … with garden tents and other outdoor joys.
La boutique pour le jardin qui donne le ton. Alta Tingle présente de façon originale des vases en verre, des livres sur la décoration, des sobres tables à plateau de pierre, des beaux sièges indonésiens, des vêtements pratiques et des outils pour tous ceux qui aiment jardiner ou en rêvent. Antiquités asiatiques d'esprit zen, pots de terre cuite venus d'Italie. Style classique mais original à la fois. Voir également la nouvelle boutique de Healdsburg, avec ses tentes pour le jardin et autres accessoires pour la vie au grand air.

Das wunderbare, betriebsame Geschäft von Alta Tingle setzt Trends. Exzellent präsentierte Glasvasen, Designbücher, Tische mit Steinplatten, indonesische Stühle, asiatische Antiquitäten im Zen-Look, italienische Terrakottatöpfe, Arbeitskleidung und Geräte für Gartenfreunde und solche, die es werden möchten. Konsequent origineller und gleichzeitig klassischer Stil. Besuchen Sie auch den neuen Country Store in Healdsburg mit Zelten, Gartenmöbeln und anderen Gartenaccessoires.

Omega Too
2204 San Pablo Avenue
Also: Omega Salvage
2407 San Pablo Avenue
First founded in the 60s as a hippie collective – and still thriving. Hard-to-find treasures from salvaged houses. Building materials, brass fixtures, rewired lighting, plus old tiles. Some aficionados mine the stores weekly.
Fondé dans les années 60 sous forme de collectif hippie, et toujours en pleine forme! Trouvailles récupérées dans des maisons en démolition. Matériaux de construction, accessoires en laiton, appareils électriques réélectrifiés et vieux carrelages. Certains aficionados viennent régulièrement y fouiller.
In den 60er Jahren von einem Hippie-Kollektiv gegründet, ist dieser Laden immer noch aufregend: Baumaterialien, Messingarmaturen, neu verkabelte Leuchten, alte Kacheln und schwer zu findende Fundschätze aus Abrißhäusern. Manch Süchtiger schürft hier einmal pro Woche.

Prize
2363 San Pablo Avenue
A charming, feminine collection of vintage accessories and painted furniture. Flowery fabrics, sunbright accents, fresh styling. A great stop after visiting rare booksellers in Berkeley – such as Serendipity, Mo's, and Turtle Island Books.
Sélection aussi charmante que féminine d'accessoires anciens et de meubles peints. Tissus fleuris, style frais et ensoleillé. A voir après une viste aux marchands de livres rares de Berkeley, comme Serendipity, Mo's et Turtle Island Books.
Eine charmante, feminine Auswahl an alten Accessoires, bemalten Möbeln und Blumenstoffen, sonnenhell und frisch präsentiert. Wunderbar geeignet für eine kurze Pause, nachdem man bei Serendipity, Mo's oder Turtle Island Books in Berkeley nach seltenen Büchern gestöbert hat.

Tail of the Yak
2632 Ashby Avenue
Alice Hoffman Erb and Lauren Adams Allard have created a magical mystery store that is always worth a detour – across the bay or across the Pacific. Whimsical accessories, wedding gifts, Mexican furniture, fabrics, ribbons, notecards, Lauren's hand-printed cards, linens, and antique English jewelry.
Alice Hoffman Erb et Lauren Adams Allard ont créé cette boutique magique et pleine de mystère qui vaut toujours le voyage (que ce soit traverser la Baie ou le Pacifique). Accessoires étranges, cadeaux de mariage, mobilier mexicain, tissus, rubans, cartes imprimées à la main, linge et bijoux anglais anciens.
Alice Hoffman Erb und Lauren Adams Allard haben einen magischen, verzauberten Laden geschaffen, der jederzeit einen Umweg lohnt, sei es quer über die Bucht oder auch über den Pazifik. Hier verkaufen sie schrullige Accessoires, Hochzeitsgeschenke, mexikanische Möbel, Stoffe, Bänder, Laurens handgedruckte Karten, Bettwäsche und alten englischen Schmuck.

Erica Tanov
1627 San Pablo Avenue
Also: Claremont Avenue, Berkeley
Linen pajamas, romantic bed accessories. Erica's lace-edged sheets and shams, and linen duvet covers are quietly luxurious. While in the Cedar Street neighborhood, drop in to Kermit Lynch Wine Merchants, Acme Bread and Café Fanny.
Pyjamas de lin, accessoires de chambre à coucher romantiques. Les draps à bordures de dentelle, les coussins et les housses de couette en lin sont assez luxueux. Pendant que vous vous trouvez dans le quartier de Cedar Street, arrêtez-vous chez Kermit Lynch Wine Merchants, la boulangerie Acme Bread, et au Café Fanny.
Leinenpyjamas und romantische Bettaccessoires. Ericas spitzenbesetzte Bettwäsche und Zierkissen sowie Bettbezüge sind unaufdringlicher Luxus. Sind Sie schon in der Cedar Street, sollten Sie auch die Weinhandlung Kermit Lynch Wine Merchants, der Bäckerei Acme Bread und dem Café Fanny einen Besuch abstatten.

Zia Houseworks
1310 Tenth Street
Colin Smith's colorful gallery-store offers a vivid variety of hand-crafted furniture designs and art. Maine Cottage and Mike Furniture Studio collections. Also Colin's sculptures and assemblages.
Coloré et ensoleillé, le magasin-galerie de Colin Smith propose toute une variété d'objets d'art et de mobilier artisanal. Collections de Maine Cottage et de Mike Furniture Studio. Egalement sculptures et assemblages de Smith.
Die farbenfrohe Galerie von Colin Smith bietet eine temperamentvolle Auswahl an Kunstwerken und handgefertigten Möbeln, außerdem die Kollektionen von Maine Cottage und Mike Furniture Studio sowie Colins Assemblagen.

Big Sur

The Phoenix
Highway One
Linger for hours, mesmerized by the sound of the sea and wind chimes. Hand-crafted jewelry, decorative objects, candles, glassware, French soaps, crystal, local history books, wood sculptures, woven wool throws, seductive hand-knit sweaters by Kaffe Fassett who grew up in Big Sur. Coast and fog views from all windows. Visit Nepenthe restaurant up the hill.
Vous pouvez vous y promener des heures, hypnotisé par le bruit de l'océan et les effluves marins. Bijoux artisanaux, objets décoratifs, bougies, verrerie, savonnettes françaises, cristaux, livres sur l'histoire locale, sculptures en bois, jetés de lit en laine tricotée, pull-overs tricotés main si séduisants de Kaffe Fassett qui a grandi à Big Sur. De toutes les fenêtres, vues sur la côte et le brouillard. Restaurant Nepenthe en haut de la colline.
Hier kann man Stunden verbringen, hypnotisiert vom Rauschen des Meeres und dem Klingen der Glockenspiele. Handgefertigter Schmuck, dekorative Objekte, Kerzen, Glas, französische Seifen, Kristallglas, Bücher über Lokalgeschichte, Holzskulpturen, gewebte Tagesdecken aus Wolle und verführerische handgestrickte Pullover von Kaffe Fassett, der aus Big Sur stammt. Von allen Fenstern sieht man nur Küste und Nebel. Das Restaurant Nepenthe auf dem Hügel ist ebenfalls einen Besuch wert.

Carmel

Carmel Bay Company
Corner Ocean and Lincoln
Tableware, books, glassware, furniture, prints.
Arts de la table, livres, verrerie, meubles et gravures.
Alles rund um den Tisch, dazu Bücher, Glas, Möbel und auch Drucke.

Luciano Antiques
San Carlos and Fifth Streets
Cosmopolitan antiques. Wander through the vast rooms to view furniture, lighting, sculpture, and handsome reproductions.
Antiquités: Promenez-vous dans ses vastes salles: meubles, luminaires, sculptures et belles reproductions.
Antiquitäten mit kosmopolitischem Touch. In den großen Räumen stöbert man nach Möbeln, Leuchten, Skulpturen und hübschen Stilmöbeln.

Carmel Valley

Tancredi & Morgen
Carmel Valley Road
Easy-going country style with painted furniture, old-fashioned fabrics in handsome colors, painted flower vases, candles, furniture. Just across the road from Quail Lodge, site of the annual spring Carmel Garden and Flower Show.
Style campagne décontractée, meubles peints, tissus à motifs anciens dans de belles couleurs, vases à fleurs peints, bougies et meubles. Juste en face de Quail Lodge, site du célèbre festival annuel, le Carmel Garden and Flower Show.
Unkomplizierter Landhausstil mit bemalten Möbeln, Stoffen in hübschen Farben, bemalten Blumenvasen, Kerzen und Möbeln. Direkt gegenüber befindet sich der Quail Lodge, wo jedes Jahr die Carmel Garden and Flower Show stattfindet.

Fort Bragg

Studio Z Mendocino
711 North Main Street
Perfectionist interior designers like Barbara Barry, and stars like Jamie Lee Curtis love glamorous Zida Borcich. She's one of the last letterpress printers. And she has style. Zida handsets old letterpress ornaments on fine papers and prints on antique presses. Her goldfoil and black logos – flowers, teapots, bees, dragonflies, a chef, a watering can – are chic and smart for modern correspondence and letter-writing in bed. Phone ++1–707–964–25 22 for an appointment.
Des décoratrices perfectionnistes comme Barbara Barry et des stars comme Jamie Lee Curtis apprécient Zida Borcich au charme et au glamour. Elle est une des dernières à utiliser une presse ancienne à main pour imprimer d'élégantes en-têtes de lettres sur de beaux papiers. Ses logos noir et or – fleurs, théières, abeilles, libellules, chef, arrosoir – sont chics et élégants pour ce type de lettres que l'on écrit au lit. Téléphonez au ++1–707–964–25 22 pour prendre rendez-vous.
Interior-Designer wie die perfektionistische Barbara Barry und Stars wie Jamie Lee Curtis lieben die glamouröse Zida Borcich. Zida ist eine der letzten, die die Kunst des Hochdrucks beherrscht. Stilbewußt bedruckt sie mit alten Bleiornamenten feines Papier. Ihre Logos in Goldfolie und Schwarz – Blumen, Teekannen, Bienen, Libellen, ein Koch oder eine Gießkanne – eignen sich bestens für die elegante Korrespondenz und für Briefe, die man im Bett schreibt. Nach telefonischer Anmeldung: ++1–707–964–25 22.

Glen Ellen

The Olive Press
Jack London Village
14301 Arnold Drive
Everything pertaining to olives including handblown martini glasses. Olive oils, cooking equipment, tableware, linens.

Tout ce qui entretient un rapport avec l'olive, y compris les verres à martini. Huiles d'olive, matériel de cuisine, arts de la table et linge de maison.

Alles, was mit Oliven zu tun hat, inklusive mundgeblasener Martinigläser. Olivenöl, Küchenutensilien, Tischdekor und -wäsche.

Healdsburg

The Gardener
516 Dry Creek Road, off Highway One

Now Alta Tingle's The Gardener goes country. Citrus trees in terracotta pots, Indian pleasure tents, bamboo trellises, the best tools, recycled redwood outdoor furniture – and the "Gardener Club chair" – reminiscent of a wheelbarrow – designed by Ted Boerner. Open only Thursday, Friday, Saturday.

La boutique d'Alta Tingle'devient de plus en plus campagnarde. Citronniers en pots de terre cuite, tentes indiennes pour le jardin, treillis en bambou, superbes outils, mobilier d'extérieur en bois rouge recyclé, et le «Gardener Club Chair» en forme de brouette, dessiné par Ted Boerner. Ouvert jeudi, vendredi et samedi seulement.

Alta Tingles »The Gardener« zieht aufs Land. Zitrusbäume in Terrakottatöpfen, indische Lustzelte, Spaliere aus Bambus, die besten Gartengeräte, aufgearbeitete Gartenmöbel aus Redwood und natürlich der »Gardener Club Chair«, der an eine Schubkarre erinnert und von Ted Boerner entworfen wurde. Nur donnerstags, freitags und samstags geöffnet.

Jimtown Store
6706 State Highway 128

Bicycle along country roads among the vineyards to J. Carrie Brown and John Werner's friendly store in the Alexander Valley. Sample the new preserves. The Mercantile & Exchange sells cheerful and very well-priced vintage Americana.

Partez en vélo à l'aventure parmi les vignes pour découvrir l'accueillante boutique de J. Carrie Brown et John Werner's dans l'Alexander Valley. Goûtez les dernières confitures. Le département Mercantile & Exchange vend des souvenirs américains amusants à prix doux.

Nach einer Fahrradtour über Landstraßen und zwischen Weinbergen kommen Sie zu dem freundlichen Laden von John Werner im Alexander Valley. Testen Sie die frischen Marmeladen. In der Abteilung Mercantile & Exchange gibt es fröhliche und günstige Amerikana.

Malibu

Room at the Beach
23410 Civic Center Way

Silken sheets in fine Egyptian long-staple cotton are even more impor-

tant if you've spent all day carefully cultivating a tan or lying beside the pool. Super bed linens, all very glamorous, along with Italian silk velvet throws and blankets.

Les draps soyeux en fin coton d'Egypte à longues fibres sont encore plus nécessaires lorsque vous avez passé des heures à cultiver votre bronzage au bord de la piscine. Superbes parures de lit, dessus de lit en velours de soie italien et couvertures.

Seidige Bettlaken aus fein gekämmter, langfaseriger ägyptischer Baumwolle sind unverzichtbar, wenn man den ganzen Tag zum Bräunen im Liegestuhl oder am Pool liegt. Wunderbar glamouröse Bettwäsche, Tagesdecken aus italienischem Seidensamt und prächtige Decken.

Mendocino

The Golden Goose
Main Street

Delicious bedroom decor, furnishings. Superb, pristine classic linens, antiques, armoires, all overlooking the Headlands and the roiling ocean. Baby linens, cashmere and merino throws. The most stylish decor store in Mendocino.

Style délicieux pour le décor de la chambre à coucher. Superbe linge de maison classique, antiquités, armoires. Vue sur les terres hautes des Headlands et les vagues de l'océan. Linge de maison pour enfants, jetés en cachemire et mérinos. La plus stylée des boutiques de décoration de Mendocino.

Feine Schlafzimmerausstattungen. Exzellente Bettwäsche in klassischem Stil, Antiquitäten, Schränke – das alles gibt es hier mit Blick auf den Ozean und die Hochebene der Headlands. Babywäsche sowie Tagesdecken aus Kaschmir und Merino. Das eleganteste Geschäft in Mendocino.

Lark in the Morning
10460 Kasten Street

Hand-crafted musical instruments to display and play. Traditional harps, guitars, violins, as well as ethnic instruments from around the world: Arab "ouds", bagpipes, pennywhistles, flutes and CDs.

Instruments de musique faits à la main pour jouer ou comme objets décoratifs. Harpes traditionnelles, guitares, violons, et instruments du monde entier: ouds arabes, cornemuses, flutes, sifflets et CD.

Dieser wundervolle Shop bietet handgefertigte Musikinstrumente zum Spielen und Dekorieren an: traditionelle Harfen, Gitarren und Violinen, aber auch Instrumente aus der ganzen Welt: arabische Ouds, Dudelsäcke, Pfeifen, Flöten und CDs.

Sticks
45085 Albion Street

The refreshing "twigs and branches" store of Bob Keller. Rus-

tic furniture, decor and accessories – without the cliches. Great chairs, willow headboards.

Boutique rafraîchissante, très «charmille et branchages» de Bob Keller. Mobilier, objets et accessoires de décoration rustiques, sans clichés. Superbes sièges et têtes de lit en osier.

In dem erfrischenden Laden von Bob Keller ist alles aus Holz: rustikale Möbel, Dekor und Accessoires jedweder Form. Großartige Stühle und Kopfenden fürs Bett aus Weidengeflecht.

Wilkes Sport
10466 Lansing Street

In addition to fine Italian sportswear, Wilkes Bashford offers Northern California craft talent – plus antiques, crafts of the region, and fine paintings.

En dehors d'un choix de mode sportive italienne, Wilkes Bashford propose quelques exemples du talent des artisans de Californie du nord, des antiquités, objets artisanaux de la région et de beaux tableaux.

Wilkes Bashford verkauft italienische Sportmode, nordkalifornische Handwerkskunst sowie Antiquitäten, regionales Kunstgewerbe und Gemälde.

Menlo Park

Millstreet
1131 Chestnut Street

Continental antiques, Ann Gish bed linens and silks, Tuscan pottery, tapestries, orchids, mirrors, botanical prints, silk and cashmere throws.

Antiquités européennes, parures de lit et soies d'Ann Gish, poteries toscanes, tapisseries, orchidées, miroirs, gravures botaniques, jetés de lit en cachemire et soie.

Antiquitäten aus Europa, Bettwäsche und Seide von Ann Gish, Keramik aus der Toskana, Wandteppiche, Orchideen, Spiegel, botanische Drucke sowie Tagesdecken aus Kaschmir und Seide.

Mill Valley

Mill Valley Sculpture Gardens
219 Shoreline Highway

Artistic outdoor sculpture arranged in garden rooms. Owned and curated by the talented Schwartzes: Isis Spinola Schwartz, her husband David, and his parents, Howard, a rare plants expert, and Leah, an artist. Sculptors Barton Rubinstein, Lucia Eames of Design Demetrios are standouts among the 45 artists. Fountains, kinetic works, and furniture.

Sculptures mises en scène dans des pièces-jardin. Propriété de la famille Schwartz aux multiples talents: Isis Spinola Schwartz, son mari David et ses parents aussi bien que Howard, expert de plantes rares, et l'artiste Leah. Les sculpteurs Barton Rubinstein, Lucia Eames de Design

Demetrios font partie des 45 artistes représentés. Fontaines, œuvres cinétiques et mobilier.

Kunstvolle Skulpturen, präsentiert in Wintergärten. Geführt werden die Gärten von der talentierten Familie Schwartz: von Isis Spinola Schwartz, Ehemann David und seinen Eltern, Howard, einem Experten für seltene Pflanzen, und der Künstlerin Leah. Unter den 45 ausgestellten Künstlern ragen die Werke von Barton Rubinstein und Lucia Eames von Design Demetrios heraus. Brunnen, kinetische Arbeiten und Möbel.

Smith & Hawken
35 Corte Madera

The first and original garden S&H style store ... now much-copied. Plant nursery began under horticulturist Sarah Hammond's superb direction. Everything for gardens. Also in Pacific Heights, Berkeley, Palo Alto, Los Gatos, Santa Rosa and points beyond. Catalogues.

Première boutique style S&H créée, et beaucoup copiée depuis. Pépinière sous la direction éclairée de l'horticultrice Sarah Hammond. Tout pour le jardin. Même maison à Pacific Heights, Berkeley, Palo Alto, Los Gatos, Santa Rosa et autres lieux. Catalogues.

Der erste und originale S&H-Laden, mittlerweile oft kopiert. Die Gärtnerei gedeiht unter der hervorragenden Leitung von Sarah Hammond. Alles für den Garten. Auch in Pacific Heights, Berkeley, Palo Alto, Los Gatos, Santa Rosa und vielen anderen Orten. Kataloge.

Summer House Gallery
21 Throckmorton Street

Scented with candles and hand-crafted soaps. Impossible to leave empty-handed. Artist-crafted accessories and (to order) comfortable sofas and chairs. Witty hand-crafted frames, glassware, candlesticks, colorful accessories, slipcovered loveseats, vases. Also now adding style to the bustling Fourth Street neighborhood in Berkeley, along with George – chic and fun outfits, health food, and accessories for pets – and Erica Tanov who now has a mini-empire of sheets, pajamas, accessories, dresses, sweet sweaters, and kiddie outfits.

Le magasin embaume l'odeur des bougies et des savons artisanaux. Impossible de repartir les mains vides. Accessoires pour la maison réalisés par des artistes et confortables canapés et fauteuils (sur commande). Cadres faits à la main amusants, verrerie, bougeoirs et objets décoratifs très colorés. Housses, vases. Cette galerie participe à la montée en style du quartier de plus en plus animé de Fourth Street à Berkeley, en compagnie de George – tenues chics et fun, aliments bio et accessoires pour animaux – et Erica Tanov qui possède maintenant un vrai petit empire de draps, pyjamas, accessoires, robes,

sweaters et vêtements pour les plus petits.

Es duftet nach Kerzen und selbstgemachten Seifen. Hier kommt man nie mit leeren Händen heraus: von Künstlern hergestellte Accessoires, bequeme Sofas und Sessel auf Bestellung, ungewöhnliche, handgefertigte Rahmen, Glas, Kerzenständer und farbenfrohe Accessoires. Zweisitzer mit Überzug und Vasen. Die Summer House Gallery bringt Stil in die geschäftige Fourth Street von Berkeley. Direkt in der Nachbarschaft bietet George elegante und witzige Outfits, Reformhauslebensmittel und Accessoires für Haustiere, während Erica Tanov über ein Minireich an Laken, Pyjamas, Accessoires, Anzügen, Sweaters und Kinderkleidung herrscht.

Montecito

Bill Cornfield Gallery
539 San Ysidro Road

Antiques – from Europe, India, etc.

Antiquités d'Europe, Inde, etc.

Antiquitäten, unter anderem aus Europa und Indien.

Michael Haskell Antiques
539 San Ysidro Road

Serious antiques, including Mexican silver and ceramics, 18th-century Spanish colonial furniture, early prints, religious paintings.

Antiquités sérieuses, y compris céramiques et argenterie mexicaines, mobilier colonial espagnol du 18e siècle, gravures et peintures religieuses.

Antiquitäten, darunter mexikanisches Silber und Keramiken, spanische Kolonialmöbel aus dem 18. Jahrhundert, frühe Drucke und religiöse Gemälde.

Pierre Lafond/Wendy Foster
516 San Ysidro Road

Handsomely-displayed linens, household furnishings, books, accessories and South American and Malabar Coast furniture.

Linge de table de présentation raffinée, accessoires pour la maison, livres, mobilier d'Amérique du Sud et de la côte de Malabar.

Hübsch präsentierte Bettwäsche, Haushaltswaren, Bücher, Accessoires sowie Möbel aus Südamerika und von der Malabarküste.

William Laman
1496 East Valley Road

Country antiques, casual furniture, garden accessories.

Antiquités rustiques, mobilier pour le quotidien et accessoires de jardin.

Rustikale Antiquitäten, Möbel für jeden Tag und Gartenaccessoires.

Oakville

Oakville Grocery
7856 St. Helena Highway

Wine Country Central. No visit to

the Napa Valley would be complete without a long stop here. Extraordinary wine selection, prepared foods, local olive oils, herbs, international cheeses, organic coffees, and locally-baked artisan breads. Everything for picnics, parties. Find Dean & DeLuca's food hall just north, in St. Helena.
Au centre du pays du vin. Aucune visite de la Napa Valley ne serait complète sans un long arrêt dans cette épicerie. Sélection de vins, de plats préparés, d'huiles d'olive locales, d'herbes, de fromages de tous les pays, de cafés biologiques et de pain artisanal. Tout pour les pique-niques et les réceptions. Le «food hall» de Dean & DeLuca se trouve un peu plus au nord, sur St. Helena.
Mitten im Wine Country. Kein Besuch in Napa Valley ist vollständig, ohne hier ausgiebig zu verweilen. Exzellente Auswahl an Weinen, Speisen zum Mitnehmen, Olivenöl aus der Region, Kräutern, internationalen Käsespezialitäten, ökologisch angebauten Kaffeesorten und Brot aus der örtlichen Bäckerei. Alles für Picknick und Party. Im nahen St. Helena befindet sich die Food Hall von Dean & DeLuca.

Pacific Grove

The Grove Homescapes
472 Lighthouse Avenue
Thomas Finklang and his two sons, Beau and Thompson, have turned an outmoded 1927 industrial laundry building into a striking and highly successful new home design store. There are orchids, style and art books, painting, wrought-iron tables, vases, handmade candles, and upholstered furniture in the atrium gallery, along with Turkish, Indonesian and Chinese antiques upstairs. A gazebo in the garden displays garden tools, plants.
Thomas Finklang et ses deux fils, Beau et Thompson, ont transformé un ancienne blanchisserie industrielle en un étonnant magasin de décoration qui connaît un grand succès. On y trouve des orchidées, des livres sur les styles et l'art, des peintures, des tables en fonte, des vases, des bougies artisanales et des sièges rembourrés dans la galerie de l'atrium ainsi que des antiquités de Turquie, d'Indonésie et de Chine à l'étage. Dans le jardin, une gloriette est bourrée d'outils de jardin et de plantes de tous les pays.
Thomas Finklang und seine beiden Söhne Beau und Thompson haben das altmodische Gebäude von 1927, das ursprünglich eine Industriewäscherei war, in einen wunderbaren und sehr erfolgreichen Laden für Interior-Design umgebaut. In der Galerie im Atrium findet man Orchideen, Lifestyle- und Kunstbücher, Gemälde, schmiedeeiserne Tische, Vasen, handgefertigte Kerzen und Polstermöbel, im ersten Stock Antiquitäten aus der Türkei, Indonesien und China, in dem Pavillon im Garten Gartengeräte und Pflanzen.

Palm Springs

La Galleria Consignment
71-500 Highway 111, Rancho Mirage
Hit and miss, in this town of daily estate sales. Worth a trip for vintage furniture.
A voir, à tout hasard, car dans cette ville les maisons ne cessent de se vendre et de se revendre. Vaut le voyage si vous cherchez des vieux meubles.
Wie russisches Roulette, weil hier täglich prächtige Villen ausverkauft werden. Eine Reise wert, wenn man alten Möbeln auf der Spur ist.

John's Resale Furnishings
891 North Palm Canyon Drive
Names like Harry Bertoia, Knoll and Herman Miller, along with Eames and his ilk. An only-in-Palm-Springs experience. And don't forget to visit Vintage Fest, every Thursday night, nor to try fresh dates at the farmers' market.
Harry Bertoia, Knoll et Herman Miller, les Eames et leurs émules. Une atmosphère que l'on ne peut trouver qu'à Palm Springs. Ne pas oublier de passer au Vintage Fest, tous les jeudis soir, ni de goûter aux dattes fraîches du Farmers' market.
Markennamen wie Harry Bertoia, Knoll und Herman Miller sowie Eames und Gefolge. So etwas findet man nur in Palm Springs. Vergessen Sie nicht, das Vintage Fest (jeden Donnerstag) zu besuchen oder die frischen Datteln vom Bauernmarkt zu testen.

Verandah
461 North Palm Canyon Drive
Vintage chic. Laces and linens, old silver. Dripping with glamour-Palm Springs style.
Chic d'une époque. Dentelles et draps, vieille argenterie. Tout le glamour d'un certain Palm Springs.
Die Eleganz vergangener Zeiten. Spitzen und Leinen, altes Silber. Glamouröser Palm-Springs-Stil im Überfluß.

Palo Alto

Hillary Thatz
Stanford Shopping Center
A long-time favorite. It's a dreamy view of the interiors of old England, as seen by interior designer Cheryl Driver. Traditional accessories, furniture, frames, and decorative objects. Garden furnishings.
Quasi-institution, cette vision rêvée de la vieille Angleterre vue par le décorateur Cheryl Driver. Accessoires traditionnels, meubles, encadrements et objets décoratifs. Meubles de jardin.
Seit langem eine Top-Adresse. Ein verträumter Blick in das von der Interior-Designerin Cheryl Driver interpretierte »Old England«. Accessoires in traditionellem Stil, Möbel, Rahmen und Dekoratives. Gartenmöbel.

Pasadena

Hortus
284 East Orange Grove Boulevard
Gary's superbly selected perennials, antique roses, and a full nursery. Handsome collection of antique garden ornaments. Request to receive catalogues and mailings – very inspiring. Excellent seminars.
Gary a sélectionné une superbe gamme de plantes vivaces et de roses anciennes. Beaux ornements anciens pour le jardin. Demandez les catalogues et les mailings, intéressantes sources d'inspiration. Pépinière. Excellents séminaires.
Garys ausgewählte Stauden und alte Rosen. Hübsche alte Gartendekorationen. Baumschule. Fragen Sie nach den inspirierenden Katalogen und Wurfsendungen. Exzellente Seminare.

Petaluma

Petaluma Bluestone Main
120 Petaluma Boulevard North
Victoria Card loves gardening. And she likes to bring fresh fragrances and a feeling for nature indoors. Her sun-filled, season-reflecting store features garden tools, rattan furniture, bird baths, whacking-great iron chandeliers, garden benches, glass vases, Aromatherapy of Rome (the best) candles, and always armfuls of flowers.
Victoria Card adore jardiner. Et elle aime rapporter dans ses maisons les odeurs fraîches et le sentiment de la nature. Son magasin ensoleillé vit au rythme des saisons et propose des outils de jardin, des meubles en rotin, des bains d'oiseau, de superbes lustres en fer, des bancs de jardin, des vases en verre, des bougies Aromatherapy of Rome (les meilleures) et toujours des brassées de fleurs.
Victoria Card liebt das Gärtnern, aber auch Innenräume mit frischen Düften und Outdoor-Flair. Ihr sonnendurchfluteter Laden, der sich mit den Jahreszeiten ändert, bietet Gartengeräte, Rattanmöbel, Vogelbäder, fantastische Kronleuchter aus Eisen, Gartenbänke, Glasvasen, Kerzen von Aromatherapy of Rome (die besten!) und immer große Mengen Schnittblume n an.

Chelsea Antiques
148 Petaluma Boulevard North
Saturday afternoons, this antiques collective buzzes with activity – and many of the visitors are San Francisco decorators and their chums looking for vintage accessories and furniture. Antiques dealers like Laura Rombauer bring in garden antiques, Americana, French flea-market treasures, lovely porcelain, old glass jars, funky toys, graceful turn-of-the-century furniture. Two floors for browsing.
Chaque samedi après-midi, ce marché d'antiquaires bourdonne d'activité et beaucoup de ses visiteurs sont des décorateurs de San Francisco et leurs copains à la recherche d'accessoires et de meubles. Des antiquaires comme Laura Rombauer proposent des accessoires de jardin anciens, des trouvailles en provenance directe des marchés aux puces français, de charmantes porcelaines, de vieilles jarres en verre, des jouets rigolo, de gracieux meubles fin-de-siècle. Deux étages de découvertes.
Am Samstag nachmittag wimmelt es in diesem Antiquitätenladen von Interior-Designern aus San Francisco und ihren Anhängern, die hier nach alten Accessoires und Möbeln fahnden. Antikenhändler wie Laura Rombauer bringen alte Gartendekorationen, Amerikana, Fundstücke von französischen Flohmärkten, wunderschönes Porzellan, alte Glaskrüge, eigenartiges Spielzeug und anmutige Möbel aus der Jahrhundertwende vorbei. Stöbern total auf zwei Etagen.

Placentia

Denman & Company
1202 East Pine Street
This is the kind of great, old-fashioned store everyone longs to find. It has true style, but it also sells things you really, truly need. Connoisseurs of great garden tools drive from all over California to visit Denman & Company. Bob and Rita Denman have assembled more than 800 implements, including 25 different hoes, 14 spades, rakes, and a push plow that dates back 100 years. Denman and his blacksmith will also handcraft old-fashioned tools, and custom manufacture special sizes of tools. Bob calls a spade a spade.
C'est le style même de magasin démodé que l'on a envie de découvrir. Il a son style bien à lui, mais vous n'y trouverez pas moins ce dont vous avez vraiment besoin. Les connaisseurs en outils de jardin viennent de toute la Californie. Bob et Rita Denman ont réuni ici plus de 800 accessoires, dont 25 houes différentes, 14 bèches, des râteaux, une charrue à bras vieille d'un siècle. Bob et son forgeron peuvent également réaliser des outils traditionnels ou de dimensions spéciales.
Einer dieser großartigen, altmodischen Läden, die jeder liebt. Er ist stilvoll und führt Dinge, die man wirklich braucht. Kenner guter Gartengeräte reisen quer durch Kalifornien, um hier einzukaufen. Bob und Rita Denman haben über 800 Geräte auf Lager, darunter 25 verschiedene Hacken, 14 Spaten, Rechen und einen 100 Jahre alten Pflug. Denman und sein Schmied fertigen auf Wunsch traditionelle Gerätschaften und Werkzeuge in Spezialausfertigung. Bei Bob heißt ein Spaten noch Spaten.

San Anselmo

Modern i 1950
500 Red Hill Avenue
Steven Cabella is passionate about Modernism and time-warp mid-century (1935–1965) furnishings. Vintage furnishings, Eames chairs, furniture by architects, objects and artwork. Located in a restored modernist architect's office building. Take a detour to this sleepy town to find a trove of antiques shops, antiques collectives, rare book galleries, used book shops. Stay for dinner on the patio at Bradley Ogden's Lark Creek Inn in Larkspur.
Steven Cabella est un passionné du modernisme et des meubles légèrement fatigués des années 1935 à 1965. Vieux meubles, sièges Eames, mobilier d'architectes, objets et œuvres d'art. Situé dans un immeuble moderniste restauré qui servait de bureaux d'architecte. Faites le détour par cette petite ville assoupie, et vous serez récompensé par la présence d'un multitude de boutiques d'antiquités, d'objets de collection anciens, de vieux livres rares ou de livres d'occasion. Dînez dans le patio de la Lark Creek Inn de Bradley Ogden à Larkspur.
Steven Cabella hat eine Leidenschaft für die Moderne und vom Lauf der Zeit leicht gezeichnetes Mobiliar von 1935 bis 1965. In dem restaurierten modernistischen Gebäude, in dem sich früher Architektenbüros befanden, verkauft er alte Möbel, Stühle von Eames, Möbel von Architekten, Objekte und Kunstwerke. Ein Umweg durch das verschlafene Örtchen lohnt sich, denn hier gibt es ein Vielzahl an Antiquitätenläden, Antiquariaten und Geschäften für seltene Bücher. Das Dinner sollten Sie in Bradley Ogdens Lark Creek Inn in Larkspur einnehmen.

San Rafael

Restoration Hardware
1700 Redwood Highway
Men love the tools. Women love the sofas. Kids love the toys. Try to leave empty-handed! Excellent displays of traditional-style hardware and lighting, easy-going furniture, tools, frames, practical garden accessories. Always a thorough and definitive collection of design and style books. Also in Palo Alto, and all points north and south.
Les hommes adorent les outils. Les femmes les canapés. Les enfants les jouets. Inutile d'essayer de repartir les mains vides! Superbe exposition de quincaillerie et de luminaires de style traditionnel, mobilier sympathique, outils, cadres, accessoires de jardin. Un choix définitif de livres sur le design et la décoration. Même maison à Palo Alto et diverses adresses dans tout l'Etat.
Männer lieben die Werkzeuge, Frauen die Sofas und Kinder das

Spielzeug. Versuchen Sie einmal, hier mit leeren Händen herauszukommen! Exzellentes Angebot an traditionellen Haushaltswaren und Lampen, schlichten Möbeln, Werkzeugen, Rahmen und praktischen Dingen für den Garten. Gute Design- und Lifestyle-Bücher. Auch in Palo Alto und anderen Orten in Süd- und Nordkalifornien vertreten.

Santa Monica

Thomas Callaway Bench Works, Inc.
2929 Nebraska Avenue
Interior designer and actor Thomas Callaway designs, makes and offers custom-made star-quality armchairs, sofas, and ottomans with deep-down comfort and timeless glamour. These are future heirlooms. By appointment only: ++1-310-828-93 79.
Acteur et décorateur, Thomas Callaway conçoit, réalise et vend des fauteuils, des canapés et des poufs sur commande, d'un confort aussi profond que leur charme intemporel. Des meubles à transmettre à vos héritiers. Sur rendez-vous seulement au ++1-310-828-93 79.
Der Interior-Designer und Schauspieler Thomas Callaway entwirft und verkauft bequeme und zeitlose Armsessel, Sofas und Hocker, dier er auch auf Bestellung anfertigt. Alles künftige Erbstücke. Nur nach telefonischer Absprache: ++1-310-828-93 79.

Hennessy & Ingalls
1254 Third Street, Promenade
Late-night crowds bustle in for browsing. Architects and designers flock to this book store, which specializes in the widest range of architecture and design and style books.
On y vient tard le soir pour jeter un coup d'œil. Architectes et décorateurs affluent vers cette librairie spécialisée dans les ouvrages les plus variés sur l'architecture, le design et le style.
Nachteulen stöbern hier gerne. Architekten und Designer pilgern zu dieser Buchhandlung mit der größten Auswahl an Architektur-, Design- und Lifestyle-Titeln.

Kathryn Ireland Fabrics and Furnishings
1118 Montana Avenue
Kathryn Ireland first created "le style anglais" for Anglophile Angelenos. Now she has her own handsome block-printed and classic fabrics. Special cushions, lamps.
Kathryn Ireland avait à l'origine créé «le style anglais» pour les Angéliniens anglophiles. Aujourd'hui, elle édite ses propres tissus classiques et imprimés au pochoir. Coussins intéressants et lampes.
Zunächst kreierte Kathryn Ireland »le style anglais« für anglophile Angelenos. Inzwischen fertigt sie ihre eigenen bedruckten Stoffe in klassischem Stil. Ungewöhnliche Kissen und Leuchten.

Jasper
1646 19th Street
Interior designer Michael Smith's brilliant atelier. In a cool high-ceilinged studio Michael displays bold vignettes of antiques, accessories gathered around the world, linens, art glass, and his own superb furniture designs. Worth a detour.
Le superbe studio du décorateur Michael Smith. Dans une pièce à hauts plafonds, il présente des antiquités, des accessoires divers venus du monde entier, de la verrerie d'art et ses propres créations de meubles. Vaut le détour.
Das brillante Atelier von Interior-Designer Michael Smith präsentiert in den hohen Räumen kühn zusammengestellte Antiquitäten, Accessoires aus der ganzen Welt, Bettwäsche, kunstvolles Glas und natürlich seine eigenen wunderbaren Möbelentwürfe. Einen Umweg wirklich wert.

Museum of Contemporary Art Store
2447 Main Street
In a Frank O. Gehry-designed complex. Best contemporary designs, including furniture, books, gifts.
Dans un complexe dessiné par Frank O. Gehry. Sélection du meilleur du design contemporain, y compris meubles, livres et cadeaux.
Der Laden in dem von Frank O. Gehry entworfenen Komplex bietet das beste aktuelle Design an, darunter Möbel, Bücher und Geschenke.

Shabby Chic
1013 Montana Avenue
Also: 3075 Sacramento Street
San Francisco
Rachel and partners defined this style. A long-time classic. Yes, they still do smooshy, ruffly sofas, but they've also moved on to tailored upholstery and a new line of vintage-style fabrics. Trim as well as fat furniture.
Rachel et ses associés ont défini leur style. Du classique durable. Oui, ils continuent à fabriquer leurs canapés profonds et moelleux, mais proposent également une nouvelle ligne de tissus à motifs anciens. Grands et petits meubles.
Rachel und ihre Partner haben diesen Stil erfunden, der schon seit langem ein Klassiker ist. Sie fertigen zwar immer noch rüschenbesetzte Sofas, führen aber auch Polsterstoffe nach Maß, neue Stoffe in traditionellem Stil, schlanke und üppige Möbel.

Santa Rosa

Randolph Johnson Studio
608 Fifth Street
Master craftsman and designer Randy Johnson makes dreamy furniture and accessories with superb detail in a wide range of styles. Draperies, painted finishes. Finest custom artistry.
Le maître-artisan et designer Randy Johnson réalise avec talent de merveilleux meubles et accessoires dans toute une gamme de styles et de finitions. Tentures. Remarquable travail de professionnel.
Der Handwerksmeister und Designer Randy Johnson fertigt Traummöbel und Accessoires, perfekt bis ins letzte Detail sowie in vielen Stilarten und Oberflächenbehandlungen. Vorhänge. Allerbeste Maßarbeit.

Sonoma

Studio Sonoma
380 First Street West
Designer Robin Nelson offers beautifully edited home furnishings, paintings, slipcovers, lighting. Seasonal delights – including hammocks for summer, quilts for winter.
Le designer Robin Nelson propose de superbes accessoires pour la maison, tableaux, dessus de lits, luminaires. Il tient compte des saisons: hamacs pour l'été et quilts pour l'hiver.
Der Designer Robin Nelson verkauft wunderschöne Inneneinrichtungen, Gemälde, Möbelüberzüge und Leuchten sowie saisonbedingte Schmankerl wie Hängematten für den Sommer und Quilts für den Winter.

St. Helena

St. Helena St. Helena Antiques
1231 Main Street
Yes, the name is intentionally repetitious. Rustic furniture, vintage wine paraphernalia, vintage accessories.
Oui, la répétition dans le nom est volontaire. Mobilier rustique, tout ce qu'il faut pour le vin, accessoires anciens.
Ja, der Name ist absichtlich gedoppelt. Er führt rustikale Möbel, alles über Wein und alte Accessoires.

Showplace North
1350 Main Street
Interior design, fabrics, custom furniture. Stores also in Santa Rosa and Carmel.
Décoration, tissus, mobilier sur mesure. Même maison à Santa Rosa et Carmel.
Inneneinrichtung, Stoffe sowie maßgefertigte Möbel. Auch in Santa Rosa und Carmel vertreten.

Tantau
1220 Adams Street
Charming atmosphere. Hard to leave empty-handed. Decorative accessories, furniture, hand-painted furniture, toys, gifts.
Atmosphère de charme. On y trouve toujours quelque chose. Accessoires de décoration, mobilier, meubles peints, jouets, cadeaux.
Charmant. Hier kommt man nie mit leeren Händen raus. Dekorative Accessoires, Möbel, handbemalte Möbel, Spielzeug und Geschenke.

Tivoli
1432 Main Street
In a former mortuary, Tom Scheibal has created a sunny indoor and outdoor garden furniture and accessories store. Tables and chairs and occasional pieces in iron, aluminum, concrete and recycled redwood. Antique garden ornaments.
Dans un ancien magasin de pompes funèbres, Tom Scheibal a créé un lieu ensoleillé où il présente meubles et accessoires de jardin ou d'intérieur. Tables, sièges, et quelques pièces en fer, aluminium, béton et bois rouge de récupération. Ornements de jardin anciens.
Tom Scheibals sonnendurchfluteter Laden für Wohn- und Gartenmöbel sowie Accessoires befindet sich in den Räumen eines ehemaligen Bestattungsinstituts. Tische, Stühle und gelegentlich Objekte aus Eisen, Aluminium, Beton oder wiederverwendetem Redwood. Gartendekorationen.

Vanderbilt & Co.
1429 Main Street
The best! Extensive collections of luxury bed linens, books, French glassware, Italian ceramics, handmade accessories. A year-round favorite in the wine country. Also at the Stanford Shopping Center, Palo Alto.
Le meilleur! Immense sélection de draps de luxe, de livres, de verrerie française, de céramiques italiennes, d'accessoires faits main. Un lieu très fréquenté toute l'année. Même maison au Stanford Shopping Center, Palo Alto.
Vom Allerfeinsten! Riesenauswahl an luxuriöser Bettwäsche, Büchern, französischem Glas, italienischer Keramik und handgemachten Accessoires. Im Wine Country das ganze Jahr über beliebt. Auch im Stanford Shopping Center in Palo Alto.

I. Wolk Gallery
1235 Main Street
Ira Wolk's excellent gallery shows sculpture and paintings. Uncommon artists. Also visit the Olive Grove Sculpture Garden at Auberge du Soleil, Rutherford, curated by Ira Wolk.
La remarquable galerie de sculptures et de peintures d'Ira Wolk. Artistes hors du commun. Visitez également le Olive Grove Sculpture Garden de l'Auberge du Soleil, à Rutherford, que gère également Ira.
Ira Wolks exzellente Galerie zeigt Skulpturen und Gemälde von ungewöhnlichen Künstlern. Besuchen Sie auch Iras Olive Grove Sculpture Garden bei der Auberge du Soleil in Rutherford.

Summerland

Flotsam and Jetsam
2496 Lillie Avenue
Neil Korpinen and Eric Erickson's cottage-selling American furniture of the 20th century. Art deco, Monterey-style furnishings.
Le quasi-vide grenier de Neil Korpinen et Eric Erickson propose du mobilier américain du 20e siècle et des accessoires Art Déco et Monterey style.
Neil Korpinen und Eric Erickson verkaufen amerikanische Cottage-Möbel aus dem 20. Jahrhundert, außerdem Art-déco-Mobiliar und Möbel im rustikalen Monterey-Stil.

Tiburon

Ruth Livingston Design
72 Main Street
Interior designer Ruth Livingston's studio, with elegant art, furniture, crafts. Also custom design.
C'est le studio de la décoratrice Ruth Livingston. Art, mobilier, artisanat, le tout choisi avec élégance. Egalement modèles sur commande.
Das Studio der Interior-Designerin Ruth Livingston bietet elegante Kunst, Möbel und Kunsthandwerk an. Auch Maßanfertigungen.

Venice

Bountiful
1335 Abbott Kinney Boulevard
By appointment only: ++1-310-450-36 20. Sue Balmforth's vintage Edwardian and Victorian painted furniture, lamps, old beds, quirky "objets". This is a street and a neighborhood to explore. Sue's is a destination store and there are others worth discovering along this sun-struck stretch of boulevard.
Exclusivement sur rendez-vous: ++1-310-450-36 20. Meubles peints anciens edouardiens et victoriens de Sue Balmforth, lampes, lits anciens et objets curieux. Explorez cette section ensoleillée du boulevard.
Nur nach telefonischer Absprache: ++1-310-450-36 20. Hier verkauft Sue Balmforth alte, bemalte, edwardianische und viktorianische Möbel, Leuchten, alte Betten und skurrile Objekte. Auf dem Weg zu Sues Laden sollten Sie unbedingt auf dem sonnigen Boulevard und in der Nachbarschaft auf Entdeckungsreise gehen.

Flea Markets

On weekends, flea-marketeers and connoisseurs of kitsch pore over newspapers for listings of tag sales, garage sales, seasonal collector shows, and special auctions, such as those by Butterfield & Butterfield. On the hunt for cool stuff, they find antiques sales, estate sales, weekend flea markets, and occasional vintage and antique furniture shows. Where else can you unearth old garden tools that are no longer manufactured – or hippie posters, old sepia photos of long-gone civic-pride buildings, rusted hardware, weird medical drawings or poetic conchological prints?

There are fleas to keep everyone hopping. A swing through the world of junk and vintage stuff could take in San Francisco, Alameda and San Bernadino each Sunday, Pasadena (second Sunday of each month and more than 2 200 vendors), Long Beach (third Sunday of every month) or Ventura, Santa Monica (fourth Sunday of each month).

In dusty, cob-webbed shops in small towns, the persistent may find Eames chairs, precious laces, hippie-ish brass beds, artsy chairs, René Lalique vases, and hand-bound books, busted tools, smelly tins, and funny signs. Every Sunday the action is at San Francisco's Alemany Flea Market (junction of Highways 280 and 101) but that sortie could also take in Mission thrift shops.

Dealers come prepared, and collectors descend early, armed with backpacks for treasures, cash, a magnifying glass, and a patient knowledge that sooner of later they will find something remarkable. The dilettanti among us watch for famous film directors, French and German art dealers, Lesbian latte makers, rare jade jewelry, kitschy pottery, Bakelite bracelets, embroidered linens, and amazingly wonderful and junky junk among the treasures.

Marchés aux puces

Le week-end, les amateurs de marchés aux puces et les spécialistes du kitsch se précipitent sur les journaux pour repérer les annonces de ventes de greniers, de «garage sales», d'expositions-ventes pour collectionneurs, de marchés, de brocantes et de ventes aux enchères telles celles organisées par Butterfield & Butterfield. Puis ils partent en chasse, car ils savent qu'ils ne pourraient trouver ailleurs les outils de jardin qui ne sont plus fabriqués, les posters hippies, les vieilles photos sépia de bâtiments disparus, les objets de fer rouillés, les planches médicales illustrées un peu bizarres ou les gravures poétiques sur les champignons.

Les marchés aux puces répondent à tous les espoirs. On en trouve à San Francisco, Alameda et San Bernardino chaque dimanche, à Pasadena au second dimanche de chaque mois avec plus de 2 200 stands, à Long Beach au troisième dimanche de chaque mois ou à Ventura et Santa Monica au quatrième dimanche de chaque mois.

Dans les boutiques poussiéreuses de petites villes à l'écart des grands axes, vous pourrez trouver, avec un peu de courage et d'opiniâtreté, des sièges de Charles Eames, des dentelles précieuses, des lits de cuivre style hippie, des sièges qui jouent à l'œuvre d'art, des vases de René Lalique, des livres reliés, des outils cassés, des pots de toute sorte aux senteurs mystérieuses et des panneaux publicitaires amusants. Chaque dimanche, il faut absolument se rendre à l'Alemany Flea Market de San Francisco (au croisement des Highways 280 et 101), et continuer par les boutiques de brocante de Mission.

Les marchands sont sur le pied de guerre, et les collectionneurs arrivent en rang serrés, armés de sacs à dos (pour rapporter leurs découvertes), d'argent liquide, de loupes et de la certitude de trouver un jour ou l'autre l'objet remarquable. Les dilettantes repéreront au milieu des bijoux rares en jade, des poteries kitsch, des bracelets de Bakélite, du linge brodé, de célèbres réalisateurs de films, des serveuses de café lesbiennes, des marchands d'art allemands et français.

Flohmärkte

Jedes Wochenende durchstöbern Flohmarktfans und Kitschkenner die Zeitungsanzeigen auf der Suche nach Räumungsverkäufen, saisonbedingten Sammlermärkten und Sonderauktionen, wie zum Beispiel bei Butterfield & Butterfield. Sie sind immer auf der Jagd nach Schätzen, die man nur bei Wohnungsauflösungen, Wochenendflohmärkten und gelegentlichen Trödel- und Antikmärkten finden kann. Wo sonst stöbert man alte Gartengeräte auf, die längst nicht mehr hergestellt werden? Oder Hippie-Poster, alte sepiagetönte Fotografien von längst abgerissenen Gebäuden, verrostete Gegenstände, merkwürdige medizinische Zeichnungen oder poetische Drucke mit Muschelmotiven?

Für jeden Geschmack gibt es etwas. Eine Reise durch die Welt des Trödels und der Antiquitäten führt jeden Sonntag durch San Francisco, Alameda, San Bernardino, jeden zweiten Sonntag im Monat nach Pasadena, wo sich mehr als 2 200 Verkäufer versammeln, jeden dritten Sonntag im Monat nach Long Beach und jeden vierten Sonntag nach Ventura und Santa Monica.

Besonders Hartnäckige wühlen sich durch staubige, mit Spinnenweben behangene Läden in den Kleinstädten und finden dort möglicherweise einen Stuhl von Eames, wertvolle Spitzen, Messingbetten aus der Hippie-Ära, kunstvolle Stühle, Vasen von René Lalique, handgebundene Bücher, defektes Werkzeug, merkwürdig riechende Kanister und eigenartige Schilder. Jeden Sonntag brodelt es auf dem Alemany Flohmarkt in San Francisco (an der Kreuzung von Highway 280 und 101), aber auch in den Geschäften im Mission District.

Händler kommen grundsätzlich gut vorbereitet. Sammler stehen früh auf, bewaffnen sich mit Bargeld, Lupen und Rucksäcken, um die Beute heimtragen zu können, und machen sich mit der geduldigen Gewißheit auf den Weg, daß sie früher oder später etwas Bemerkenswertes finden werden. Amateure hingegen halten Ausschau nach einem berühmten Filmregisseur, einer lesbischen Kellnerin im Café sowie französischen und deutschen Kunsthändlern. Oder sie suchen seltenen Jadeschmuck, kitschige Keramik, Armbänder aus Bakelit, bestickte Bettwäsche und andere erstaunliche und wunderbare Trödelschätze.

Bibliography / Bibliographie

Alexander, Christopher, *The Timeless Way of Building*, Oxford University Press 1979

Alexander, Christopher, Sara Ishikawa, Murray Silverstein et al., *A Pattern Language: Towns, Buildings, Construction*, Oxford University Press 1977 (German edition: *Eine Muster-Sprache*, Löcker Verlag 1995)

Bachelard, Gaston, *The Poetics of Space*, Beacon Press 1969 (Reprint 1994; German edition: *Poetik des Raumes*, Fischer 1997; French edition: *Poétique de l'espace*, French & European Publications 1992)

Boutelle, Sara Holmes, *Julia Morgan Architect*, Abbeville Press 1988 (revised edition 1995)

Dunham, Judith, *Details of Frank Lloyd Wright. The California Work: 1909–1974*, Chronicle Books 1994

Gill, Brendan and Derry Moore, *The Dream Come True: The Great Houses of Los Angeles*, Lippincott & Crowell 1980

Gössel, Peter (Editor), *Julius Shulman. Architecture and its Photography*, Benedikt Taschen Verlag 1998 (German edition: *Julius Shulman. Architektur und Fotografie*; French edition: *Julius Shulman. L'architecture et sa photographie*)

Hart, James D., *A Companion to California*, Oxford University Press 1978

Jennings, James, *Jim Jennings Architecture. Ten Projects, Ten Years*, William Stout Publishers 1999

Jodidio, Philip, *Contemporary American Architects I–IV*, Benedikt Taschen Verlag 1995

Jodidio, Philip, *Contemporary California Architects*, Benedikt Taschen Verlag 1993–1998

Johnson, Paul C. (Editor), *The California Missions*, Sunset Books 1964

Kahn, Lloyd, Sarah Hammond et al., *Shelter*, Shelter Publications 1996 (first published 1973)

Kerouac, Jack, *Big Sur*, various editions

Kirkham, Pat, Charles and Ray Eames, *Designers of the Twentieth Century*, MIT Press 1998 (first published 1995)

Massey, James and Shirley Maxwell, *Arts & Crafts Design in America: A State-By-State Guide*, Chronicle Books 1998

McCarter, Robert et al., *Constructed Reality. The work of Tanner, Leddy, Maytum and Stacy, Architects*, William Stout Publishers 1998

McCoy, Esther and Randell L. Makinson, *Five California Architects*, Hennessey & Ingalls 1987 (first published 1960)

Power, Nancy Goslee and Mick Hales (Photographer), *The Gardens of California: Four Centuries of Design from Mission to Modern*, Clarkson Potter 1995

Saeks, Diane Dorrans and John Vaughan (Photographer), *San Francisco: A Certain Style*, Chronicle Books 1988 (New edition 1999)

Saeks, Diane Dorrans and John Vaughan (Photographer), *California Country: Interior Design, Architecture and Style*, Chronicle Books 1992 (New edition 1999)

Saeks, Diane Dorrans and Alan Weintraub (Photographer), *San Francisco Interiors*, Chronicle Books 1996

Saeks, Diane Dorrans and Alan Weintraub (Photographer), *California Cottages: Interior Design, Architecture and Style*, Chronicle Books 1997

Saeks, Diane Dorrans and Alan Weintraub (Photographer), *California Wine Country: Interior Design, Architecture and Style*, Chronicle Books 1997

Saeks, Diane Dorrans, *Design Library: Bathrooms, Bedrooms, Living Rooms, Kitchen*, Chronicle Books 1997/1998

Smith, Bruce and Alexander Vertikoff (Photographer), *Greene & Greene: Masterworks*, Chronicle Books 1998

Street-Porter, Tim, *The Los Angeles House: Decoration and Design in America's Twentieth Century City*, Clarkson Potter 1997

Woodbridge, Sally Byrne and John Woodbridge, *San Francisco Architecture. The Illustrated Guide to over 1 000 of the Best Buildings, Parks, and Public Artworks in the Bay Area*, Chronicle Books 1991

Acknowledgements / Remerciements / Danksagung

This book is dedicated to my son, Justin, with love, always.

Sincerest thanks to Ursula Fethke who has steadily and expertly guided the photography and texts, first in Paris, later in Cologne. Thanks, also, to the superb talents that Taschen has brought together: Nazire Ergün, Ute Wachendorf, Jacques Bosser, Corinna von Bassewitz, Sue Rose, Michèle Schreyer.

Grey Crawford's photography graces these pages, and I am most grateful for his technical skills, focus, and good humor. Warmest thanks to his assistants, Kristen Loken, Tom Bachand and Sharon Cavanaugh.

Barbara Thornburg, senior editor with the "Los Angeles Times" magazine, was generous and gracious with time and sources.

Bouquets and warmest thanks to the eloquent and wonderful owners of all the apartments, houses, studios, lofts, cottages, houseboats, cabins, ranches, trailers, guest-houses, villas, penthouses, and one former swimming club that bring the pages of this book alive. My special thanks go to Eames Demetrios (eamesd@eamesoffice.com). The work of many talented designers and architects shine throughout this volume. They create the exterior and interior landscapes that inspire us all to dream, imagine, go forward, rest, meditate, and live enriched lives. Thank you all.

Heartfelt gratitude to all the photographers whose work appears on these pages: Klaus Baier, Gilles de Chabaneix, Todd Eberle, John Ellis, John Reed Forsman, Thibault Jeanson, David Duncan Livingston, Russell MacMasters, Michael Mundy, Anthony Peres, Cesar Rubio, Julius Shulman, René Stoeltie, Tim Street-Porter, Dominique Vorillon, Alan Weintraub, Edina van der Wyck.

Special thanks to talented editors: Donna Warner, Michael Lassell, Margaret Kennedy, Louis Gropp, Jody Thompson Kennedy, Marian McEvoy, Dorothy Kalins, Sarah Gray Miller, Newell Turner, Louise Farr, Paul Fortune, and Barbara Graustark.

As always, I send love, bouquets and thanks to dearest friends, colleagues and family who have encouraged me in my endeavours: Theadora van Runkle, Geraldine Paton AO and Brian Ferrari in Sydney; Robert Harvey QSO in Waitakere City; Dorothy Tanis Saeks, Ron and Louise La Palme Mann, Andrew Virtue, Myra and Wade Hoefer, Mary Grant, Melissa Wallace Deitz, Connie Ballard, Michael Bauer, Ruth St. John Grant, Julie Clerou Riegel, Sue Fisher King, Tim Street-Porter, Mish Tworkowski, Kate and Odom Stamps, Michael Smith, and Ryann Abeel.

Diane Dorrans Saeks